WAR STUDIES READER

War Studies Reader

*From the Seventeenth Century
to the Present Day and Beyond*

EDITED BY
GARY SHEFFIELD

continuum

Published by the Continuum International Publishing Group

The Tower Building
11 York Road
London SE1 7NX

80 Maiden Lane
Suite 704
New York, NY 10038

www.continuumbooks.com

Copyright © Gary Sheffield, 2010

First published 2010

British Library Cataloguing-in-Publication Data
A catalogue record for this book is available from the British Library.

ISBN: 978-0-8264-2186-9 (HB)
ISBN: 978-0-8264-2070-1 (PB)

Designed and typeset by Newgen Imaging Systems Pvt Ltd, Chennai, India
Printed and bound by CPI Antony Rowe, Chippenham, Wiltshire

Contents

Editor's Acknowledgements

My primary thanks go to Mr Michael LoCicero, PhD candidate at the University of Birmingham, who very kindly acted as my research assistant. Without his help this book would not have happened. At Continuum, thanks are due to Robin Baird-Smith and Rhodri Mogford.

Introduction

The discipline of War Studies in its current form is a comparatively recent development, but its origins go back many years. Much of the earliest historical writing concerned war in some shape or form. Both Herodotus (c.480–425 BC) and Thucydides (c.460–396 BC) took war as their subject. In *The History of the Peloponnesian War,* Thucydides had a particularly sophisticated approach. He not only gave details of military operations but discussed such matters as human nature, power, Athenian democracy, and the underlying causes of the war: Sparta feared the growing strength of Athens, and took the decision to fight while they still had a chance to win. Thucydides cast the whole in the form of literature. In today's terms, Thucydides adopted an inter-disciplinary approach to explain the causes and conduct of a war, employing elements of history, philosophy, literature, and political science.

If Herodotus is the 'father of history', Thucydides is the ancestor of War Studies, a discipline that seeks to understand the phenomenon of war by using a wide variety of approaches. Most university War Studies courses in the UK have military history, broadly defined, at their centre, but draw upon political science, economics, law, ethics, philosophy, literature, theology, anthropology, sociology and indeed other disciplines. From this it can be seen that War Studies is not synonymous with military history as is sometimes assumed, and is a relative of Strategic (or Security) Studies. Practitioners of Strategic Studies focus on contemporary defence and security issues, although some draw upon history and other disciplines to inform their work.

There is no single template for a War Studies course or department. Some have evolved in the direction of a primary focus on international relations and contemporary security, while others concentrate on military history. My Chair at the University of Birmingham is in War Studies, and I am a military historian by background and inclination. The approach to War Studies at this university is best described as 'military history plus'. The main concern is the history of war, covering topics that are normally associated with 'traditional' military history such as generalship, battles, and strategy, but also matters such as the organization of armed forces; 'home fronts', the impact of war on politics and society; the literature of war; law and ethics – and indeed many other things. This Reader follows a similar pattern of 'military history plus', seeking to demonstrate the breadth and diversity of War Studies while keeping the history of war at its core.

What is 'war'? At its simplest, war is the use of force by a state in order to achieve political objectives. Clearly this definition needs to be modified to take into account Non-State Actors such as revolutionary guerrilla movements and terrorist organizations, such as the Chinese Communist forces during the Chinese Civil War (1927–49), or Al Queda today. Would-be states seeking to break away from an existing political structure, such as the 13 colonies in the American War of Independence (1776–83), also need to be encompassed within the definition of war. So do conventional armies attempting to seize control of a state, be it the contending forces of Octavian and Mark Antony battling for the late Roman Republic, or the Royalist and Parliamentarian armies in England in the 1640s.

The key elements in any definition of war must be 'violence' and 'politics'. Remove them and the phenomenon ceases to be war and becomes something else. Take away 'violence' and it becomes, perhaps, diplomacy, which can be defined as 'a non-lethal method of achieving political aims, used instead of, or in conjunction with, armed force'. The great insight of the nineteenth century Prussian military thinker Karl von Clausewitz (1780–1831) was that war was essentially a political act, 'an act of force to compel the enemy to do our will'. Omit politics and one is left with mere banditry or organised crime, not war.

Moreover, as Clausewitz argued, the *nature* (as opposed to the *conduct*) of war is unchanging. That means that there are some things that can be taken for granted across vast swathes of history. Although the conduct of war has changed greatly – the move from chariots to tanks via horsed cavalry makes the point – the bedrock of war has not. For instance, three elements are common to battles from ancient times to the present day: missile weapons (from arrows to smart bombs); melees (close quarter fighting); and morale. More often than not, a battle will be decided by the resolve to fight of one side or the other giving way, such as at Waterloo in 1815. The reason for the strategic defeat of the USA in the Vietnam War (1965–73) was not that its forces were beaten in the field but that the will to fight of the US government had been eroded by the prolonged attritional campaign fought by its Communist enemies.

The unchanging nature of war means that some analytical tools can be used across the centuries. Current British military doctrine gives three components of 'Fighting Power'. The first is the 'physical'; that is the means to fight, normally divided into 'teeth arms' – combat units such as infantry, armour, and artillery – and the 'tail', that is logistic and support units. Second is the 'conceptual', which deals with thinking and military culture. In some armed forces this is formally expressed as 'doctrine', well described by the twentieth century British military theorist J.F.C. Fuller as the 'central idea of an army'. Finally, there is the moral component, or what makes people fight. This includes such factors as morale, leadership, and motivation. This concept of fighting power provides a useful, although not infallible, model which can be used to analyse armed forces at any point in history, providing suitable adjustments are made: substituting cavalry for armour, for instance.

There are many other examples of continuities in military history. The importance of logistics – the art and science of moving troops and equipment from place to place and keeping them in supply once they arrive there – has always been fundamental to military operations. Similarly, the statement of the Chinese military thinker Sun Tzu (c. 544 BC – 496 BC) 'If you know your enemies and know yourself,

you will not be imperilled in a hundred battles' points to the importance of military intelligence, and also of self-knowledge. Intelligence
is at the heart of the modern concept of 'Information Warfare'.

One should never lose sight of one of the fundamental facts about
war. It is a tragedy that brings about the death and maiming of
human beings, creates widows and orphans, destroys homes and
communities, and wrecks lives. The negative effects of war can be
very long lasting indeed. As late as 1980, in Britain there were 27,000
men drawing pensions as a result of the psychiatric damage done to
them during the First World War. The last British survivor of the
Western Front, Harry Patch, died in 2009, aged 111. He was affected
by the memory of his comrades killed in 1917 until the very end.

Yet the fact that war is so dreadful has not prevented it from
being a constant factor in history. The first organized battle that we
know much about was fought at Kadesh (c. 1275 BC), between the
Egyptian and Hittites in what is now Syria. To list, let alone describe,
the wars, battles and campaigns that have occurred since then would
take a thick book. The reason why war has been so prevalent perhaps rests in the aggressive impulses of humans, particularly males;
but an undeniable factor is that war can change things dramatically.
Millennia ago Sun Tzu wrote:

> The art of war is of vital importance to the State. It is a matter
> of life and death, a road either to safety or to ruin. Hence it is
> a subject of inquiry which can on no account be neglected.

War can decide the fate of tribes, states, nations and empires. It can
bring about freedom or slavery, prosperity or penury. It can be used
to smash one social and political system and impose another. The
'futility of war' is a phrase that is frequently heard in Britain. While
I would not say that there has never been a futile conflict, any objective study would surely conclude that war does change things, for
good or ill. The idea that is sometimes heard that *all* war is futile can
be rebutted by reference to the American Civil War (1861–65). The
Civil War is laden with ambiguities. Abraham Lincoln and the North

certainly did not enter the war determined that the South's 'Peculiar Institution' would be ended by force of arms; the war began as a conflict over whether the USA would split in two. Yet as the war evolved, the North sought to hurt the South by attacking the institution of slavery, resulting in the ending of human bondage across the restored United States. Although released from slavery, African-Americans did not achieve full civil rights for another century. Like every war, the war between the States caused untold misery, but this conflict brought about an undoubted good. Whatever else it may have been, the American Civil War was not 'futile'.

The Soviet revolutionary Leon Trotsky declared that 'war was the locomotive of history'. He was right. War, especially the total wars of the nineteenth and twentieth centuries, has been inextricably linked with revolutionary change. Revolutions have brought about wars, and wars spawn revolutions. The French Revolution of 1789 set in train a series of events that by 1793 had led to the new Republic being at war with most of *Ancien Regime* monarchical Europe. The revolutionary ideas of liberty, fraternity and equality were exported by French bayonets, and newly conquered territories had puppet governments of republican form imposed upon them. A similar process took place in 1944–45, when the Red Army of the Soviet Union imposed Marxist-Leninist regimes on the states of eastern Europe 'liberated' in the course of its advances at the end of the Second World War. Likewise, it is impossible to understand the rise of Fascism and Nazism in Italy and Germany without comprehending the importance of the First World War. The liberal regime in Italy was fatally weakened by the war. Imperial Germany was destroyed, and its liberal democratic successor of the Weimar Republic was built on shaky foundations. Italian and German society was radicalised and brutalised by the Great War and proved fertile ground for extremist political movements.

It should also be said that liberal democracy can result from war. Democratic West Germany and modern Japan arose from the ruins of their wartime predecessors, with the victorious Western allies, especially the USA, ensuring that the successor states followed a democratic, capitalist path. Perhaps surprisingly, the outcome of the Cold War (1945–91) was the collapse of Marxist-Leninist regimes across much of Eastern Europe and their replacement by more-or-less democratic political systems. By contrast, the overt attempt by the USA and UK to bring about 'regime change' in Iraq in 2003, to replace Saddam Hussein's Baathist rule with a pluralist democracy, appears at the time of writing (2009) to have been a failure.

A Case Study: Armed Forces

The breadth of the subjects included in the portmanteau term War Studies can be illustrated by examining the institution of armed forces. Armed forces come in different varieties such as volunteer professional troops, conscripts, part-time militia, paramilitaries (such as the frontier guards or riot police of some states) and mercenaries. Regular, professional armies, navies and air forces are 'total' organisations. Their members are under discipline, committed to serve the state 24 hours a day, seven days a week. The single most important factor is that they have 'unlimited liability'. Their very lives are at the service of the state. They volunteered in knowledge that they may be wounded or die as a result of their service. There have been many conscript forces in history in which 'National Servicemen' or 'draftees' have become part of total organisations with unlimited liability, regardless of their personal motivations to fight. The study of armed forces has attracted sociologists, anthropologists and political scientists as well military and social historians, while combat motivation has engendered a plethora of studies approaching the subject from a number of angles, including interdisciplinarity.

As for the apparently simple question 'what are armed forces for?' one simple and obvious answer is that they are Clausewitzian instruments of national policy, used by governments to achieve political aims such defeating an external enemy. That is certainly one of the uses of armed forces, but not the only one. They can also be used as for internal security, to crush rebellion: actual, as in the French

Revolution, or potential, as when the Chinese People's Liberation Army, bloodily destroyed the pro-democracy protests in Tiananmen Square in 1989. A milder use of armed forces is the deployment of military units to lend assistance to the civil authorities. Such aid can be armed or unarmed, and range from support to police faced by riot, crime and terrorism, to humanitarian work such as rescue from floods or other natural disasters, operating essential services in times of crisis (such as the use of the army in Britain to man 'Green Goddess' fire engines during the 1978 fireman's strike), to out-and-out strike breaking.

This list does not exhaust the uses of armed forces. Even if they do nothing other than stay in their barracks, mere possession of armed forces can be prestigious, on the grounds that a state isn't really a state without them. The acquisition of nuclear weapons by India and Pakistan was arguably as much about national prestige as security. Armed forces can have maintenance of the government regime in power as their primary task. The reluctance of Napoleon to commit his Imperial Guard to battle owed much to this fact, as did the role allocated to Saddam Hussein's Iraqi Republican Guard.

Another essentially political rather than military role for armed forces is as instruments of national cohesion and social control. Mass conscription in nineteenth century Europe allowed the French state to attempt to use the army to inculcate patriotism and approved cultural values, to turn 'peasants into Frenchmen'. Similarly, the post-Second World War West German state used the *Bundeswehr* as a means of transmitting liberal democratic values to generations of young men.

Moreover, armies, being inherently political bodies, can become significant actors in national politics. Senior officers' jobs demand that they exercise a political role. It is but a short step from legitimate engagement in the political process to active intervention. In his classic work *The Man on Horseback* (1962) S.F. Finer set out four levels of military activity in politics. In ascending order of seriousness, they were: 'Influence'; 'Blackmail'; 'Displacement'; and 'Supplantment'.

Terms such as 'Praetorianism' and 'Bonapartism' given to varieties of military activity in politics are testimony to the prevalence of the problem across time and space. They refer to the ability of the Roman Praetorian Guard to make and unmake emperors, and the achievement of one of the most successful generals of the French Revolutionary wars in seizing power in a coup (and in later crowning himself emperor). In modern post-colonial states, the army has often proved to be the best organised, best educated, and most technologically advanced part of the new country. The virtually inevitable result was that in states such as Pakistan and Nigeria the military has played an active role in politics, intervening to establish military regimes.

The study of armed forces thus demonstrates the variety of academic approaches encompassed in the term 'War Studies'. Building on traditional military history, it draws upon a variety of disciplines to create a holistic, and nuanced, view of the subject.

The Development of War Studies

Authors from Thucydides onwards have adopted an approach to scholarship that we would now see as sitting within the field of War Studies. The discipline has emerged in its present configuration since 1945. In part this was a response to the Cold War, when academic study was called upon to inform decision-makers. It was also a way of repackaging military history at a time, in the 1960s and 1970s, when it was deeply unfashionable in academia, being considered by some as intellectually disreputable. This reflected much liberal academic opposition to the Vietnam War, as well as a reaction to the old-fashioned 'drum and trumpet' tradition of military history. A new school of historians of 'war and society' grew up as this subject was seen as having intellectual validity. Thus the study of war crept onto the syllabus of the university history department.

The establishment of the Department of War Studies at King's College London in the 1960s was a significant step, not least because it brought together a diverse group of scholars of war, whose eclectic interests almost defined the discipline. Other groupings at universities and military academies across the Anglophone world developed, although the study of war never entirely overcame the negative connotations it had in some academic circles. One unhealthy trend of the 1970s and 1980s was the marginalisation of military history by some scholars and institutions that specialised in contemporary issues: to some extent it continues to this day. This was particularly evident in the educational curriculum of the British army, although considerable steps have been taken towards a more balanced approach.

War Studies can be an applied subject. Practitioners can influence government policy and help to develop military doctrine. The levels of war are recognised by British and American militaries owe much to the study of military history. They are: Strategy (often divided into grand strategy, the use of all instruments of power to achieve national goals, and military strategy, the use of military resources to those ends); the Operational level, the use of campaigns and operations to achieve strategic goals, and Tactics, the fighting of battles and engagements. Moreover it is no coincidence that the panel appointed in 2009 by the British government to conduct an enquiry into the 2003 Iraq War included a Professor of War Studies at King's College London, and a distinguished war historian and biographer of Winston Churchill. Neither should anyone be surprised to find that the British armed forces' senior operationally focused course for future high commanders includes three military historians as an integral part of the team. This emphasis on the relevance and usefulness of War Studies sets it aside from many cognate subjects in the arts and humanities.

At the end of the Cold War in the early 1990s, there was a brief period of optimism about the future which manifested itself in the so-called 'peace dividend'. Such optimism proved to be short lived, as the world moved from one phase of conflict into another. The evolution of War Studies has reflected this change, as a heavy emphasis on Cold War security and nuclear strategy gave way to different concerns (and some academics hastily reinvented themselves as contemporary historians). Today, in the era of wars in Iraq and Afghanistan, the long-neglected subject of counter-insurgency is enjoying a new lease of life among academics. War Studies has moved to embrace theology and religious affairs, as religion has emerged as a major force in international relations and as a source of conflict.

In a parallel development, the more historical branch of War Studies has not stood still. A recent and very welcome development is the partial bridging of the gulf between scholars who concentrate on the operational side of the First World War and those who study its cultural history. The result is the gradual creation of a more inclusive and altogether richer history of the war. War Studies, then, has evolved and will continue to evolve. At a time when armed conflict remains endemic, when governments and Non-State Actors alike continue to adhere to Clausewitzian policies of using violence as a means of attaining political goals, War Studies retains its relevance as a vehicle for understanding the world in which we live.

The Essays

The collection of essays in this Reader has been selected to demonstrate the breadth and diversity of the subject. The first, by Peter W. Gray, lays essential foundations by posing the deceptively simple question 'Why study military history'? He is not the first person to address this subject, and he not only provides a very useful synthesis of some previous thinking in the area, but also moves the debate forward. Gray wrote from the perspective of a serving senior officer in the Royal Air Force (he is now Senior Research Fellow in Air Power Studies at the University of Birmingham). Writing in part at least for a military audience, he argues for the utility of military history as providing 'analytical tools' for decision makers, but warns against the dangers of cherry-picking examples to support particular ideas or cases. Gray, in short, sees military history as being useful for the military practitioner, but he is realistic about its limitations. He quotes Michael Howard's dictum that 'Clio is like the Delphic oracle; it is only in retrospect, and usually too late, that we understand what she was trying to say', although the tone of Grey's argument suggests that he is not as pessimistic as this quotation would suggest.

In our second article a distinguished Anglo-American scholar, Colin S. Gray, tackles another apparently straightforward subject. 'Why is Strategy Difficult' is an inter-disciplinary piece. Gray, who is currently Professor of International Politics and Strategic Studies at the University of Reading, is a political scientist who uses military history to very good effect. The argument of the article can be summed up in a telling quotation he takes from Clausewitz: 'everything in strategy is very simple, but that does not mean that everything is very easy'. Gray's incisive analysis of why simple things can be very difficult to achieve addresses a subject that runs through history, as his choice of examples from the Hannibal to Kosovo in 1999 indicates. At its centre is the Clausewitzian concept of friction, which can be crudely described as the idea (born out by experience) that anything that can go wrong in war, does. Gray is scathing about optimists who believe that technology can solve problems of strategy, as the nature of the problem has not fundamentally changed over the years. His article is a useful corrective to those who judge strategy on its artistic merits, as it were. Two much-praised generals, Hannibal and Napoleon, Gray points out, won battles but ultimately lost their respective wars. 'You do not have to win elegantly; you just have to win'.

One peculiar form of strategy is the waging of total war. Definitions of total war vary, with some scholars seeing it as a synonym for a large war, or for a 'modern' conflict. Others focus on its bloodiness and the removal of moral constraints. However a total war is best viewed as an 'all out' conflict in which all available national resources are directed towards the defeat of the enemy with extreme ruthlessness. Total war is essentially a twentieth century phenomenon, although elements of totality can be detected in earlier wars. Whether or not the American Civil War (1861–65) was a true total war is a contentious point. John Bennett Walters' 1948 article 'General William T. Sherman and Total War' is one of the seminal treatments of the topic. He was writing in the aftermath of the most destructive war in history, at a time when the prospect of an even worse conflict appeared very real. Bennett saw Sherman as deliberately waging war on Southern civilians during his 1864–65 march through Georgia and the Carolinas. His men destroyed the economy of the Confederacy and demoralized the population, thus indirectly attacking the morale of Confederate soldiers. Walters was a Southerner, and viewed Sherman's methods as effective but counterproductive, in that they left a legacy of hatred in the Southern states of the reunited union. Although dated, Walters' article remains worthwhile as an introduction to some of the key themes in debates on total war, which remains a controversial subject in War Studies. It is also an important reminder that historians' ideas cannot be divorced from their influences and environment.

Coalition warfare has been an enduring facet of strategy, and the fundamental challenges of bringing together two or more states, sometimes on an *ad hoc* basis, to make war on a common enemy have changed little over the centuries. Even successful coalitions, like the Anglo-Americans in the Second World War or the US-led coalition in the First Gulf War, are invariably beset by political and military problems. Unsuccessful coalitions can be extremely vulnerable to disintegration followed by recriminations and even hostilities between the erstwhile partners. In the aptly entitled 'Disjointed Allies', Holger H. Herwig of the University of Calgary examines the Austro-Hungarian/German coalition in 1914. In spite of having been allies before the war, the Germans and Austrians did not find coalition warfare easy. In an insightful article, Herwig argues that the problems experienced by the two powers were not institutional but rather 'political and personal'. Both powers 'pursued national strategies that were not mutually beneficial', and the senior soldiers on either side, Moltke and Conrad, failed to develop the sort of personal relationship which might have overcome some of the problems. Placing Herwig's work into a wider perspective, such problems have been experienced in many other coalitions.

As noted earlier, irregular conflict, particularly in its forms of guerrilla warfare and terrorism, has risen high on the War Studies agenda in recent years. In '"Freies Deutschland" Guerrilla Warfare in East Prussia, 1944–1945', Perry Biddiscombe provides an unusual sidelight on the subject by examining anti-Nazi guerrillas parachuted into East Prussia by the Soviets. Whereas successful guerrilla organizations, such as Mao's Communists during the Chinese Civil War, were able to thrive because they were 'fish' operating in the 'sea' of a friendly population, these anti-Nazi partisans were isolated from the wider population, lacked popular support and hence were unsuccessful. Biddiscombe's analysis of the reasons for the failure of this attempt at stirring up an insurgency, especially the fact that the 'mood, psychology and culture of the population' in East Prussia was inimical to active opposition to the regime, can be applied more widely. Certainly, there are obvious parallels with Che Guevara's failed attempt to create an insurgency in Bolivia in the 1960s.

In the 1990s a lively debate developed about the existence or otherwise of a contemporary 'Revolution in Military Affairs' (RMA), spurred on by the Coalition victory in the First Gulf War of 1991. The debate became entangled in an older historical debate about 'military revolutions'. In his article reproduced here, Andrew N. Liaropoulos makes the point that there is no accepted definition of an RMA, and provides a useful overview of the paradigms of the subject. He goes on to give two case studies, based on existing literature: the Napoleonic Wars and the First World War. Here he unwittingly underlines the difficulty of using military history for contemporary purposes, for his polarised characterization of the German and British armies in 1914–18 (the former opting for developed command, the latter for centralization) would not be accepted by all historians, myself included. He concludes that RMAs are 'sociopolitical' phenomena as well as 'war-fighting models', and places technology into a proper perspective. The article is both a sensible contribution to the historical debate and a useful corrective to some contemporary military thinking.

The legal and ethical dimensions of war, and its brutal realities, are discussed by Barbara Donagan in 'Atrocity, War Crime and Treason in the English Civil War'. As she noted, this seventeenth century conflict is not usually regarded as a particularly savage war – certainly not in comparison with the contemporaneous Thirty Years War on the continent. English soldiers were well aware of the horrors being perpetrated in Germany, and clung to 'the norms of war', deliberately exercising restraint, by for instance insisting on the protection of women and children, and humane treatment for prisoners. Nonetheless, atrocities did occur, and Donagan argues that over time the codes that helped moderate behaviour in war were observed less. This article gives a nuanced view of some aspects of an early modern example of a perennial challenge: war is brutal and destructive, so how can its brutality and destructiveness be limited? Behind that headline are a whole range of problems that continue to face armed forces and governments to the present day. Does the reason for fighting a war, and its conduct, conform to classic principles of just war theory? Once armed conflict begins, how is it to be controlled? How can the impact on civilians be minimized? Without consideration of the ethics and laws of armed conflict, War Studies is woefully incomplete.

One of the most significant developments in War Studies in recent years has been the fruitful engagement of cultural and military historians. Jay Winter, now of Yale University, is the doyen of cultural historians of the Great War, and his examination of shell shock and cultural history is a typically stimulating piece. It was originally an introduction to a collection of essays (not reproduced here) but stands alone as a piece of scholarship in its own right, arguing that shellshock could 'turn from a diagnosis into a metaphor' for the type of trauma-inducing industrialised war endured between 1914 and 1918. He links it to British political culture between the wars, social class and the idea of a 'lost generation'. The article stands as an excellent introduction to an important sub-genre of War Studies.

War, as we have seen is an inherently political activity, but studies of politicians and war tend to look at the highest levels – heads of government, cabinets, ministers, presidents, prime ministers. Yet wars affect politics, and politicians, at all levels, and this is particularly important in liberal democracies where the need to maintain popular consent is paramount. America's major period of involvement in the Vietnam War from 1965 to 1973 is a particularly fruitful area of study. Three American academics, Scott Sigmund Gartner, Gary M. Segura and Bethany A. Barratt in 'War Casualties, Policy Positions, and the Fate of Legislators' examined elections to the US Senate from 1966 to 1972. They conclude that military deaths, among other factors, did affect the stance that candidates took on the war in Vietnam and had a measurable impact on the elections themselves, although local circumstances were important. Their argument that 'citizens are well informed of local costs and sensitive to the positions of locally elected leaders' has important implications for democratic states waging wars, particularly when the conflict is controversial.

The collection concludes with a thoughtful piece that deals with a major sub-theme in War Studies: the interface between international relations and strategy. The final essay discusses an issue that threatens to be a major factor in the twenty-first century: the emergence of China as a superpower, with military might to match its economic strength; and how the USA will react to such a development. Although major inter-state war currently seems a distant possibility, Colin S. Gray and others have warned that it simply cannot be ruled out in the future. Jonathan D. Pollock of the US Naval War College gives a sober assessment of the state of play of the Sino-American relationship. He argues that 'the latent elements of strategic rivalry (if not outright confrontation)' are already in place. At present, neither Washington nor Beijing have fully thought through their strategy vis-a-vis the other, leaving the door open to either future insecurity or cooperation.

1

Why Study Military History?

AIR COMMODORE PETER W. GRAY, RAF

The lessons of history are never clear. Clio is like the Delphic oracle: it is only in retrospect, and usually too late, that we understand what she was trying to say.

Michael Howard[1]

It's the steady force-feeding of the same old horse pills of history.

An anonymous naval captain[2]

In his essay on 'The Use and Abuse of Military History', Professor Sir Michael Howard highlighted the problems of drawing from history and either failing to heed the lessons, or drawing the wrong ones. He notes a 'depressingly close analogy' between the mistakes made by Austrian commanders in their conflict with Napoleon in Italy in 1796 and 1797 and those committed by the British in the desert operations against Rommel in 1941 and 1942; both were overly concerned with security, or what today may be called 'force protection' – an analogy with potentially very worrying overtones.

The scope for the misuse of history was typified by the classic situation in which the French General Staff applied the lessons of World War I trench warfare in their preparations for their defence against the Third Reich. At first sight this may seem excusable, but a more detailed examination shows that the French actually applied the lessons of 1916 rather than the more relevant ones of 1918. Ironically the staffs of the Wehrmacht and the embryo Luftwaffe expended considerable energy in the interwar years analysing the lessons of history, trends in technology and their likely impact on warfare.[3] In some instances the ensuing doctrine, such as Blitzkrieg, has been given almost mythical status.

There is a further problem in this area and that is one of proving causal links. It is very easy to say that because an individual was present at a given juncture of time, he must have been influenced by concurrent events, and this therefore was key to the formulation of future policy. This is particularly relevant to the likes of Lord Trenchard and Sir Arthur Harris. It is very easy to draw casual conclusions from the latter's experiences in colonial policing duties and apply then to his thinking on the strategic bomber offensive. It may actually be more instructive to look at Harris's experiences operating over Passchendaele, or attempting to shoot down Zeppelins over London. A rigorous historical approach should highlight the truth of the matter; and if this is too optimistic an outlook, then awareness of the pitfalls will at least help.

If the study of history is so fraught with problems, and either so easy to get wrong or difficult to get right, depending on one's view of the contents of the glass, why bother at all? To many military men and women, the benefits of the allied disciplines of doctrine, strategy and military history could either be summarised on the back of the proverbial cigarette packet, or more likely consigned to a broom cupboard at the end of a corridor only to surface when a search is undertaken for some arcane piece of memorabilia that had once been donated by a venerable senior officer now scheduled to revisit the haunts of his former glory. The concept of recording today's events with an eye to the interests of future historians combing the archives seems to many to be preposterous[4] – particularly in an era where capacity for routine staff work is occupied by the latest management fad or the accumulation of apparently meaningless statistics.

These practical constraints on the acquisition and retention of primary source material are further exacerbated by the limits on intellectual capacity; the modern serviceman or woman needs an almost encyclopaedic knowledge of everything from their operational systems through to the latest legislation on health and safety or individual rights.

It could therefore be argued that all that is required from history is the accumulation of the recent experiences of the latest operations, detachments and trials. The reality, however, is that this distillation of 'what has worked best' is the seed corn of tactical level doctrine.[5] The same academic approach produces operational doctrine and so on. By stealth, therefore, history, albeit recent history, is an indispensable part of everyday military business – even if many would deny their link with either doctrine or study of the past! With the rate of change of technology so marked in all areas of warfare from network enabled operations to air power, it is particularly important that we develop the analytical skills necessary to sort wheat from chaff. Even if we accept the de facto omnipresence of military history, is there a requirement to study the discipline more formally? The real danger in not doing so is evident from the transition between the deceptively simple accumulations of 'what has worked best' to the calamitous pitfalls described by Professor Howard.

The question 'Why study the history of a particular campaign or operation?' or the somewhat broader debate on why we should study military history is of interest to more than just the potential military historian. The question has equal validity for academics across a range of fields, diplomats, officials, journalists and indeed anyone who is likely to cite history, or even a humble precedent, in the course of their routine business. Such a wide-ranging audience is entitled to a comprehensive answer, starting with an examination of why we should study history at all. This article will then look at the nuances of military history as an extension of the discipline prior to reappraising the benefits and pitfalls of the subject in the wider field of strategy and doctrine.

Why Study History (and what is it)?

This question is at the heart of all historical endeavour and is the essence of the study of the past. At the same time, it is the bane of student historians at all levels; those in schools can attempt to duck the issue by explaining away their choice of studies because of a dislike of maths, or whatever the alternatives may be. But undergraduates and the vast majority of their more learned peers will have had to give some thought to this issue and the wider discipline of historiography. The literature is inevitably extensive and, almost equally inevitably, much of it is impenetrable on first inspection. Some authors seek to ascertain what history actually 'is'.[6] Others 'pursue' the subject or write 'on history' itself.[7] Yet more actively 'defend their studies'[8] while their colleagues ally history to social theory.[9] An exhaustive review of these theories is well beyond the scope of this analysis, with only room for a cursory examination; the curious are recommended to consider the works endnoted as useful starters.

Professor Howard has argued that there is no such thing as 'history'.[10] He contends that the subject is merely what historians have written and that they, by their very nature, are an integral part of the process. This means that no matter how objective they attempt to be, historians imbue their work with their own values and cultural perspectives – and this is before perceptions and prejudices are superimposed. The historiography of the bombing of Dresden is a stark example of this, especially as one of the earliest accounts was published by the highly controversial David Irving.[11] There can therefore be no absolute account of history and nor can it be considered to be a closed box. The Dutch historian Pieter Geyl famously suggested that 'history is an argument without end'.

Historical research can be pursued by a logical method in which a thesis is postulated, tested against the evidence, and reviewed if necessary. History is, however, very much a humanity rather than a science, not least because the principle of repeatability cannot be applied; successive generations of scientists should be able to replicate the findings of their predecessors – historians approach what are ostensibly equivalent occurrences from vastly differing perspectives with the ensuing ranges of interpretations. The historian must consider not only what may have happened in the past, but also attempt to infer what conditions were like. In this emerging context, the historian can begin to postulate how the social, intellectual and political structures developed.

From this, the logical progression is to begin to analyse why events then occurred. At no stage, however, can the historian actually know what people thought; even supposed contemporaneous diaries are fraught with potential difficulties. But this does not render the process of enquiry any the less worthwhile. An analytical approach is, of course, essential in any academic endeavour; the postulation of a thesis and the subsequent arguing of evidence are fundamental.

Professor Arthur Marwick takes recourse in the dictionary definition of history – learning or knowing by enquiry. History is therefore an interpretation of the past in which 'a serious effort has been made to filter *out* myth and fable'.[12] It should therefore come as no surprise to confirm that not all that purports to be history is any more than myth, fable and legend. It is worth dwelling on the meanings of these terms. A myth is defined as a 'traditional narrative usually involving supernatural or imaginary persons'; a fable is a 'story, especially a supernatural one, not based on fact'; and a legend is a 'traditional story sometimes popularly regarded as historical but unauthenticated'.[13]

If we combine Howard and Marwick it becomes immediately evident that some of what we may have solemnly considered to be history is no more than earlier scholars' interpretation of myth and legend – the tales of King Arthur and his Knights of the Round Table spring instantly to mind, but there are arguably as many legends emanating from the Strategic Bomber Offensive in World War II or the Vietnam War.[14] Human nature is such that we are intrinsically fascinated by the past, by myths and legends, history and archaeology (or at least as depicted on popular television series[15]). Unless we are content to swallow unthinkingly this diet of what may potentially be fables, we must have recourse to a more scholarly approach to the past.

It is not, however, sufficient to take the works of an eminent scholar down from their dusty position on the library shelves and be confident that we have a work of pure history in our hands – no matter how eminent the historian. In his biography of A. J. P. Taylor, Adam Sisman describes one of the most famous (and controversial) historians of the twentieth century. His subject was the author of major works of considerable learning such as *The Struggle for Mastery in Europe* (Oxford: OUP 1954); he was also described, somewhat disparagingly, as being the 'star in his studio' referring to his hugely successful television appearances.[16] Taylor also wrote *The Origins of the Second World War;*[17] this was immediately controversial, not least because of its thesis that Hitler had stumbled into his foreign conquests rather than them being part of a pre-ordained plan. The controversy and debate continue today with books reappraising his work.[18] Woe betide the putative history student who only reads one book on a given subject![19]

The complexities of the discipline should not, however, act as a deterrent. Knowledge of the past is an essential part of our attempts to understand the present. Marwick compares the history of the community to the memory of an individual.[20] In a complex society, the analogy can arguably be extended to a comparison between a sophisticated system of historical analysis and the genetic detail recorded on DNA. The direct implication is that without such collective memory, a society would be little more than an amorphous mass. In the same way that DNA can be 'fingerprinted', so a society, from its earliest beginnings in a cave, will bear the imprints of its collective experience. In its earliest guise this will have been a mix of practical experience on hunting and fire making techniques. These will, in time, have been embellished with superstition, ritual, songs and legends.

As society has matured, these have become more complex, with neighbouring clans telling of their conquests, rivalry and battles whilst lamenting hard times and defeats. Some of these have been committed to text, others have been passed down orally, in song and verse.[21] So tradition has oft matured into a primitive form of history that has, in turn, served to solidify the faultlines between societies; a glance at the use and misuse of history in the Balkans highlights the dangers of this process. An understanding of the rifts, nursed grievances and remembrance of earlier glories became essential fodder for the embryo statesmen and warriors. The direct inference, therefore, is that the better an understanding we require of the situation in which we find ourselves depends crucially on our appreciation of the route taken by all concerned. This provides a more than sufficient justification for the study of history as a window on the past through which we can interpret contemporary actions more rationally.

If we hope to take our efforts one step further and learn lessons from history, the study will almost certainly need to be more precise and more exacting. Thucydides apologised for the lack of romance in his history of the Peloponnesian War, pointing out that he would be content if his work was to be 'judged useful by those inquirers who desire an exact knowledge of the past as an aid to the understanding of the future'; in short, it was to be a possession for all time.[22] The search for lessons from history is almost as frustrating a task as seeking to find the Holy Grail or Camelot.

For some students, historical lessons are analogous to a legal precedent that can be applied with precision and certainty. The reality of the technical application of legal precedent, however, shows that this is far from being a simple process. The case has to be studied in full and the judgement analysed to reveal the *ratio decidendi* (that which was decided) and separate this from the clutter of what was also said (*obiter dicta*). The circumstances of the case have to be directly similar and relevant to those on which our learned counsel is seeking to rely. This is genuinely frustrating in law (or highly remunerative depending on one's standpoint), but can be almost impossible in history. One can learn principles of strategy from Karl von Clausewitz or Baron Henri Jomini, but the opportunity to replicate Napoleon's victories is unlikely beyond the sandtable or the wargame.

Exact comparisons across the decades provide neither a blueprint for action[23] nor precise guidance around the pitfalls to be avoided.

But this does not mean that an examination of the processes involved by which a group of nations arrived at the brink of war is not worthy of study. By the same token, analysis of the structure of a society may offer valuable insight into the forces at work that resulted in the events that subsequently evolved. This latter French-originated school of thought (known as *Annales* after their journal) emphasised the importance of the study of humanity and mankind as an intrinsic part of the study of history.

History may therefore be studied for a range of reasons from the eradication of myth and legend through to the impact of human nature on the development of society. Whatever theory is chosen to justify the chosen course of study, it could be argued that the intellectual exercise is worth the while *in its own right*. In the same way that an athlete trains by running or in the gym, rather than because of a need to get from A to B, so the historian is exercising powers of judgement, analysis and dedication that have relevance both to enhancing our understanding of the past and to improving our appreciation of society. Mankind's continuing reliance on force as an instrument of policy makes warfare as enduring a part of society as economic or social order. Although it is also therefore worthy of study in its own right, it has other claims on our attention.

Why Military History?

At the simplest level, military history is worthy of study for pure entertainment value alone. A glance through the schedules of even the terrestrial television channels will attest to the popularity of the genre ranging from collections of rare colour footage of World War II ('Because war is not black and white') through to reappraisals of key events – often on their anniversaries. Similarly, the local high street bookstore (in the United Kingdom and North America at least – it is less popular in Germany for example) will almost invariably contain well-stocked sections on military history. Specialist military history book clubs flourish and there is a lively trade in secondhand material from enthusiasts' colour guides featuring the camouflage of their favourite aircraft type to the memoirs of air marshals like Lords Tedder and Douglas. War walks remain popular events as do re-enactments of famous or local conflicts.

There is a duty beholden to most servicemen to have some knowledge of military history. This can take the form of natural pride in the activities of the regiment or squadron of which the individual has become part. The more cynical approach points out the occasional passing of examinations may act as a spur for the study of military history. Beyond the parochial detail of battle honours and key dates, a wider knowledge of the particular form of warfare quickly follows with, for example, considerable study into air or sea power and its application. At its most basic level, this takes the minimalist form of merely knowing (or being interested in, or entertained by) the story – in other words, basic narrative history detailing the sequence of events and describing the factors evident to the participants.

The newcomer to military history who is seeking to research a given topic may be well advised to seek out an authoritative account to act as a platform from which to branch out. John Terraine's *The Right of the Line: The Royal Air Force in the European War 1939–1945*[24] is a classic example that has been recommended to generations of staff college students and of course has considerable appeal to a wider readership. Following this example, an alternative could be the official history written shortly after the event by Denis Richards and Hilary St George Saunders and published in 1953/54.[25] The virtue in following such a route is that it is often well trodden having served so many as a common starting point.

Military history (and indeed history more generally) can go beyond the entertaining, inspirational,[26] descriptive and informative. It can also be critical, educational and prescriptive.[27] The critical application of history is essential if we are to avoid the myths and legends – or what J.F.C. Fuller referred to as the 'Obsession of Traditions'.[28] Myths inevitably arise for many reasons. On one hand there is a natural reluctance to speak ill of the dead – especially when they may have paid the ultimate cost with the loss of their own

lives and those of their colleagues. The counter argument is that some
history is written specifically to excoriate the subject (Field-Marshal
Lord Haig being a prime example). Some myths are maintained as
part of either an ongoing, or long expired, information operation
(propaganda in old money) or campaign; it may well be that it suits
most concerned to continue this as could be argued with nuclear
deterrence theory or coercion.[29] Others have arisen from an uncritical acceptance of cinema renditions of famous events such as the
Battle of Britain,[30] or more recently, the capture of Enigma machines
and codes from German U-boats.[31] The elimination of myths – past
and present – is essential if history is to be used in a genuinely educational sense.

Knowledge of history, or its influence on decision-makers, is frequently cited. Winston Churchill wrote, and was in turn influenced by,
history. Anthony Eden was determined not to follow 'The Appeasers'
and this was evident in his approach to Nasser in the lead up to the
1956 Suez crisis. Social scientists have developed their theories in the
uses and abuses of history in decision making with *Thinking in Time:
The Uses of History for Decision-Makers* by Neustadt and May as
a classic example.[32] Detailed analysis of a single event (The Cuban
Missile Crisis) is painstakingly described in *Essence of a Decision* by
Graham T. Allison. [33] But this process is fraught with difficulties if
the wrong lessons of history are even identified, let alone learned
and then internalised. Professor Howard sides with the old adage,
pointing out that 'History does not repeat itself – historians repeat
one another.'[34]

It is also extremely easy for historians to raid 'the storehouse', to
use Professor Colin Gray's analogy, in order to locate examples that
will immediately support virtually any hypothesis.[35] The controversy
that surrounded the publication of Robert A. Pape's *Bombing to
Win – Air Power and Coercion in War*[36] is highlighted by the follow-on
book edited by Benjamin Frankel – *Precision and Purpose, Debating
Robert A. Pape's Bombing to Win.*[37]

The reality is that cause-and-effect is often very difficult to prove
with no 'directing staff pink solution' to every episode. Even where
linkages appear to be either present or logical, there is a lamentable

tendency for historians to join events where no connection exists. Rather the historian should highlight the dynamic processes where the Clausewitzian frictions of weather, faulty decisions and personalities impact on unique sets of circumstances. That no blueprint emerges does not make the study any less worthwhile. Professor Geoffrey Till has suggested that 'the chief utility of history for the analysis of present and future lies in its ability not to point out lessons, but to isolate things that need thinking about'.[38] A refinement of this view would be to suggest that historical examples can, and indeed should, be used as a set of intellectual tools. These may be pertinent to every putative user of history, but it could be readily suggested that the military practitioner has more need of historical example than most.

In the first instance history, or rather historians, are only too willing to use the discipline to criticise soldiers, sailors and airmen for their failings in battle whether real or imagined. Alan Clark's emotively entitled book on World War I is a suitable example whereby the British (and Empire) leadership on the Western Front in 1915 was unfavourably compared with the men 'who fought like lions',[39] but were led by the 'Donkeys'. The shelves are inevitably full of autobiographies; some are merely bland while many more, equally inevitably, are self-serving. The biographies, with notable exceptions (especially when the subject and his or her immediate family have long departed and are therefore unlikely to be awkward guests at the book launch), tend towards being hagiographies leaving hapless readers to wonder how the war in question was not won earlier by the noble deeds of the subject.[40] Willingness to pronounce on failure is part of human nature.

By the same token, it is equally natural to select the lesson from history that supports the chosen thesis. The new recruit at Sandhurst, Dartmouth or indeed Cranwell, now that some history has been restored to the syllabus of the latter, is faced with an unenviable morass of material to ingest if all of the collected wisdom is to be distilled into a bedrock of experience.

Most, if not all, military practitioners willingly extol the virtues of both education and training as being necessary throughout their careers. But training will only cover some 80 per cent of the ground as there is no substitute for the 'real thing' with lives at stake and much else to be lost or won. No amount of simulation, special effects or exercise injects can replicate this – no matter how realistic the training may be. Professor Howard equates this to a surgeon whose only operation is a life saving one after a career spent practising on dummies.[41] Although this may seem somewhat far-fetched, he goes on to suggested that fixation on running an army (or elements thereof) may become an end in itself – process becomes all-important.

Howard advocates the study of past conflicts as one possible way in which the inexperienced practitioner can prepare him or herself for the acid test. General Sir Miles Dempsey, who commanded a corps in North Africa and Italy (and later the Second Army in Normandy) under Montgomery, was a keen exponent of the battlefield tour and an officer who had developed an extremely well honed sense of the terrain on which he was about fight.[42]

History must be studied in breadth, depth and arguably most importantly in a proper context, not least because conflict is essentially between societies or elements thereof. Even a cursory inspection of the writings of Machiavelli reveals as much about the world in which he lived and operated as it does about his own thinking – the two are totally intertwined.

Strategy

The inevitable refinement on the use of military history and its influence on operations at all levels is to consider the history of martial thought (as opposed to General Hindsight). In his book, *Studies in British Military Thought, Debates with Fuller and Liddell Hart,* Professor Brian Holden Reid has described the 'gray area' (*sic*) between military history and the history of ideas.[43] Later in the same chapter, Holden Reid goes on to discuss the importance of Fuller's work *The Foundations of the Science of War*[44] in which the latter proclaimed that the art of war was actually founded on definite principles and laws. This attempt to order the chaos of the so-called

'Great War' was not an isolated phenomenon; there was a marked revival of interest in eighteenth century philosophers as well as burgeoning study of relatively original work. Nor was the aftermath of conflict a stranger as a catalyst for thinking on the principles of war. Clausewitz and Jomini both wrote extensively on Napoleon's victories in the years after Waterloo. Their work still repays the reading because of the scope and depth of their analysis.

Clausewitz defined strategy as being the 'use of the engagement for the purpose of the war'.[45] He goes on to point out that the strategist will define the aim for the entire operational side of the war. Without either wishing or needing to disappear down the proverbial rabbit-hole of definitions, it is worth citing Colin Gray's adaptation of Clausewitz, with strategy being 'the use that is made of force and the threat of force for the ends of policy'.[46] Given the importance of both deterrence theory, and coercion, in modern warfare the distinction is worth making. What is arguably more important to the scholar and military practitioner alike is the subsequent influence of their writings.

Some scholars, such as Clausewitz and Jomini, have been studied and read by countless generations of students in military colleges and wider academe. It has, however, to be said that few actually read, or understand, the whole works with many content to regurgitate the same old tired clichés – often out of context. Clausewitz's work has been subject to much secondary analysis, and comprehensive treatment of this is outside the scope of this paper. Those interested could do worse than to read the introductory essays by Michael Howard and Bernard Brodie in Howard and Peter Paret's translation of *On War*.[47]

The air power student will be aware of the writings of the Italian theorist General Guilio Douhet whose *Command of the Air* (1921) is widely considered to have been an influential tome in the interwar years. Dr Philip Meilinger points out that translations of excerpts of this book were available in US Air Service circles as early as 1923 and that Brigadier General William Mitchell (the famous US air power theorist) had met Douhet the year before.[48] *Command of the*

Air was, however, never required reading at the RAF Staff College and arguably had no influence on strategic air power thinking in the inter-war years in the United Kingdom.[49]

Given the undoubted influence of the Army Staff College at Camberley on its infant sibling (not least the new Commandant's yearning to replicate the stables and opportunities for riding) it is highly likely that Fuller would be at least as widely read at Andover as at Camberley. Fuller's suggestions, in 1923, that henceforth land and sea forces could be used to occupy territory 'after a moral victory had been won on land by aircraft' was an early taste of the strategic bombing debate that continues to arouse controversy.[50]

Further discussion on the development of this theory is again outside our scope, but it is worth differentiating what writing was influential *at the time* as opposed to what subsequent authors have taken from contemporary library shelves and then ascribed to earlier times. The need to situate events in their own context is, after all, at the heart of military history and thinking.

Conclusions

The answer as to why we should study history, military history or strategic thinking varies from an intellectual exercise in its own right, through the need to know the story and on to Dominick Graham's 'spectrum of categories: entertaining, informative, descriptive, inspirational, critical, educational and prescriptive'.[51] If we extend this to encompass the notion of history as an interpretation of the past in which a serious attempt is made to filter out myth and legend, the role of the discipline becomes both more demanding and more necessary. Given mankind's continuing reliance on the use of force as an instrument of policy, our interest in the past is ever more important. We need to shed the myths, fables and legends, of which military history has more than its fair share, if we are to learn anything from history. Tradition and fable have often matured into the fault lines between nations and between peoples. If we are to have anything approaching a reasonable understanding of the complex situations in which we are increasingly likely to find ourselves, dexterity with the analytical tools provided by the study of history is essential.

Notes

1 Michael Howard, 'The Use and Abuse of Military History', in *The Causes of War and other essays* (London: Temple Smith 1983) p. 195.
2 The unfortunate naval captain quoted was a student on the Higher Command and Staff Course at the Joint Services Command and Staff College. The article by Robert Fox, 'Combined college launches Forces into a new era', *Daily Telegraph*, 28 Feb. 2001, was published to coincide with the formal opening of the new building by HRH Prince Philip.
3 For a snapshot of the lessons on tank warfare see Alex Danchev, *Alchemist of War, the Life of Basil Liddell Hart* (London: Weidenfeld 1998) p. 226. On the Luftwaffe see James S. Corum, *The Luftwaffe, Creating the Operational Air War 1918–1940* (Lawrence: UP of Kansas 1997) Chapters 1 and 2. See in particular page 58ff. for the establishment of the air doctrine process.
4 Interview with Mr Sebastian Cox, Head of the Air Historical Branch for the Royal Air Force. It remains a constant bane of Branch life trying to ensure that RAF Form 540 Operational Record Books are submitted in a comprehensive, timely and usable format. An example that emanates from the other end of the spectrum occurred when this author was specifically tasked with writing the 29 (F) Squadron records when the unit was deployed to the Falklands in 1982.
5 For a more detailed review of the nature of doctrine see Peter W. Gray, 'Air Power and Joint Doctrine, An RAF Perspective' in *The Royal Air Force Air Power Review* 3/4 (Winter 2000) p. 5.
6 See for example, E. H. Carr, *What Is History?*, first published by Macmillan in 1961; a second edition followed in 1987 and has been reprinted many times.
7 John Tosh, *The Pursuit of History: Aims Methods and New Directions in the Study of Modern History*, 2nd edn. (London: Longman 1991) and Eric Hobsbawm, *On History* (London: Weidenfeld 1997).
8 Richard J. Evans, *In Defence of History* (London: Granta Books 1997).
9 Peter Burke, *History and Social Theory* (Cambridge: Polity Press 1992).
10 Michael Howard, *The Lessons of History* (Oxford: OUP 1991) p. 11.
11 David Irving, *The Destruction of Dresden*(London: Kimber 1963).
12 Arthur Marwick, *The Nature of History*, 3rd edn.(London: Macmillan 1989) p. 3.

[13] *Concise Oxford Dictionary*, 9th edn.

[14] For an excellent and scholarly review of Arthur in myth and reality see Leslie Alcock, *Arthur's Britain, History and Archaeology AD 367 – 634* (London: Penguin 1971).

[15] Take the *Timewatch* history series for example. Alternatively, on the date of writing the fact that terrestrial TV broadcast three archaeological programmes, *Meet the Ancestors* (BBC2 22 Jan. 2001), and two programmes based on maritime studies highlights the popularity of the genre.

[16] These did little to endear Taylor to the Oxford University establishment. The quotation was taken from an article in the *New Statesman* cited in Adam Sisman, *A.J.P. Taylor, A Biography* (London: Mandarin 1995) p. 265.

[17] A.J.P. Taylor, *The Origins of the Second World War*, first published by Hamish Hamilton in 1961 and still in print the world over.

[18] Gordon Martel (ed.), *The Origins of the Second World War Reconsidered: The A.J.P. Taylor Debate after Twenty-Five Years* (London: Routledge 1986).

[19] For what it is worth, a better bet on the subject would be either P.M.H. Bell, *The Origins of the Second World War in Europe* (London: Longman 1986) or R.J. Overy, *The Origins of the Second World War* (Harlow: Addison Wesley Longman 1987).

[20] Marwick, *The Nature of History* (note 12) p. 14.

[21] An excellent example of this genre includes *Beowulf* which was composed near to the end of the first millennium of our era; it is a great tale of epic proportions. An excellent translation by Seamus Heaney was published by Faber and Faber in 1999.

[22] Taken from *The Landmark Thucydides, A Comprehensive Guide to the Peloponnesian War*, Robert A. Straser (ed.) (New York: Touchstone 1998) p. 16.

[23] Tosh, *Pursuit of History* (note 7) p. 17.

[24] Published by Hodder and Stoughton, London, 1985.

[25] *The Royal Air Force 1939–1945: Vol. 1 The Fight at Odds, Vol. 2 The Fight Avails, Vol. 3 The Fight is Won*, HMSO, London, 1953ff.

[26] See for example, Air Cmdre Graham Pitchfork, *Men Behind the Medals* (London: Leo Cooper 1998).

[27] Dominick Graham, 'Stress Lines and Gray Areas: The Utility of the Historical Method to the Military Profession', in David A. Charters, Marc Milner and J. Brent Wilson (eds.), *Military History and the Military Profession* (Westport, CT: Praeger 1992) p. 147.

[28] Col. J.F.C. Fuller, *The Foundations of the Science of War* (London: Hutchinson 1926) p. 24.

[29] See the extensive list of air power myths offered by Noel F. Parrish in 'The Influence of Air Power upon Historians' in Lt. Col. Harry R. Borowski (ed.), *The Harmon Memorial Lectures in Military History, 1959–1987* (Washington DC: Office of Air Force History, USAF 1988) p. 31: these myths include Douhet, Dresden, Linebacker Losses and so forth.

[30] For a full analysis of this see Tony Aldgate, 'The Battle of Britain on Film' in Paul Addison and Jeremy A. Craig (eds.), *The Burning Blue: A New History of the Battle of Britain* (London: Pimilico 2000) p. 207.

[31] For an analysis of the former, see Peter W. Gray, 'The Battle of Britain – So We Already Know the Story?', *Royal Air Force Air Power Review 3/3* (Autumn 2000) p. 17.

[32] Published by Free Press, New York, 1986.

[33] Graham T. Allison, *Essence of Decision: Explaining the Cuban Missile Crisis* (London: Longman 1971). Hutchinson

[34] Howard, 'The Use and Abuse of Military History', in *Causes of War* (note 1) p. 191.

[35] Colin S. Gray, 'History for Strategists' in Geoffrey Till (ed.), *Seapower: Theory and Practice,* first published by Frank Cass as a special issue of *The Journal of Strategic Studies* 17/1 (March 1994) p. 10.

[36] Published by Cornell University Press, Ithaca, 1996.

[37] Published by Frank Cass, 2001.

[38] Geoffrey Till, *Maritime Strategy and the Nuclear Age* (Macmillan: London 1982) pp. 224–5.

[39] Alan Clark, *The Donkeys* (London: Hutchinson 1961). Even more remarkably Clark apparently made up the donkeys part of the quotation ascribed to German generals.

[40] A worthwhile example of a biography that aimed to balance many years of vilification was John Terraine, *Douglas Haig, The Educated Soldier,* first published by Hutchinson in 1963 and reissued in 2000 by Cassell, London. Andrew Boyle's biography of *Trenchard* is now very dated and such a worthy subject is due to be revisited. The title alone confirms the trend with Anthony Furse, *Wilfrid Freeman, The Genius Behind Allied Survival and Air Supremacy 1939 to 1945* (Staplehurst, Kent: Spellmount 1999).

[41] Howard (note 1) p. 194.

[42] Carlo D'Este, *Decision in Normandy: Unwritten Story of Montgomery and the Allied Campaign* (London: HarperCollins 1983) p. 60.

[43] Brian Holden Reid, *Studies in British Military Thought, Debates with Fuller and Liddell Hart* (Lincoln: Univ. of Nebraska Press 1998) p. 33.

[44] Fuller, *Foundations of the Science of War* (note 28).

[45] Carl von Clausewitz, edited and translated by Michael Howard and Peter Paret, On War, originally published by Princeton University Press in 1976 and subsequently included in the Everyman Library in 1993, p. 207. This version is used for page numbering and can be recommended for the introductory essays.

[46] Colin S. Gray, *Modern Strategy* (Oxford: OUP 1999) p. 17.

[47] Howard and Paret (note 45).

[48] Colonel Philip S. Meilinger (ed.), *The Paths of Heaven, The Evolution of Airpower Theory* (Maxwell AFB, ALA: Air UP 1997) p. 33

[49] Ibid. p. 32. See also Robin Higham, *The Military Intellectuals in Britain, 1918–1939* (New Brunswick, NJ: Rutgers UP 1966) pp. 257–9 and Wing Commander R.A. Mason, *The Royal Air Force Staff College 1922–1972* (Bracknell Staff College Pamphlet 1972) p. 5 in which Trenchard is described as using the words 'Command of the Air' in his inaugural address long before Douhet had been heard of on these shores.

[50] Col. J.F.C. Fuller, *The Reformation of War* (London: Hutchinson 1923) p. 148.

[51] Graham, 'Stress Lines and Gray Areas' (note 27) p. 147.

2

Why Strategy Is Difficult

COLIN S. GRAY*

My aim is to relate the nature of strategy to the character of its artistic application and to the unknowable context of the 21st century. The immodesty, even arrogance, of this endeavor is best conveyed through an anecdote about a meeting between Hannibal Barca and an armchair strategist. Hannibal suffered from what in this last century has been the German failing—winning battles but losing wars. Hannibal won all of his battles in the Second Punic War except, sadly for a Carthage that did not deserve him, the last one, against Scipio Africanus at Zama in 202 BC. He is reported to have had little patience with amateur critics.

> *According to Cicero (de Oratione), the great general when in exile in Ephesus was once invited to attend a lecture by one Phormio, and after being treated to a lengthy discourse on the commander's art, was asked by his friends what he thought of it. "I have seen many old drivellers," he replied, "on more than one occasion, but I have seen no one who drivelled more than Phormio."[1]*

The theme of this article lurks in the ancient strategic aphorism that "nothing is impossible for the man who does not have to do it." When I was contributing to the *Defense Guidance* in the early 1980s

---

* Colin S. Gray is director of the Centre for Security Studies at the University of Hull; among his books is *The Leverage of Sea Power: The Strategic Advantage of Navies in War.*

its basic direction for the Armed Forces could be reduced to "be able to go anywhere, fight anyone, and win." To repeat my point, to those who do not have to *do* strategy at the sharp, tactical end of the stick, the bounds of feasibility appear endless.

True wisdom in strategy must be practical because strategy is a practical subject. Much of what appears to be wise and indeed is prudent as high theory is unhelpful to the poor warrior who actually has to do strategy, tactically and operationally. Two classic examples make the point.

Carl von Clausewitz advised us that there is a "culminating point of victory," beyond which lies a decline in relative strength.[2] Great advice—save, of course, that political and military maps, let alone physical terrain, do not come with Clausewitz's "culminating point" marked. Imagine that you are a German and that it is anytime between late June 1941 and late August 1942. You have read Clausewitz. Where is the culminating point—at Minsk or Smolensk, on the Dnieper, Don, or Volga? How can you find a culminating point of victory until adverse consequences unmistakably tell you where it was?

The other example of great strategic wisdom that is difficult to translate into practical advice is the insistence of Clausewitz (and Jomini) that "the best strategy is always to be very strong; first in general, and then at the decisive point."[3] Naturally the challenge is not to comprehend the all but sophomoric point that one needs to be very strong at the decisive point. Rather it is to know the location of that point. What did Clausewitz's advice mean for Germans in the late summer and fall of 1941? Did they need to concentrate their dissipating strength on the Red Army in the field, on the road to Moscow, or both?

For a tougher call, consider the American military problem in Southeast Asia in the second half of 1965. General William Westmoreland somehow had to identify military objectives to match and secure the somewhat opaque political objectives. Mastery of the arguments in the classics of strategic theory was unlikely to be of much practical help.

The Argument

Before expounding the central elements of my argument, which appear pessimistic, let me sound an optimistic note. Terrible though the 20th century has been, it could have been far worse. The bad news is that the century witnessed three world wars—two hot, one cold. The good news is that the right side won each of them. Moreover, threats to peace posed twice by Germany and then by the Soviet Union were each seen off at a cost that, though high, was not disproportionate to the stakes nor inconsistent with the values of our civilization. Western statecraft and strategy in two world wars was not without blemish. One needs to remember the wisdom of Lord Kitchener who said during World War I: "We wage war not as we would like but as we must." Strategically, notwithstanding errors, the Western World did relatively well. Now for a darker view.

My key argument is organized around three reasons why it is difficult to do strategy well:

- its very nature, which endures through time and in all contexts[4]
- the multiplicity and sheer variety of sources of friction[5]
- it is planned for contexts that literally have not occurred and might not occur; the future has not happened.

This argument is essentially optimistic, even though that claim may appear unpersuasive given that the high-quality strategic performance is always challenged by the nature of strategy—not only by its complexity but by the apparent fact that whatever can go wrong frequently does. Also, strategy can fail because it may apply the wrong solutions to incorrectly framed questions because guesses about the future were not correct. If, despite this, the bad guys were beaten three times during the course of the 20th century, there are grounds for hope.

Before explaining the many sources of difficulty for strategy, it is necessary to highlight the recurrence of a serious fallacy. Lest this point appear unfairly focused on the United States, I will sugar coat the pill by citing an American who got it right, and two others—one

American and one German—who got it wrong. Samuel Griffith, who got it right, was a scholar of Chinese military theory from Sun Tzu to Mao. He once observed that "there are no mechanical panaceas" when commenting on a *Newsweek* report in July 1961 about a fuel-air explosive to destroy bunkers.[6] The American and German, who got it wrong, allowed themselves to be seduced by the promise of "mechanical panaceas." One must hasten to add that these two warrior-theorists were exceptionally able men. The point is that, writing ninety years apart, they made almost the same mistake.

The issue underlying both views is whether much of the fog and thus friction that undoes applied strategy can be thwarted by modern technology. Writing in 1905, Lieutenant General Rudolf von Caemmerer, a member of the great general staff working under Field Marshal Alfred Graf von Schlieffen, offered this claim:

> *The former and actually existing dangers of failure in the pre-concentrated action of widely separated portions of the army is now almost completely removed by the electric telegraph. However much the enemy may have succeeded in placing himself between our armies, or portions of our armies, in such a manner that no trooper can get from one to the other, we can still amply communicate with each other over an arc of a hundred or two hundred or four hundred miles. The field telegraph can everywhere be laid as rapidly as the troops marching, and headquarters will know every evening how matters stand with the various armies, and issue its orders to them accordingly.*[7]

Caemmerer proceeded to admit that the telegraph might dangerously diminish the initiatives allowed to army commanders. The irony is that poor communications, lack of coordinated action, and a general loss of cohesion by the all important armies on the right wing of the German assault in early September 1914 allowed an Allied victory with the miracle on the Marne.[8] The telegraph was a wonderful invention, but it could not reliably dissipate the fog of war.

An American example of a functionally identical error is drawn from the magical "system of systems" invoked by Admiral William Owens, former Vice Chairman of the Joint Chiefs of Staff. In 1995 he wrote, "The emerging system . . . promises the capacity to use military force without the same risks as before—it suggests we will dissipate the fog of war."[9]

New technology, even when properly integrated into weapons and systems with well trained and highly motivated people, cannot erase the difficulties that impede strategic excellence. A new device, even innovative ways to conduct war, is always offered as a poisoned chalice. Moreover, scarcely less important, strategy cannot be reduced to fighting power alone.[10] Progress in modern strategic performance has not been achieved exclusively through science and technology.

Consider this argument: strategists today have at their disposal technological means to help dissipate the fog of war and otherwise defeat friction that previous generations could only imagine. Modern strategists can see over the hill, communicate instanteously with deployed forces around the world, and in principle rapidly destroy enemy assets wherever they are located—at least in fine weather and provided no innocent civilians are colocated with the targets. The problem is that war can't be reduced simply to the bombardment of a passive enemy.

Despite electro-mechanical marvels it is no easier—in fact it is probably harder—to perform well as a strategist today than a century ago. Consider the utility of railroads, telegraph, radio, and aircraft to the strategist. The poison in the chalice of each is that other polities have acquired them; each has distinctive vulnerabilities and worse (recall the radio intercepts of World Wars I and II); and none of them can address the core of the strategist's basket of difficulties.

Strategy is not really about fighting well, important though that is. To follow Clausewitz, it is about "the use of engagements for the object of the war."[11] The fog of war and frictions that harass and damage strategic performance do not comprise a static set of finite challenges which can be attrited by study, let alone by machines. Every new device and mode of war carries the virus of its own technical, tactical, operational, strategic, or political negation.[12]

To tackle the fog and friction of strategy and war is not akin to exploring unknown terrain, with each expedition better equipped than the last to fill in blanks on the map. The map of fog and friction is a living, dynamic one that reorganizes itself to frustrate the intrepid explorer.

Why So Difficult?

Field Marshal Helmuth Graf von Moltke—victor in the wars of German unification—had it right when, in *Instructions for Superior Commanders*, he wrote that "strategy is the application of common sense to the conduct of war. The difficulty lies in its execution. . . ."[13] The elder Moltke was rephrasing the words of the master. Clausewitz advises that "everything in strategy is very simple, but that does not mean that everything is very easy."[14] Why should that be so? Five reasons can be suggested.

First, strategy is neither policy nor armed combat; rather it is the bridge between them. The strategist can be thwarted if the military wages the wrong war well or the right war badly. Neither experts in politics and policymaking nor experts in fighting need necessarily be experts in strategy. The strategist must relate military power (strategic effect) to the goals of policy. Absent a strategic brain—as was the case of the United States and NATO vis-à-vis Bosnia and Kosovo— one is left with an awkward alliance of hot air (policy statements) and bombardment possibilities (the world is my dartboard view of aerial strategists).[15] Strategy is difficult because, among other things, it is neither fish nor fowl. It is essentially different from military skill or political competence.

Second, strategy is perilously complex by its very nature. Every element or dimension can impact all others. The nature of strategy is constant throughout history but its character continually evolves with changes in technology, society, and political ideas. Success in strategy is not really about securing a privileged position in any one or more of its dimensions—such as technology, geography, or leadership—because it is always possible an enemy will find ways to compensate for that strategic effect from its special strengths. This is a major reason why information dominance in a technical-tactical sense cannot reliably deliver victory. Triumph in war does not correlate with superior technology nor mastery in any allegedly dominant dimension of conflict.

Third, it is extraordinarily difficult, perhaps impossible, to train strategists. Consider these words of Napoleon Bonaparte:

> *Tactics, evolutions, artillery, and engineer sciences can be learned from manuals like geometry; but the knowledge of the higher conduct of war can only be acquired by studying the history of wars and the battles of great generals and by one's own experience. There are no terse and precise rules at all; everything depends on the character with which nature has endowed the general, on his eminent qualities, on his deficiencies, on the nature of the troops, the technics or arms, the season, and a thousand other circumstances which make things never look alike.*[16]

Napoleon was in a position to know. Like Hannibal he was good at winning battles, but he failed catastrophically as a strategist. Like Imperial Germany, Nazi Germany, and the Soviet Union, Imperial France pursued political goals that were beyond its means. That is a failure in strategy.

Basic problems in training strategists can be reduced to the fact that no educational system puts in what nature leaves out, while the extraordinary competence shown by rising politicians or soldiers in their particular trades is not proof of an aptitude for strategy. The strategist has to be expert in using the threat or use of force for policy ends, not in thinking up desirable policy ends or in fighting skillfully.

Fourth, because strategy embraces all aspects of the military instrument (among others), as well as many elements of the polity and society it serves, the maximum possible number of things can go wrong. To illustrate, sources of friction that can impair strategic performance include those familiar to the military realm (incompatibilities among the levels of military activity and specialized functions such as operations, logistics, and weapons production) and, conceivably the most lethal of all, a mismatch between policy and military capabilities. In the world of strategists, as opposed to that of tacticians, there is simply much more scope for error.

Finally, it is critical to flag an underrecognized source of friction, the will, skill, and means of an intelligent and malevolent enemy. Andre Beaufre defines strategy as "the art of the dialectic of force or, more precisely, the art of the dialectic of two opposing wills using force to resolve their dispute."[17] Recall Clausewitz's dictum: "War is thus an act of force to compel our enemy to do our will."[18] Yet it is easier to theorize about new ways of prevailing than to speculate honestly and imaginatively about possible enemy initiatives and responses.

Further Thoughts

There is a sense in which this article reinvents the wheel. It is no great achievement to appreciate that strategy is difficult to do well. Indeed, my point is not dissimilar from that made by Lawrence Freedman, who takes 433 pages in *The Evolution of Nuclear Strategy* to state that there is no truly strategic solution to the dilemmas of nuclear strategy.[19] When armchair strategists tell military practitioners that their task is difficult on the level of strategy, they should not expect much praise. After all, strategy does have to be done. Academics can vote undecided and write another book. Practicing strategists must make decisions regardless of the uncertainty.

Next, one must stress the strategic ignorance of even practical people. Clausewitz wrote:

> *It might be thought that policy could make demands on war which war could not fulfill; but that hypothesis would challenge*

the natural and unavoidable assumption that policy knows the instrument it means to use.[20]

The challenge is that before undergoing trial by battle, no one really knows how effective military power will be. Every passage of arms remains unique. A capability that appears lethally effective in peacetime exercises will not translate automatically into a violent elixir to solve political issues. That the Armed Forces appear lethally potent against a conventional enemy in open warfare could prove irrelevant or worse in urban areas. In peacetime, militaries train against themselves, and that has to comprise a major source of uncertainty concerning future effectiveness.

It is vital to recognize potential tension in three sets of relationships: between politicians and commanders, between commanders and planners, and between commanders and theorists (recall Phormio's efforts to educate Hannibal). Military professionals must simplify, focus, decide, and execute. Politicians, by virtue of their craft, perceive or fear wide ramifications of action, prefer to fudge rather than focus, and like to keep their options open as long as possible by making the least decision as late as feasible. Although commanders are gripped by operational requirements, planners—especially if unschooled by real operational experience—are apt to live in an orderly world where a model of efficiency and compromise is acceptable, indeed is a driver.

The tension becomes acute when a soldier who is only a planner finds himself in a position of high command. The classic example is Dwight Eisenhower, a superb staff officer and military politician who lacked the experience and the aptitude for command, let alone supreme command.[21] As to the terrain between theorists and doers of strategy, the former are skilled in the production of complexity and are unlikely to enjoy the empathy for operational realities that makes strategic ideas readily useful. For example, the nuclear strategist might conceive of dozens of targeting options yet be unaware that his theory passed its "culminating point of victory"—actually its "culminating point of feasibility"—at a distinctly early stage. A President thoroughly uninterested in matters of nuclear strategy until suddenly confronted at dawn some Christmas with the necessity for choice can't likely cope intellectually, morally, politically, and strategically with many options. Probably he would find it useful to have alternatives: shall we go now, shall we go later, shall we go big, or shall we go small. But those broad binaries may be close to the limits of Presidential strategic thinking. Many strategists have presented seemingly clever briefings to policymakers and senior officers whose eyes crossed and brains locked at the sight of the third PowerPoint slide.

The many reasons why strategy is so difficult to do well can be subsumed with reference to three requirements. For strategic success:
forces :

- forces must be internally coherent, which is to say competently joint
- be of a quantity and provide a strategic effect scaled to the tasks set by high policy
- be employed coercively in pursuit of military objectives that fit political goals.

Competence cannot offset folly along the means-ends axis of strategy. Military history is littered with armies that won campaigns in the wrong wars.

Since the future is unforeseeable—do not put faith in the phrase "foreseeable future"—we must use only assets that can be trusted. Specifically, we plan to behave strategically in an uncertain future on the basis of three sources of practical advice: historical experience, the golden rule of prudence (we do not allow hopes to govern plans), and common sense. We can educate our common sense by reading history. But because the future has not happened, our expectations of it can only be guesswork. Historically guided guesswork should perform better than one that knows no yesterdays. Nonetheless, planning for the future, like deciding to fight, is always a gamble.

To conclude on a positive note, remember that to succeed in strategy you do not have to be distinguished or even particularly competent. All that is required is performing well enough to beat an enemy. You do not have to win elegantly; you just have to win. *Rugby!*

Same – Passchendaele!

Notes

1. J.F. Lazenby, *Hannibal's War: A History of the Second Punic War* (Warminster, UK: Aris and Phillips, 1978), p. 275.
2. Carl von Clausewitz, *On War*, edited and translated by Michael Howard and Peter Paret (Princeton: Princeton University Press, 1976), pp. 566–73. See also Antulio J. Echevarria II, "Clausewitz: Toward a Theory of Applied Strategy," *Defense Analysis*, vol. 11, no. 3 (December 1995), pp. 229–40.
3. Clausewitz, *On War*, p. 204; Antoine Henri de Jomini, *The Art of War* (London: Greenhill Books, 1992), p. 70.
4. This argument is the central theme of Colin S. Gray in *Modern Strategy* (Oxford: Oxford University Press, 1999).
5. Clausewitz, *On War*, pp. 119–21.
6. Samuel B. Griffith, *On Guerrilla Warfare* (New York: Praeger, 1961), p. 31.
7. Rudolf von Caemmerer, *The Development of Strategical Science During the 19th Century*, translated by Karl von Donat (London: Hugh Rees, 1905), pp. 171–72.
8. Holger H. Herwig, *The First World War: Germany and Austria–Hungary, 1914–1918* (London: Arnold, 1997), pp. 96–106, is excellent.
9. Williamson Murray, "Does Military Culture Matter?" *Orbis*, vol. 43, no. 1 (Winter 1999), p. 37.
10. See Martin van Creveld, *Fighting Power: German and U.S. Army Performance, 1939–1945* (Westport, Conn.: Greenwood, 1982).
11. Clausewitz, *On War*, p. 128.
12. For lengthy musings, see Edward N. Luttwak, *Strategy: The Logic of War and Peace* (Cambridge: Harvard University Press, 1987). Luttwak argues that what works well today may not tomorrow exactly because it worked well today. Because Clausewitz insists war is essentially a duel, one may face an enemy capable of reacting creatively to one's moves and perhaps even anticipate them.
13. Caemmerer, *Strategical Science*, p. 276.
14. Clausewitz, *On War*, p. 178.
15. This is a fair reading of the underlying premise of airpower theory. See Giulio Douhet, *The Command of the Air*, translated by Dino Ferrari (New York: Arno Press, 1972), p. 50; and John A. Warden III, "Success in Modern War: A Response to Robert Pape's *Bombing to Win*," *Security Studies*,

vol. 7, no. 2 (Winter 1997/98), pp. 174–85. To the air strategist targeting is strategy.

[16] Caemmerer, *Strategical Science*, p. 275.

[17] André Beaufre, *An Introduction to Strategy* (London: Faber and Faber, 1965), p. 22.

[18] Clausewitz, *On War*, p. 75.

[19] Lawrence Freedman, *The Evolution of Nuclear Strategy* (New York: St. Martin's Press, 1981), p. 433.

[20] Clausewitz, *On War*, p. 75.

[21] Dominick Graham and Shelford Bidwell, *Coalitions, Politicians and Generals: Some Aspects of Command in Two World Wars* (London: Brassey's, 1993), chapters 9–16, is pitilessly Anglo-Canadian in its critical view of Eisenhower as commander and serves as a partial corrective to the "patriotic" school of military history of the European campaign that finds undue favor among American writers such as Stephen E. Ambrose in *The Victors: Eisenhower and His Boys: The Men of World War II* (New York: Simon and Schuster, 1998).

3

General William T. Sherman and Total War

JOHN BENNETT WALTERS

Within recent years the term "total war" has been so definitely accepted as a part of the everyday vocabulary that there is danger of losing sight of the fact that the concept has not always prevailed in its twentieth-century form. In a measure, of course, all wars have involved more than the clash between armed forces, but with the development of the modern state war became an instrument of national policy waged by specially organized units, either recruits or mercenaries, according to more or less generally recognized rules. By the nineteenth century the laws of land warfare, established by long usage, had begun to take form as a definite body of international jurisprudence, violations of which were subject to diplomatic protest and to reprisal. Prominent among the problems which received cognizance in the course of this development were those dealing with the status and the rights of that part of the population of a belligerent state who did not participate in the hostilities. Although effective sanction was not always present, it was generally understood that the noncombatant or civilian population should be free from all violence or constraint other than that required by military necessity. In the case of the American Civil War, for example, the Federal government officially recognized the distinction between combatants and noncombatants in the Confederacy by incorporating in its famous "Instructions for the Government of Armies of the United States in the Field" (General Orders No. 100) specific provisions concerning the treatment of the civilian population in the zones of military operations. "As civilization has advanced during the last centuries," stated Article 22 of those instructions, "so has likewise steadily advanced, especially in war on land, the distinction between the private individual belonging to a hostile country and the hostile country itself, with its men in arms. The principle has been more and more acknowledged that the unarmed citizen is to be spared in person, property, and honor as much as the exigencies of war will admit." Succeeding articles proceeded to explain that in contrast with the practice of barbarous armies, where "the private individual of the hostile country is destined to suffer every privation of liberty and protection, and every disruption of family ties," in modern civilized warfare "protection of the inoffensive citizen of the hostile country is the rule; privation and disturbance of private relations are the exceptions." Article 44 then specified that "All wanton violence committed against persons in the invaded country, all destruction of property not commanded by the authorized officer, all robbery, all pillage or sacking, even after taking a place by main force, all rape, wounding, maiming, or killing of such inhabitants, are prohibited under the penalty of death, or such other severe punishment as may seem adequate for the gravity of the offense."[1]

Paradoxically, it was in that same conflict that a Union general, William Tecumseh Sherman, gradually evolved his own personal philosophy of war along lines which were clearly at variance with the official pronouncements, and in his practical application of that philosophy became one of the first of the modern generals to revert to the idea of the use of military force against the civilian population of the enemy. While this represents only a part of the present concept of total war, its significance lies in Sherman's demonstration of the effectiveness of a plan of action which would destroy the enemy's economic system and terrify and demoralize the civilian population.

---

[1] These instructions, issued as General Orders No. 100, April 24, 1863, are in *The War of the Rebellion: A Compilation of the Official Records of the Union and Confederate Armies* (129 vols, and index, Washington, 1880–1901), Ser. III, Vol. III, pp. 148–64. This collection is cited hereinafter as *Official Records*.

By paralyzing the enemy's economy he destroyed its ability to supply its armies; and by despoiling and scattering the families of the soldiers in the opposing army, he undermined the morale of the military forces of the Confederacy. Because the lessons which it taught were not likely to be ignored in the conduct of future wars, the process by which his plan was developed, applied, and rationalized is perhaps worthy of special examination.[2]

On the eve of the Civil War, Sherman could look back upon a career of dependence, frustrations, and failures. Brought up in the family of Thomas Ewing, Ohio politician, United States senator, and cabinet member, he was indebted to his foster father for his early education, for appointment to the United States Military Academy, and, after his marriage to Ewing's daughter, for providing a home for his wife and children. Graduated from West Point in 1840, he was given a series of routine assignments and failed to receive promotion during the Mexican War because his service was too far removed from the seat of hostilities. Resigning from the army to become the manager of a bank in San Francisco, he saw both it and its New York office to which he was transferred close their doors within three years. Joining his brothers-in-law in Kansas, he read law and was admitted to the bar, but abandoned the legal profession after losing the only case in which he acted as counsel. "I am doomed to be a vagabond, and shall no longer struggle against my fate," he wrote his wife from Kansas in 1859. "I look upon myself as a dead cock in the pit, not worthy of further notice and will take the chances as they come."[3]

---

[2] No attempt is being made in this study to present either a biography of General Sherman or a narrative of his military operations during the Civil War. It represents, instead, an effort to examine the relation between certain aspects of his activities and the development and application of his philosophy of war. The most successful attempt at a biographical study is Lloyd Lewis, *Sherman, Fighting Prophet* (New York, 1932), in which some of the matters considered here have been given a somewhat different emphasis.

[3] Sherman to Mrs. Sherman, April 15, 1859, in M. A. DeWolfe Howe (ed.), *Home Letters of General Sherman* (New York, 1909), 158–59.

Later in that year the chance seemed to have come when Sherman applied for and received the appointment as superintendent of the newly-established Louisiana State Seminary, soon to be transformed into a military academy and later to become Louisiana State University. Entering into this work with enthusiasm, he won the confidence of the state authorities as well as the good will of the students and the general public to such an extent that he began to feel that he had at last found security and a place of contentment in which he could forget the failures in his military and business career. "If Louisiana will endow this college properly, and is fool enough to give me $5,000 a year," he wrote Mrs. Sherman, "we will drive our tent pins, and pick out a magnolia under which to sleep the long sleep."[4] But before he could move his family to the new home, this dream was shattered by the coming of secession; and when Louisiana cast its lot with the Confederacy he promptly resigned. As he traveled northward late in February, 1861, to face once more the prospect of renewed dependence upon his father-in-law, his brooding over the ghosts of his own failures became mingled with gloomy forebodings concerning the future of the nation itself. Passing from the South, where it seemed to him that the people showed unanimity of purpose and a fierce, earnest determination in their hurried organization for action, into Illinois, Indiana, and Ohio, where he found no apparent signs of preparation nor any great concern over the trend of events, he began to develop the conviction that he was one of the few people who understood the real state of affairs.[5] It was only a short step from there to resentment against those who seemed unwilling to heed his warning or advice.

After spending a few days with his family, he proceeded to Washington in response to suggestions from his brother, John Sherman,

---

[4] Sherman to Mrs. Sherman, February 13, 1860, *ibid.*, 176–77. For a valuable collection of documentary material on this phase of Sherman's career, see Walter L. Fleming (ed.), *General W. T. Sherman as College President* (Cleveland, 1912).

[5] William T. Sherman, *Memoirs* (2 vols., New York, 1875), I, 166–67.

newly-elected senator from Ohio, that a desirable position might be obtained for him in the government service. Here he was shocked at the carefree air and the lack of preparation for the crisis which he had predicted, and his concern was heightened to indignation when President Lincoln seemed not to be interested in hearing what he wanted to tell about the attitude of the South. As he and his brother left the interview, he railed out at the politicians, who, he said, "have got things in a hell of a fix," and in his disappointment and anger announced that so far as he was concerned the government would have to get along wthout his services.[6] Accepting an offer to become president of a street railway company in St. Louis at the meager salary of $2,000, he turned his back on Washington and before the end of March had moved his family to the new location.

Although he was successful in his new position, the flow of events around him served to aggravate his emotional condition. Because he had a feeling of being left on the side lines while others who in his opinion were not as well qualified played the game, he became restless, irritable, and moody. His uneasiness was increased during April by letters from his brother urging him to get into the army, "where you will at once put yourself in high position for life." Whether with studied intent or by accident, the Senator's letters carried the unmistakable implication that now was the opportune moment for Sherman to redeem himself in his own estimation as well as that of his family, his friends, and the world. They contained no appeal to a sense of patriotism or service of country, but concentrated instead on the possibility of self-advancement which might be realized by raising a regiment or brigade for the volunteer army and getting himself chosen as its commanding officer.[7]

---

[6] See *ibid.*, 167–68, for Sherman's own later account of this incident. For his brother's version see John Sherman, *Recollections of Forty Years in the House, Senate, and Cabinet* (2 vols., Chicago, 1895), I, 241–42.

[7] John Sherman to Sherman, April 12 and 14, 1861, in Rachel S. Thorndike (ed.), *The Sherman Letters* (New York, 1894), 110–11, 112–13.

Equally self-centered in his calculation and still resentful toward the President, Sherman replied that his earlier offer of his services had been spurned and that he would not volunteer again. "The time will come in this country," he wrote, "when professional knowledge will be appreciated, when men that can be trusted will be wanted, and I will bide my time." In justifying this decision he expressed his distrust of volunteers and militia and went on to say: "The first movements of the government will fail and the leaders will be cast aside. A second or third set will arise, and among them I may be, but at present I will not volunteer as a soldier or anything else. If . . . the regular army be put on a footing with the wants of the country, [and] if I am offered a place that suits me, I may accept."[8] In short order he rejected an offer of a chief clerkship in the War Department and one for appointment as brigadier general of volunteers, and in a letter to the secretary of war, which he later explained as having been written to counteract rumors concerning his loyalty, he said, "I hold myself now, as always, prepared to serve my country in the capacity for which I was trained. . . . I will not volunteer because rightfully or wrongfully I feel unwilling to take a mere private's place, and having for many years lived in California and Louisiana, the men are not well enough acquainted with me to elect me to my appropriate place."[9] The records of the War Department, he added, would show where he could render the most service. A few days later he received and accepted a commission as colonel of the Thirteenth Regular Infantry.

Because the apparent singleness of purpose with which Sherman had cut his way through diverting factors to the attainment of a regular army appointment may be considered as the first stage in the

[8] From an undated excerpt from a letter to John Sherman, obviously written in April, 1861, *ibid.,* 111–12. The same fragment appears also in John Sherman, *Recollections,* I, 244, where it is designated as a reply to his own letters.

[9] Sherman to Simon Cameron, May 8, 1861, in the William T. Sherman Papers (Division of Manuscripts, Library of Congress). See also Sherman, *Memoirs,* I, 171–72, where the second sentence quoted above was made to read: "I will not volunteer as a soldier, because. . . ."

development of his attitude toward the conduct of the war, it perhaps deserves further analysis. Looking back at it in the light of subsequent events, there is a temptation to explain it as the result of a superior foresight which enabled him to see more clearly than others what ought to be done. Such reasoning, however, overlooks those elements in the situation which caused him to view things as he did. Of outstanding importance was undoubtedly the cumulative effect of his own personal background of failure and frustration, out of which had come both an extreme sensitiveness to criticism and an impelling desire to attain security. As a defense against criticism he had developed a tendency to exaggerate the difficulty of problems in which he was concerned and to blame the failures to lack of understanding on the part of others. In the matter of security he had become convinced that the essential requirement was permanence of position and income. Thus as he considered the possibility of his own participation in the war, his emphasis on the magnitude of the task and the shortcomings of the government's plans may have been prompted as much by a desire to prepare a basis for explaining possible failure as by a power of prophecy; and his insistence upon a commission in the regular army should perhaps be attributed to the obvious fact that nowhere else in the public service could he expect the permanence which he sought.

With the acceptance of his commission and the beginning of active military service Sherman also moved into a new phase of his attitude toward the conduct of the war. As a private citizen he had been free to criticize and to offer advice without having to assume responsibility, but in his new status as an officer in the army he became one of those against whom criticism could be directed. Thus in gaining the prospect of permanent position he had not been relieved of the haunting dread of the consequences of failure. Torn between a desire to prove to himself and others that he could succeed and a lingering fear that he might fail, he apparently decided to proceed cautiously in order to avoid being precipitated into responsible assignments before he was ready for them. Following a brief period of routine inspection duties, he went into the battle of Bull Run in July, 1861, as the commander of a brigade, seemingly content to follow orders as effectively as possible and to let others do the planning. Although he felt keenly the humiliation of the defeat and the disorderly retreat, his official report and public statements contained no censure of anyone involved.[10] In writing to his wife, however, he was less reserved in expressing his opinion that lack of training and discipline was probably the chief factor in causing the Union defeat. Referring to the troops as "the armed mob we led into Virginia," he said: "Each private thinks for himself. If he wants to go for water, he asks leave of no one. If he thinks right, he takes the oats and corn, and even burns the house of his enemy. No curse could be greater than invasion by a volunteer army. No Goths or Vandals ever had less respect for the lives and property of friends and foes, and henceforth we ought never to hope for any friends in Virginia."[11]

Instead of the disgrace which he expected and the opportunity to "sneak into some quiet corner," he soon received a promotion to brigadier general and an assignment to assist General Robert Anderson in recruiting a force in Kentucky sufficiently large to protect the state against an expected invasion. Still hopeful that he could avoid responsibility and thus escape the oblivion which he had predicted would be the fate of those who reached high command in the early stages of the war, he seems to have obtained at this time a promise from President Lincoln that he would be permitted to continue "to serve in a subordinate capacity, and in no event to be left in a superior command."[12] When ill health forced General Anderson to resign from the army on October 8, 1861, however, the command

---

[10] For Sherman's later comments on the battle, together with his official report of July 25, 1861, see Sherman, *Memoirs,* I, 179–89.

[11] Sherman to Mrs. Sherman, July 24 and 28, 1861, in Howe (ed.), *Home Letters of General Sherman,* 203–10.

[12] See Sherman, *Memoirs,* I, 192–93, for his later account of the interview in which this request was made. No immediately contemporary record of the promise seems to have been made, and Sherman himself did not mention it in writing to his brother concerning the assignment. Sherman to John Sherman, August 19, 1861, in Thorndike (ed.), *Sherman Letters,* 126–27.

devolved upon Sherman, and he immediately began to bombard the authorities in Washington with appeals for men, for arms, and for recognition of the importance of Kentucky to the Union. In his apprehensive state of mind he painted a gloomy picture of utter disorganization in the Union efforts in Kentucky, greatly overestimated the size of the enemy's forces in the state, and exaggerated the possibility of an immediate Confederate attack.[13] Convinced that Washington's failure to act promptly on his requests was due either to indifference to the situation or to a willingness to sacrifice him,[14] he developed a state of nervous tension in which his irritability and his unreasonable treatment of those about him antagonized the newspaper correspondents and led some of them to publish stories questioning his sanity. At his own insistence he was relieved of the command as soon as a successor could be transferred to the post, and after a brief period of subordinate service in Missouri he was sent home for a complete rest.

It was during this period of inactivity that the full import of these charges of insanity began to bear in upon him and to create in his mind an agonizing sense of humiliation. After all his careful planning to recover his own self-confidence and to secure his future by proceeding quietly and unobtrusively toward the building of a successful military career and the gaining of public acclaim, he was again faced with the fact of having failed, to which was now added the ominous specter of disgrace. As he looked back at his actions in Kentucky, he apparently realized that his efforts to avoid being held responsible for possible failure had been carried too far. Writing to his brother early in January, he said: "I ought to have endured and

---

[13] For Sherman's correspondence of this period, see *Official Records*, Ser. I, Vol. IV, pp. 255–314; especially his letters to President Lincoln, October 10 and 14, 1861 (pp. 300, 306–307), to Secretary of War Cameron, October 20, 1861 (p. 312), and to Adjutant General Lorenzo Thomas, October 22, 1861 (pp. 313–14). Sherman, *Memoirs*, I, 199–210, presents his retrospective view.

[14] See especially Sherman to John Sherman, October 26, 1861, in Thorndike (ed.), *Sherman Letters*, 133–34, in which he says categorically: "I feel that I am to be sacrificed."

then would have been responsible only for my part, whereas by giving up the command I not only confessed my inability to manage affairs entrusted to me but placed the burden on other shoulders." And on the same subject he had said a few days earlier: "I am so sensible now of my disgrace from having exaggerated the force of our enemy in Kentucky that I do think I should have committed suicide were it not for my children. I do not think that I can again be entrusted with a command."[15] Although he admitted to his father-in-law that the newspaper charges 'will be widely circulated and will impair my personal influence for much time to come, if not always,"[16] he declined to make any public answer or to bring suit against the papers; and he seems to have returned to active duty with a dogged determination to keep his own counsel until he could again prove himself worthy of confidence.

During the early weeks of 1862 Sherman served as the commanding officer at Benton Barracks, a camp of instruction for recruits near St. Louis, where he could not hide from himself the fact that many of the officers and men coming under his command regarded him with mingled curiosity and suspicion.[17] He entered into his duties with great industry and gave his personal attention to drilling the recruits sent to him, forming regiments of them, and rebuilding the physical equipment of the camp; and after watching him furnish well-trained units at a moment's notice for service in the field, General Henry W. Halleck, in command of the Federal armies in the West, began to draw him into conferences for planning the strategy of operations in the western theater of the war. As the plans were developed for an advance up the Cumberland and Tennessee rivers, Sherman was stationed at Paducah in charge of assembling and forwarding troops and supplies to the army under General U. S. Grant, and was then placed in command of a division which joined Grant's

---

[15] Sherman to John Sherman, January 4 and 8, 1862, in William T. Sherman Papers.
[16] Sherman to Thomas Ewing, December 12, 1861, *ibid.*
[17] Sherman, *Memoirs*, I, 214–15.

army in time to participate in the battle of Shiloh. His work in that battle won high praise from both Halleck and Grant and, upon their recommendations, a promotion to major general;[18] but more important to Sherman was the fact that he had regained confidence in himself. "I have worked hard to keep down," he wrote Mrs. Sherman, "but somehow I am forced into prominence and might as well submit."[19] And within a few weeks he was citing his own successful rise from the depths of the insanity charge as an argument to persuade Grant to stay with the army in spite of the accusation of drunkenness and negligence which had been hurled at him after Shiloh.[20]

The recovery of his self-confidence seemed to remove the restraints which Sherman had imposed upon himself after the Kentucky experience, and he was soon writing vitriolic attacks on the critics of Grant on the one hand and criticizing Halleck's conduct of the Corinth campaign on the other. At the same, time his statements and plans began to reflect some of the changes which had taken place in his concept of the nature of the war. After the battle of Bull Run, for example, his attitude toward the enemy was essentially that of the orthodox professional soldier of the period—interested in the game itself as it was being played by the two armies rather than in personalizing the enemy. He was concerned over seeming violations of the rules with regard to civilian and private property rights and expressed a hope that "a common sense of decency may be inspired into the minds of this soldiery to respect life and property."[21] In Kentucky he thought he saw indications of civilian organization against the Union. "Our enemies have a terrible advantage," he wrote Adjutant General Lorenzo Thomas, "in the fact that in our midst,

---

[18] Halleck's recommendation credited Sherman with "Saving the day on the 6th, and contributing largely to the glorious victory of the 7th." Copy, dated April 13, 1862, in William T. Sherman Papers.

[19] Sherman to Mrs. Sherman, April 11, 1862, in Howe (ed.), *Home Letters of General Sherman*, 220–23.

[20] Sherman, *Memoirs*, I, 255.

[21] Sherman to Mrs. Sherman, August, 1861, in Howe (ed.), *Home Letters of General Sherman*, 214–15.

in our camps, and along our avenues of travel they have active partisans, farmers and business men, who seemingly pursue their usual
calling but are in fact spies."[22] Two months later, while drilling
recruits at Benton Barracks, he wrote to his brother that the civilian
population of the South would have to be reckoned with in the
months of war ahead, and pointed out the fact that although General
Halleck had in Missouri about 80,000 men and the organized
Confederate force was only about one-fifth of that number, "yet the
country is full of Secessionists, and it takes all of his command to
watch them." Adding that this was a type of warfare which the politicians could not understand, he continued: "These local Secessionists
are really more dangerous than if assembled in one or more bodies,
for then they could be traced out and found, whereas now they are
scattered about on farms and are very peaceable, but when a bridge
is to be burned they are about."[23]

As he watched the effectiveness with which the Confederate force
under General Sterling Price managed to control the surrounding
country while a Union force of five times its number was tied to its
base at St. Louis, he developed a serious doubt as to the wisdom of
occupying cities and expending the great energy required to retain a
tenuous hold on vital lines of communication. The cost of the effort
seemed to him to be greater than the advantages gained, especially if
the people quietly but efficiently destroyed those communications
and dispersed to blend themselves back into the surrounding scene,
where they would appear blandly incredulous as they looked up
from their plowing to answer the questions of a searching Union
patrol. Having become convinced that this destruction was being
accomplished by civilians rather than by military personnel, he found
it easy to judge the whole South on the basis of what he thought he
saw in Missouri. Here was a manifestation of his tendency to arrive
at generalizations by leaping over wide gaps of fact and reason and
to proceed on the basis of his inspirations and convictions with the

---

[22] Sherman to Thomas, November 6, 1861, in William T. Sherman Papers.
[23] Sherman to John Sherman, January, 1862, in Thorndike (ed.), *Sherman Letters*, 138.

utmost faith in the soundness of his conclusions.[24] In this case his generalization led him to visualize the people themselves as a significant factor in the conduct of the war and to think in terms of a campaign against them as well as against their armies. After the battle of Shiloh he seemed to see similar civilian activities retarding Halleck's operations around Corinth, but it was not until he was placed in command of the District of West Tennessee with headquarters at Memphis that he was in a position to test his new theories.

Sherman entered upon his duties as military commander at Memphis on July 21, 1862. The city had been one of the Confederacy's strong points on the Mississippi, and when the southern forces withdrew they left behind them countless southern sympathizers, and even members of their own families. Sherman's correspondence during the summer and fall of 1862 leaves no doubt that he was fully conscious of the hostility and enmity of the residents of both the town and the surrounding countryside. He had little difficulty with the administration of civil affairs, and he permitted the local authorities to continue their normal operations under military supervision. One of his earliest concerns grew out of the cotton-buying policy of the Federal government, as a result of which Memphis had become a center for the purchase of cotton destined for northern markets and for the distribution of supplies obtained in exchange, which in his opinion were being passed on by the civilian population to the Confederate armies.[25] To him this was a confirmation in a new form

[24] David F. Boyd, an associate of Sherman at the Louisiana State Seminary, said of him: "He could not reason—that is, his mind leaped so quickly from idea to idea that he seemed to take no account of the time over which it passed, and if he was asked to explain how he came by his conclusions it confused him. . . . His mind went like lightning to its conclusions, and he had the utmost faith in his inspirations and conviction." "General W. T. Sherman as a College President," in *American College* (New York, 1909–1910), II (April, 1910); reprinted as Vol. I (New Series), No. 10, of Louisiana State University *Bulletin* (Baton Rouge, 1910).

[25] For an extended treatment of the trading activities being carried on through Memphis, see Joseph H. Parks, "A Confederate Trade Center under Federal Occupation: Memphis, 1862–1865," in *Journal of Southern History* (Baton Rouge, 1935–), VII (1941), 289–314.

of the conclusion which he had reached in Missouri that all of the people of the South were in active resistance to the Union forces, and in a protest to the secretary of the treasury he revealed the direction which his thinking on the subject had taken. "When one nation is at war with another," he said, "all the people of the one are enemies of the other: then the rules are plain and easy of understanding." Then, apparently proceeding on the assumption that his pronouncement required no further discussion or validation, he continued: "The Government of the United States may now safely proceed on the proper rule that all in the South *are* enemies of all in the North; and not only are they unfriendly, but all who can procure arms now bear them as organized regiments or as guerrillas."[26]

As Sherman undertook to deal with the military situation around Memphis, he became more and more impressed with the disadvantages faced by an army invading enemy territory. He observed the ease with which the Confederate units moved about the country without having to guard against the civilian population, while his own larger force was rendered ineffective by the superior flexibility of action and rapidity of movement displayed by the enemy. Especially disturbing to him was the practice followed by Generals Nathan B. Forrest and Earl Van Dorn of detaching small units from their main force to strike at several different points simultaneously and to move out of reach before effective resistance could be offered. Their consistent ability to make surprise attacks wherever his force was weakest and most exposed, coupled with their elusiveness, created in him a new sense of frustration, and in trying to explain his difficulties to General Grant he expressed the belief that he was dealing with guerrillas rather than with regular troops. Apparently without taking the trouble to investigate or to weigh such evidence as he had, he quickly evolved one of his characteristic generalizations. "All the people are now guerrillas, he informed Grant, "and they have

---

[26] Sherman to Salmon P. Chase, August 11, 1862, in Sherman, *Memoirs*, I, 266. Parts of this letter appear also in *Official Records*, Ser. III, Vol. II, p. 349, with no indication of the omissions.

a perfect understanding."[27] With a rising note of conviction he wrote to his brother a few days later: "All their people are armed and at war. You hear of vast armies at Richmond, Chattanooga, and threatening New Orleans, whilst the whole country is full of guerrilla bands, numbering hundreds."[28] And finally, after a month of growing impatience at the slowness of others to respond, he fumed: "It is about time the North understood the truth. That the entire South, man, woman, and child are against us, armed and determined."[29]

While it was true that bands of guerrillas were extremely active in the region around Memphis and that unorganized civilian resistance was frequently encountered, Sherman's disposition to consider all resistance as treacherous acts of the civilian population prepared the way for the next steps in the development of his attitude on the conduct of the war. Having persuaded himself that if he failed at Memphis it would be because his foes did not play the game of war fairly, he was beginning to search for some means of counteracting their activities. An early clue to the direction in which his planning was to lead appeared in a letter written in July, 1862, to Mrs. Sherman. "We are in our enemy's country and I act accordingly," he said. "The North may fall into bankruptcy and anarchy first, but if they can hold on the war will soon assume a turn to extermination, not of soldiers alone, that is the least part of the trouble, but the people."[30] Obviously, he had come a long way since the battle of Bull Run, where he had observed the destructive tendencies of his volunteer troops with shock and disgust; and as his idea of warfare against the people crystallized, he seemed to find in those tendencies at least a partial answer to his search.

[27] Sherman to Grant, August 17, 1862, in *Official Records*, Ser. I, Vol. XVII, Part 2, p. 178. See also *ibid.*, 205, where Sherman reports an attack as having been made by civilians.
[28] Sherman to John Sherman, August 26, 1862, in Thorndike (ed.), *Sherman Letters*, 159–60.
[29] Sherman to John Sherman, September 22, 1862, ibid., 161–63.
[30] Sherman to Mrs. Sherman, July 31, 1862, in Howe (ed.), *Home Letters of General Sherman*, 229–30.

As late as mid-September, 1862, however, he was still wavering between orthodox procedure and the practical application of his newer theories. On September 21 he wrote a long letter to the editor of the Memphis *Bulletin*, in which he carefully explained that an act of Congress of 1806, which was still in force, made straggling and pillaging military crimes, and that "every officer and soldier in my command knows what stress I have laid upon them, and that, so far as in my power lies, I will punish them to the full extent of the law and orders." But he added that it was one thing to know what the law provided and quite a different matter to enforce it; and in answer to protests concerning the activities of his men he took the position that he could not punish an entire unit, but must have specific charges and complete identification "of the actual transgressor."[31] Although the tone of this letter implied adherence to the accepted rules of war, it was only three days later that he issued the first of a series of orders which indicated that he was now ready to undertake the application of his theories in a new type of warfare.

His anger had mounted steadily as he observed how effectively he was checkmated by what he insisted again and again were small guerrilla forces, and when he learned of attempts to interrupt the passage of steamboats bringing supplies down the Mississippi River to Memphis, he exploded into action. In an order of September 24 to Colonel Charles C. Walcutt, of the Forty-sixth Ohio Volunteers, he said:

> The object of the expedition you have been detailed for is to visit the town of Randolph where yesterday the packet Eugene was fired upon by a party of guerrillas. Acts of this kind must

[31] For the complete text of this letter, see Sherman, *Memoirs*, I, 276–78. It does not appear in *Official Records* with his other Memphis correspondence. It is interesting to note that a few weeks later General Grant did punish whole commands where unauthorized damage to private property was discovered. He fined the men through deductions from their pay and gave dishonorable discharges to the officers. See Grant's Special Field Orders No. 2 (November 9, 1862) and No. 6 (November 16, 1862), in *Official Records*, Ser. I, Vol. XVII, Part 2, pp. 331–32, 349–50.

be promptly punished, and it is almost impossible to reach the actors, for they come from the interior and depart as soon as the mischief is done. But the interests and well-being of the country demand that all such attacks should be followed by a punishment that will tend to prevent a repetition. . . . I think the attack on the Eugene was by a small force of guerrillas from Loosahatchie, who by this time have gone back, and therefore you will find no one at Randolph, in which case you will destroy the place, leaving one house to mark the place.[32]

All restraints were now being cast aside. The language of Sherman's order clearly indicated that no investigation had been made to ascertain the facts or to determine the complicity of the inhabitants of the town of Randolph in the attack. He had jumped to the conclusion that this attack was the action of guerrillas, and casually brushing aside the possibility that it might have been made by Confederate soldiers, he was ordering that vengeance be wreaked on the town because it happened to be near the scene of the trouble. Here he was putting into effect a theory to which his generalizations had inevitably led him—the theory of collective responsibility, based on his contention that every "man, woman, and child" in the South was "armed and at war." Under this theory it was no longer necessary to establish individual or community guilt before inflicting punishment; he could retaliate upon any who happened to be within reach. During the next few days his actions were to carry him across the narrow line between the destruction of property to punish a community and the application of punishment directly to individuals.

On September 27, three days after his order for the burning of Randolph, Sherman issued his Special Order No. 254, which read in part:

Whereas many families of known rebels and of Confederates in arms against us having been permitted to reside in peace and

---

[32] Sherman to Walcutt, September 24, 1862, in *Official Records*, Ser. I, Vol. XVII, Part 2, pp. 235–36.

comfort in Memphis, and whereas the Confederate authorities either sanction or permit the firing on unarmed boats carrying passengers and goods, for the use and benefit of the inhabitants of Memphis, it is ordered that for every boat so fired on ten families must be expelled from Memphis.

The provost-marshal will extend the list already prepared so as to have on it at least thirty names, and on every occasion when a boat is fired on will draw by lot ten names, who will be forthwith notified and allowed three days to remove to a distance of 25 miles from Memphis.[33]

By the time he reported to General Grant a week later concerning these developments, two more steamboats had been fired on, and he had added still another retaliatory measure to the list. "I caused Randolph to be destroyed," he said, "and have given public notice that a repetition will justify any measures of retaliation, such as loading boats with their captive guerrillas as targets (I always have a lot on hand), and expelling families from the comforts of Memphis, whose husbands and brothers go to make up those guerrillas."[34] Aside from the fact that in making this report to his immediately superior officer Sherman so phrased the statement that his orders seemed to apply only to guerrillas, there was no suggestion of a consciousness on his part that those orders constituted a violation of the accepted rules of war.[35] Indeed, other parts of the report contained his analysis of the problems which he faced, as well as numerous

---

[33] For the full text of this order, see *ibid.*, 240.

[34] Sherman to Grant, October 4, 1862, *ibid.*, 259–62.

[35] The standard authority on international law at the time was General Henry W. Halleck's *International Law, or Rules Regulating the Intercourse of States in Peace and War* (New York, 1861), and in view of Sherman's close association with Halleck it is hardly reasonable to assume that he was ignorant of its contents. On the question of vindictive retaliation, Halleck said: "We have no right . . . to destroy private property merely because our enemy has done this to us; for no individual is justly chargeable with the guilt of a personal crime for the acts of the community of which he is a member" (p. 296).

suggestions as to how the war should be conducted, in which he summed up his new concept of the employment of terror against the armies and the civilian population alike. "We cannot change the hearts of those people of the South," he said, "but we can make war so terrible that they will realize the fact that, however brave and gallant and devoted to their country, still they are mortal and should exhaust all peaceful remedies before they fly to war." And elsewhere in the same letter he suggested that while the people of the South "cannot be made to love us, [they] can be made to fear us, and dread the passage of troops through their country."

If Grant did not immediately grasp the full implications of the concept as he read Sherman's report, he at least could have had no doubt that its sponsor was convinced, willing, and ready to carry out the program to its ultimate conclusions. For the time being, however, he said nothing; and the next two weeks witnessed a rapid series of events. Sherman reported on October 9 that his retaliatory actions had been effective in stopping the attacks on the steamboats; but a few days later he was again stung into an angry mood by even more intensified attacks, both above and below Memphis. Ignoring the fact that this new action was too extensive to have been carried out by civilians, and choosing not to mention the fact that the boats actually carried munitions and supplies for the army as well as "passengers and goods for the use and benefit of the inhabitants of Memphis," he branded the attacks as "cowardly acts" which called for retaliation. "We will have to do something more than merely repel these attacks," he told Grant on October 18. "We must make the people feel that every attack on a road here will be resented by the destruction of some one of their towns or plantations elsewhere.

With regard to the treatment of the enemy's civilian population, he wrote: "So long as they refrain from all hostilities, pay the military contributions which may be imposed on them, and quietly submit to the authority of the belligerent who may happen to be in military possession of their country, they are allowed to continue in the enjoyment of their property, and in the pursuit of the ordinary avocations" (p. 427).

All adherents of their cause must suffer for these cowardly acts."[36] And on the same day he ordered Colonel Walcutt's Ohio volunteers, who had been so efficient in their destruction of Randolph, to "destroy all the houses, farms, and corn fields" for a distance of fifteen miles along the Arkansas bank of the Mississippi River.[37]

In calling these Confederate attacks "cowardly acts" and ordering retaliation for them, Sherman was in effect denying that the enemy had the right to resist an invasion of its country. He either failed to understand or, if he understood, refused to acknowledge that under the accepted rules of war his occupation of Memphis itself did not give him authority to exercise control over the inhabitants of surrounding territory in which the enemy continued to offer effective resistance.[38] Even if he could have proved that the attacks were made by unauthorized guerrillas, he was still bound by the rules of war to direct his retaliation against them rather than against the civilian population in general, unless complicity had been established. His theory of collective responsibility made all the people participants in the hostilities, however, and thus he considered himself absolved from following the accepted rules in dealing with them. If the resistance continued, they would be punished; and he would not be restricted in the methods he used to inflict that punishment—whether through destruction of their property or through the fear and uncertainty that are the lot of the hostage who is held responsible for acts beyond his control. Repeating his threat to expel additional "secessionist families" from Memphis and to visit summary punishment upon the neighborhood with each new act of resistance, he added: "It may sometimes fall on the wrong head, but it would be folly to

---

[36] Sherman to Grant, October 9, 1862, in *Official Records*, Ser. I, Vol. XVII, Part 2, pp. 272–74; Sherman to Major John A. Rawlins (Grant's assistant adjutant general), October 18, 1862, *ibid.*, 279–80. In the first of these two letters Sherman refuted his own characterization of one party as guerrillas by reporting the capture of all its "papers, commissions, and muster-rolls."

[37] Special Order No. 283, October 18, 1862, *ibid.*, 280–81.

[38] For an extended contemporary discussion of this principle, see Halleck, *International Law*, 778–80.

send parties of infantry to chase these wanton guerrillas."[39] Thus expediency and military necessity were being offered as the justification for the experiment in terror upon which he had now embarked.

In developing this experiment Sherman issued carefully phrased orders which not only stated concisely the nature of the operation to be carried out but also included a statement of purpose, in which he sought to inspire in both officers and men a sense of the righteousness of their cause and to justify for them the harshness of the measures they applied. On October 22, for example, in ordering several units of his command to strike separately but simultaneously at different points along the river, he said: "The people at large should be made to feel that in the existence of a strong Government, capable of protecting as well as destroying, they have a real interest; that they must at once make up their minds or else he involved in the destruction that awaits armed rebellion against the national will." Apparently concerned about the outward appearances, however, he added: "Subordinates and privates must not pillage, but commanders may do anything necessary to impress upon the people that guerrillas must be driven from their midst, else they must necessarily share the consequences."[40]

Since the officers were fully aware of their commander's attitude toward the civilian population, and since the assignments themselves were missions of retaliation and destruction, it was easy to construe such instructions as permission to authorize pillage at their own discretion. And it was even easier for soldiers who had been engaged in the work of retaliation under orders to continue to carry on such activity without orders, so long as they were unhampered by the fear of disciplinary action from their higher officers. Thus in their operations around Memphis, Sherman's troops were not only obtaining experience in destruction but were also being released from the legal and moral restraints which would have maintained their respect for

---

[39] Sherman to Rawlins, October 18, 1862, in *Official Records*, Ser. I, Vol. XVII, Part 2, p. 280.

[40] Special Order No. 285, October 22, 1862, *ibid.*, 289–90.

the sanctity of private property. Under his tutelage they learned to direct their hatred against the people of the South and to visit upon them the savage art of destruction and the disregard for human rights and dignity which the rules of war had sought to mitigate. Looking back at this experiment from the perspective of Savannah in December, 1864, he expressed the conviction that the terror inspired by his corps in the Mississippi Valley had crippled the people as much as had their actual loss of property. "It was to me manifest," he said, "that the soldiers and people of the South entertained undue fear of the Western men. . . . This was a power, and I intended to utilize it."[41]

For Sherman, therefore, the activities around Memphis during the fall of 1862 were to be considered as experimentation and rehearsal. The finished performance which was to be staged in the campaigns of the next two years in Mississippi, Georgia, and South Carolina would mean the application of his philosophy of total war on a grand scale. These states particularly would be marked by a trail of burned houses, needless destruction of the necessities of life, and the wholesale theft of private property. Whereas at Memphis ten square miles were devastated to punish a community, in Georgia a swath sixty miles wide, diagonally across the state, would be laid waste. Where the little river town of Randolph paid the penalty for its community in flames, the capital cities of Mississippi and South Carolina would be reduced to ashes to punish those states. Ten secession families were forced to move out of their homes at Memphis, but the whole city of Atlanta was to be arbitrarily depopulated without regard to the harshness involved. On the Mississippi River prisoners were to be placed on the boats exposed to the fire of their own forces, but in Georgia Sherman would force them to uncover Confederate mines by marching them over suspected areas, or, in South Carolina, would threaten to hang them if his foragers were molested. The hostage idea would be improved upon through the seizure of prominent

[41] Sherman, *Memoirs*, II, 254.

citizens as a guarantee for the safe return of prisoners captured from his line of march by Confederate forces.

The first opportunity to test the effects of the rehearsal came in December, 1862, when Sherman embarked from Memphis with 32,000 troops to go down the Mississippi River to attack Vicksburg from the rear. He ordered that wherever the Federal transports were fired on from the shore, troops were to be landed and houses and barns in the vicinity were to be burned.[42] Where the Confederates along the river had removed all their cordwood to hinder the movement of Federal boats, Sherman equipped his men with axes to be used in destroying fences and houses along the shore to supply fuel.[43] The state of Mississippi began to feel the impact of Sherman's type of warfare in earnest in May, 1863, however, when General Frank P. Blair, whom he had ordered to strip the Yazoo Valley, burned five hundred thousand bushels of corn, immense quantities of bacon, and destroyed every grist mill in the valley. In addition he drove in one thousand head of cattle, some three hundred head of horses and mules, and an army of Negro slaves.[44]

Sherman had moved into Jackson, the capital of Mississippi, for the first time in May, 1863, to drive out Confederate General Joseph E. Johnston and had remained only long enough to wreck public property. On July 4, 1863, the day Vicksburg surrendered, he was ordered by Grant to attack Jackson once more and to render it useless to the Confederacy. The Union assault on Jackson was felt throughout the northern part of the state as Mississippians fled before the Union army. In a movement described as a "stampede," they drove their horses and Negroes eastward into Alabama. The Confederates

---

[42] General Orders No. 7, December 18, 1862, in *Official Records*, Ser. I, Vol. XVII, Part 1, p. 619. See Jenkins Lloyd Jones, *An Artilleryman's Diary* (Madison, Wis., 1914), 43, for an account of an incident of this kind and the action taken in retaliation.

[43] Sherman, *Memoirs*, I, 289.

[44] Blair to Sherman, May 26, 1863, in *Official Records*, Ser. I, Vol. XXIV, Part 2, p. 436.

evacuated Jackson on the night of July 16, leaving it in the hands of soldiers who had been permitted to live off a countryside almost without effective defense and who were no amateurs in the use of the torch and wrecking bar. Three days later Sherman wrote that "Jackson, once the pride and boast of Mississippi, is now a ruined town."[45] While he gave a banquet for his officers in the governor's mansion, the Union soldiers went about the work of destruction in the town. They left the entire business section in ruins, burned most of the better residences, dragged furniture into the streets to be demolished, and looted homes, churches, and the state library. A correspondent of the Chicago *Times* reported that the only fine residences left standing were those occupied by some of the general officers; and in summing up his impression of the sack of the town, he stated that "such complete ruin and devastation never followed the footsteps of an army before."[46]

While the Union infantry was sacking and burning Jackson, other detachments moved rapidly and effectively to disrupt all lines of communication in the state, and foragers were damaging the countryside just as effectively in their destruction of foodstuffs. "The wholesale destruction to which this country is now being subjected is terrible to contemplate," Sherman said in his report to Grant, "but it is the scourge of war, to which ambitious men have appealed. . . . Therefore, so much of my instructions as contemplated destroying and weakening the resources of our enemy are being executed with rigor."[47] Wherever one of his detachments went, the story was the same—burned buildings, looted residences, and the wanton destruction of provisions vital to the civilian population. So thorough was

---

[45] Sherman to Admiral David D. Porter, July 19, 1863, *ibid.*, Part 3, p. 531.

[46] Quoted in James W. Garner, *Reconstruction in Mississippi* (New York, 1901), 12–13. For another graphic account of the extent of the damage in Jackson, see Edgar L. Erickson (ed.), "With Grant at Vicksburg, from the Civil War Diary of Captain Charles E. Wilcox," *in Journal of the Illinois State Historical Society* (Springfield, 1908–), XXX (1937–1938), 501.

[47] Sherman to Grant, July 14, 1863, in *Official Records,* Ser. I, Vol. XXIV, Part 2, p. 526.

the devastation that it became necessary for General Grant to order Sherman to assist in providing supplies of food and medicine to alleviate the suffering of the very same inhabitants who had been despoiled by his men. The operations of the Federal troops "have left the country destitute both of transportation and subsistence," Grant said, and "having stripped the country thereabouts we can do no less than supply them."[48]

In an effort to put a stop to the unrestrained looting and destruction of private property, Grant also issued a general order on August 1 for the infliction of summary punishment "upon all officers and soldiers apprehended in acts of violence and lawlessness." Branding such acts as "conduct disgraceful to the American name," he said: "Hereafter, if the guilty parties cannot be reached, the commanders of regiments and detachments will be held responsible, and those who prove themselves unequal to the task of preserving discipline in their commands will be promptly reported to the War Department for muster-out."[49] So far as the records show, Sherman's only direct response to this order was the transmittal to Grant of court-martial proceedings against a private, a sergeant, and a captain who were charged with burning a cotton gin during the operations around Jackson. He had caught these men in the act, he stated, and he regarded their act as sheer vandalism, inasmuch as "the burning of this building in no way aided our military plans."[50]

Having thus made a token acknowledgment of Grant's instructions, he showed by his subsequent actions that he had no intention of letting them dull the effect of his program of terror. Writing directly to General Halleck shortly afterward, he said:

> I would banish all minor questions, assert the broad doctrine that as a nation the United States has the right, and also the physical power, to penetrate to every part of our national

[48] Grant to Sherman, July 28 and 29, 1863, *ibid.*, Part 3, pp. 557, 559.
[49] Grant's General Order No. 50, issued from Vicksburg, August 1, 1863, *ibid.*, 570–71.
[50] Sherman to Rawlins, August 4, 1863, *ibid.*, 575.

domain, and that we will do it . . . that we will remove and
destroy every obstacle, if need be, take every life, every acre of
land, every particle of property, every thing that to us seems
proper; that we will not cease till the end is attained; that all
who do not aid us are enemies, and that we will not account to
them for our acts. If the people of the South oppose, they do so
at their peril; and if they stand by, mere lookers-on in this domestic tragedy, they have no right to immunity, protection, or share
in the final results. . . . In accepting war, it should be "pure and
simple" as applied to the belligerents. I would keep it so, till all
traces of the war are effaced; till those who appealed to it are
sick and tired of it, and come to the emblem of our nation, and
sue for peace. I would not coax them, or even meet them half-
way, but make them so sick of war that generations would pass
away before they would again appeal to it.[51]

Following a brief period of duty around Chattanooga and in East
Tennessee, where his troops aroused considerable resentment because
of their failure to distinguish between loyal Unionists and others in
their pillaging,[52] Sherman returned to Mississippi at the beginning
of 1864 to complete the subjugation of that state preparatory to
moving his army eastward for the campaign which was being
planned in Georgia. Disturbed over the return of Confederate forces
to the state and the threat they offered to Federal control of the
Mississippi River,[53] he resumed his campaign of terror on a more
extensive scale. His first move was a carefully planned and well-
executed march eastward from Vicksburg across the state to Meridian,
important to the Confederates as a railroad center and arsenal and

---

[51] Sherman to Halleck, September 17, 1863, in Sherman, *Memoirs*, I, 335–42,
especially 339–40.

[52] See, for example, a circular letter issued by General Oliver O. Howard to
his troops, December 8, 1863, in *Official Records*, Ser. I, Vol. XXXI, Part 3,
pp. 357–58. Sherman himself was forced to admit that "though we try
to forage on the enemy, I fear we take much of Union people." Sherman to
Grant, December 11, 1863, *ibid.*, 382.

as the base of supply for their operations. Finding that the Confederate forces had evacuated the place before his arrival on February 14, he lost no time in setting his men at the work of wrecking the railroads, burning public property, and unofficially destroying the town. "For five days 10,000 men worked hard and with a will in that work of destruction, with axes, crowbars, sledges, clawbars, and with fire, and I have no hesitation in pronouncing the work as well done," he reported to Grant. "Meridian with its depots, store-houses, arsenal, hospitals, offices, hotels, and cantonments no longer exists."[54]

Rigid discipline had been maintained on the march to Meridian, and foraging had been held down by the continuous presence of Confederate cavalry on the flanks of the army; but now that the Confederates had lost their base and had withdrawn from the state, Sherman once more turned his men loose on the towns, villages, and farms along the return route to Vicksburg. His *Memoirs* simply sum up the campaign by stating that he destroyed "an arsenal, immense storehouses, and the railroad in every direction,"[55] and nowhere in his official report did he mention damages other than those directed against military objectives. From other sources, however, including official reports of Confederate officers, correspondence published in both southern and northern newspapers, and revealing comments by some of his own officers, the story is one of wanton waste, arson, looting, and other indignities visited upon the defenseless citizens by a ruthless soldier.[56] "They have destroyed everything in our

---

[53] In a letter written to General John A. Logan in December, 1863, Sherman said: "To secure the safety of the navigation of the Mississippi, I would slay millions—on that point I am not only insane, but mad." Autograph Draft of W. T. Sherman's Memoirs (Division of Manuscripts, Library of Congress), which contains numerous letters and reports prepared for but not included in the published *Memoirs*.

[54] Sherman to Rawlins, March 7, 1864, in *Official Records*, Ser. I, Vol. XXXII, Part 1, pp. 173–79.

[55] Sherman, *Memoirs*, I, 392.

[56] See Garner, *Reconstruction in Mississippi*, 13–18, for a summary based on contemporary newspaper accounts.

neighborhood," wrote a refugee from Meridian. "I do not think you can hear a chicken crow for ten miles around Meridian."[57] An officer in the signal corps of Sherman's force reported that at Lake Station "the Signal Corps went through the town like a dose of salts, and just as we were leaving I noticed a man hunting around to get someone to make an affidavit that there had been a town there."[58] At Enterprise, "No place or house escaped them. Locks and bars availed nothing. Every room, trunk, wardrobe, and the beds and bedding were plundered and torn up, nor did the poor negroes, whom they came to set free, as they said, escape those low-down pilfering rascals. . . . Everything they could carry off was taken, and what they could not, was torn up and destroyed, even to servants' underclothes."[59] Writing to her husband in the Confederate army, a resident of Brandon said:

> The thieving rascals reached our premises whilst we were at the dinner table on Sunday, and kept up their plundering and steal-ing until dark. . . . Every horse and mule Papa had was taken away, hogs killed, and all the poultry taken. In the smokehouse nothing was left, except some meal which they emptied on the floor. . . . In the house there was not a trunk, drawer, wardrobe, desk or anything they did not plunder and plunder well; and the contents scattered over the house, and everything stolen they wished. Not a garment of yours did they leave. . . . What was left [of her clothing] was torn into pieces or abused in some way. Papa has nothing left but what he was wearing. Every bed was stripped of clothing. . . . For three meals we hadn't a thing but roasted potatoes to eat, and since that time what we have eaten has been done with our fingers; not a knife or fork was left, and

---

[57] Mobile *Daily Tribune*, March 5, 1864.
[58] Report of Captain Lucius M. Rose, March 8, 1864, in *Official Records*, Ser. I, Vol. XXXII, Part 1, pp. 221–23.
[59] Mobile *Daily Register*, February 27, 1864.

but little earthenware. . . . All this stealing was done before our eyes, and neither words nor tears would prevent it:[60]

The utter helplessness of the victims of such brutality, forced to stand by while humiliations and indignities were heaped upon them, left lasting scars upon the memories of those so mistreated. The closing sentence of the letter from Brandon undoubtedly expressed the sentiments of hundreds of less articulate women who had faced a similar experience: "I hate them more now than I did the evening I saw them sneaking off with all we cared for, and so it will be everyday I live." That Sherman himself had already become aware of this hatred is shown in a letter which he wrote to his wife during the earlier campaign around Jackson. "I doubt if history affords a parallel to the deep and bitter enmity of the women of the South," he said. "No one who sees them and hears them but must feel the intensity of their hate." In a revealing sentence of explanation, he continued: "Not a man is seen; nothing but women with houses plundered, fields open to the cattle and horses, pickets lounging on every porch, and desolation sown broadcast, servants all gone and women and children bred in luxury, beautiful and accomplished, begging in one breath for the soldiers' rations and in another praying that the Almighty or Joe Johnston will come and kill us, the despoilers of their homes and all that is sacred."[61] But, he added, "They have sowed the wind and must reap the whirlwind. Until they . . . submit to the rightful authority of the government they must not appeal to me for mercy or favors." Thus he had come to justify the violations of the rights of noncombatants on the ground that they had brought their fate down upon their own heads and that it was his mission to inflict punishment upon the rebellious South and all its people until they could be convinced of the error of their ways.

---

[60] Montgomery *Daily Advertiser*, February 28, 1864.
[61] Sherman to Mrs. Sherman, June 27, 1863, in Howe (ed.), *Home Letters of General Sherman*, 267–69.

As he prepared to transfer his troops to a new theater of operations in Georgia in the spring of 1864, he could view his first full-dress performance in total war with satisfaction. He had accomplished his major objectives of destroying the resources of Mississippi and paralyzing its lines of communication, and he had demonstrated to the civilian population how terrible their lot could be made in a war conducted without regard for orthodox rules. "But the great result attained," he said, "is the hardihood and confidence imparted to the command, which is now better fitted for war."[62] During the next eight months he and his men were to repeat their performance on a larger scale in Georgia and to add new refinements in the light of their experience in Mississippi.

In its first phase the Georgia campaign presented problems which Sherman had not faced in Mississippi. As he moved southward from Chattanooga toward Atlanta, he was confronted by a well-organized, battle-hardened army under the command of General Joseph E. Johnston, one of the ablest of the Confederate military leaders, and his operations were also rendered more difficult by the mountainous terrain to be traversed. Under such conditions the loose organization and lax discipline of the Mississippi campaign had to give way to compact order and carefully planned maneuvering, and thus there was less opportunity to carry the war to the civilian population. That he had not abandoned his concept of total war, however, was shown in the thoroughness of his destruction of town after town as they came within the range of his operations; in his mass deportation to Indiana of approximately five hundred women workers from the Roswell cotton and woolen mills in July, 1864; in his seizure of noncombatant citizens to be used as hostages to prevent local resistance to his foraging parties; in his condonement of pillaging wherever the opportunity presented itself; and finally, in his callous suggestion to one of his subordinates that in retaliation for attacks

[62] Sherman's Report on Operations in Mississippi, March 7, 1864, in *Official Records*, Ser. I, Vol. XXXII, Part 1, p. 177.

on Federal communications he was to "burn ten or twelve houses of known secessionists, kill a few at random, and let them know that it will be repeated every time a train is fired on.["63](#63)

With the capture and subsequent destruction of Atlanta in the early fall of 1864 and the withdrawal of the greater part of the Confederate army to the northwestward, Sherman was once more in a position to carry on the type of campaign for which his men had been trained around Memphis and in Mississippi. While the indignation of the South over his bombardment of the city and his removal of its entire civilian population was still raging, he was busily engaged in the development of plans to launch his columns into the heart of Georgia "on a worse raid than our Meridian raid was," and he calmly assured one of his officers that "you may look for a great howl against the brute Sherman."[64] As his army of 62,000 men, selected for their physical fitness, rolled into the Georgia countryside on November 15 to begin the famous "March to the Sea," there was a spirit of recklessness in its ranks which boded ill for the noncombatants deep

[63] Sherman to General Louis D. Watkins, October 29, 1864, ibid., Ser. I, Vol. XXXIX, Part 3, p. 494. In view of the extensive coverage which has been given to Sherman's Georgia and South Carolina campaigns by historians and others, it does not seem necessary to treat them in detail here or to give specific citations for general statements except in cases of direct quotation. The official reports and correspondence are to be found in *Official Records*, Ser. I, Vols. XXXVIII,' Parts 1–5, and XXXIX, Part 3 (for the Atlanta campaign); Vol. XLIV (for the march from Atlanta to Savannah); and Vol. XLVII, Parts 1-3 (for the South Carolina campaign). Sherman's own later account comprises most of Volume II of his *Memoirs*; and among the best of the many accounts by other participants are Henry Hitchcock, *Marching with Sherman* (New Haven, 1927); David P. Conyngham, *Sherman's March through the South* (New York, 1865); Theodore F. Upson, *With Sherman to the Sea* (Baton Rouge, 1943); George W. Nichols, *The Story of the Great March* (New York, 1865); George W. Pepper, *Personal Recollections of Sherman's Campaign in Georgia and the Carolinas* (Zanesville, Ohio, 1866); and Dolly Sumner Lunt, *A Woman's Wartime Journal* (Macon, Ga., 1927).

[64] Sherman to General Andrew J. Smith, November 2, 1864, in *Official Records*, Ser. I, Vol. XXXIX, Part 3, p. 596.

in the state who had thus far escaped the terrifying sound of the marching feet of an invading army.[65]

The special orders which Sherman issued for the conduct of the army on this campaign were in complete accord with the accepted rules of war. They provided that only official foraging parties were to levy on the country for supplies and that in all foraging "the parties engaged will refrain from abusive or threatening language . . . and they will endeavor to leave with each family a reasonable portion for their maintenance." Soldiers were expressly forbidden to enter the dwellings of the inhabitants or commit any trespass, "but during a halt or a camp they may be permitted to gather turnips, potatoes, or other vegetables, and to drive in stock in sight of their camp." Private property was to be destroyed only with the approval of an army corps commander, and for them the general principle was laid down that "In districts and neighborhoods where the army is unmolested no destruction of such property should be permitted; but should guerrillas or bushwhackers molest our march, or should the inhabitants burn bridges, obstruct roads, or otherwise manifest local hostility, then army commanders should order and enforce a devastation more or less relentless according to the measure of such hostility."[66]

In view of Sherman's theory of waging war against the civilian population, as evolved at Memphis and applied in Mississippi, and in the light of the well-known and fully authenticated evidence of unrestrained pillage and destruction which marked the course of this campaign, it is difficult to escape the conclusion that these orders were formulated more for the record than for the guidance of his troops. No one knew better than he that the men who were to march under the orders were hardened veterans, many of whom had participated in his first experiments in total war, and that to them waste,

---

[65] See Sherman, *Memoirs*, II, 178–79, for his description of the spirit of the men at the beginning of the march.

[66] Special Field Orders No. 120, issued at Kingston, Georgia, November 9, 1864, in *Official Records*, Ser. I, Vol. XXXIX, Part 3, pp. 713–14.

burning, and looting were an old story. They, in turn, felt that they knew their general too well to believe that he intended to bind them by the rules of orthodox warfare just at the moment they were to strike deep into the Confederacy's vitals. Even the reports, diaries, and letters of some of his officers reveal their conviction that he did not intend for these orders to be enforced;[67] and on more than one occasion Sherman himself permitted outright violations in his presence without disciplining the guilty troops.[68] In commending the spirit of the men at the end of the march, he said: "A little loose in foraging, they 'did some things they ought not to have done,' yet, on the whole, they have supplied the wants of the army with as little violence as could be expected." His official report estimated the damage done to the state of Georgia "at $100,000,000; at least $20,000,000 of which has insured to our advantage, and the remainder is simple waste and destruction." And by way of justification, he added: "This may seem a hard species of warfare, but it brings the sad realities of war home to those who have been directly or indirectly instrumental in involving us in its attendant calamities."[69]

From his own point of view, therefore, another venture in carrying the war to the civilian population had been successful. In later years he was to claim that he had considered this march merely "as

---

[67] See, for example, the Official Report of General Alpheus S. Williams (Commander of the Twentieth Army Corps), January 9, 1865, *ibid.,* Ser. I, Vol. XLIV, pp. 206–16, in which he stated frankly that "repeated instances of wanton pillage occurred on the march," and condoned these with the explanation that "the nature of the march was calculated to relax discipline" (p. 212). In writing on November 23, 1864, of his own concern over the pillaging, Major Henry Hitchcock, who served throughout the campaign as Sherman's assistant adjutant general and military secretary, stated that "the belief in the army is that General S. favors and desires it, and one man when arrested told his officer so. I am bound to say I think Sherman lacking in enforcing discipline." Hitchcock, *Marching with Sherman,* 86–87.

[68] For his own account of one such instance, see Sherman, *Memoirs,* II, 181. A graphic account of the march, based on a wide sampling of materials, is in Lewis, *Sherman, Fighting Prophet,* 438–57.

[69] Sherman's Official Report on the Savannah Campaign, January 1, 1865, in *Official Records,* Ser. I, Vol. XLIV, pp. 7–16, especially 13–14.

a means to an end, and not as an essential act of war." The purpose, he said, had been "the transfer of a strong army, which had no opponent, and had finished its then work, from the interior to a point on the sea-coast, from which it could achieve other important results."[70] Actually, however, he had accomplished much more than a shift of base from Atlanta to Savannah. By marching almost unopposed through the inner citadel of the Confederacy, he had been able to destroy the resources of one of its most productive sections and had eliminated Georgia as a possible source of supply for General Lee's army in Virginia. By applying his concept of total war in the course of that march, he had instilled in the noncombatants of Georgia the same sense of helplessness and terror that had been felt earlier in Mississippi. The ease with which such devastation and demoralization had been wrought had proved the weakness of the South and showed both sides that the end of the war was near at hand. But the success of Sherman's methods caught the imagination of an important segment of the northern public and created a feeling that before the war ended he should be permitted to extend his campaign of terror and destruction to the people of South Carolina as punishment for having started it. Even General Halleck himself reflected the blending of enthusiasm and vindictiveness when in congratulating the army on its achievement he said: "When Savannah falls, then for another wide swath through the centre of the Confederacy." Assuring Sherman that additional troops would be sent to him for the move into South Carolina, he added: "Should you capture Charleston, I hope that by some accident the place may be destroyed, and if a little salt should be sown upon its site it may prevent the growth of future crops of nullification and secession."[71]

Meanwhile, Sherman was also busily formulating his plans for the next move. Writing to Grant before the capture of Savannah, he

---

[70] Sherman, *Memoirs,* II, 220.

[71] Halleck to Sherman, December 18, 1864, *ibid.,* II, 222–23; also in *Official Records,* Ser. I, Vol. XLIV, p. 741, where the words "wide swath," quoted above, appear as "raid south"—a reading which does not fit the context.

said: "With Savannah in our possession . . . we can punish South Carolina as she deserves, and as thousands of people in Georgia hoped we would do. I do sincerely believe that the whole United States, North and South, would rejoice to have this army turned loose on South Carolina to devastate that State, in the manner we have done in Georgia."[72] On the day after he occupied Savannah, he wrote that if Grant did not need his force immediately in Virginia he "could go on and smash South Carolina all to pieces," and two days later he told Halleck: "The truth is the whole army is burning with an insatiable desire to wreak vengeance upon South Carolina. I almost tremble at her fate, but feel that she deserves all that seems in store for her."[73] This spirit of vengeance had obviously not subsided during the month of preparation which followed, and when the army finally began its march across South Carolina on February 1, 1865, both its officers and its enlisted men were ready to apply the concept of total war with a zeal which only hate could inspire and a thoroughness which represented the cumulation of two years of experience in destruction.[74] On arriving at the northern limits of the state thirty-four days later, they left behind them a trail of terror and desolation, burned homes and towns, devastated fields and plundered

[72] Sherman to Grant, December 18, 1864, in *Official Records,* Ser. I, Vol. XLIV, pp. 741–43.

[73] Sherman to Grant, December 22, 1864, *ibid.,* 6–1; Sherman to Halleck, December 24, 1864, *ibid.,* 798–800.

[74] In addition to the references listed in Note 63, above, much information on the South Carolina campaign from the point of view of minor officers appears in such accounts as the following: Julian W. Hinkley, *A Narrative of Service with the Third Wisconsin Infantry* (Madison, Wis., 1912); "Major Connolly's Letters to His Wife, 1862–1865," in *Ilinois Historical Society Publications* (Springfield, 1900-1942), No. 35 (1928), 217–383; Clement Eaton (ed.), "Diary of an Officer in Sherman's Army Marching through the Carolinas," in *Journal of Southern History,* IX (1943), 238–54; and Samuel H. M. Byers, *With Fire and Sword* (New York, 1911). An excellent account from the southern point of view is Joseph LeConte, *'Ware Sherman: A Three Months Personal Experience in the Last Days of the Confederacy* (Berkeley, Calif., 1937).

storehouses, and a record for systematic torture, pillage, and vandalism unequaled in American history. The state lay prostrate—broken, impoverished, and hopeless; and its people were filled with a deep and abiding bitterness over the viciousness of the destruction visited upon them, not only because it violated the rules of civilized warfare but also because it had gone so far beyond what was necessary to accomplish their capitulation.

The suddenness with which this orgy of destruction came to an end as the army moved into North Carolina early in March provided striking evidence of the deliberate vengeance which had determined its character in South Carolina, and indicated also that it might have been kept under control had there been any real desire to do so in earlier stages of the campaign. "The conduct of the soldiers is perceptibly changed," wrote one of Sherman's aides on March 8. "I have seen no evidence of plundering; the men keep their ranks closely; and more remarkable yet, not a single column of the fire or smoke which a few days ago marked the positions of heads of columns, can be seen on the horizon."[75] In the eyes of both the officers and the men the people of North Carolina had been more reluctant to leave the Union than had those of the other states through which they had passed. Consequently, they were ready to accept without question the prohibition which was now issued against wanton destruction of property or unkind treatment of citizens, and thus the operations of Sherman's army were returned to the normal channel of waging war against military objectives and the armed forces of the enemy.

The three years since Sherman had assumed command at Memphis and had first experimented with the concept of carrying the war to the civilian population of the South had seen the evolution of that concept through its early proving ground in Mississippi into a movement which had gained momentum and effectiveness in Georgia and had swelled into a relentless campaign of vengeance in South Carolina. Although the concept itself was not in accord with the

[75] Nichols, *Story of the Great March*, 222.

accepted rules of his own time, his success in using it as a means of destroying the enemy's resources and undermining his morale was to influence the strategy of future wars and to bring at least a tacit adjustment in the rules under which they were to be fought. That his campaigns contributed materially in hastening the final defeat of the Confederacy can hardly be denied; but since the principal purpose of the conflict from the Federal point of view was to bring back into the fold those states which had attempted to withdraw, good policy would seem to have required that it be accomplished with as little cause for future hatred as possible. In the case of Mississippi, Georgia, and South Carolina, however, the wanton destruction and the outrages and indignities to which their people were subjected in Sherman's application of his concept of total war created wounds which would remain sensitive for generations to come. Although they came back into the Union, other causes of estrangement would pass away and be forgotten long before the crime committed by him against the spirit of their people would be forgiven.

4

Disjointed Allies: Coalition Warfare in Berlin and Vienna, 1914

HOLGER H. HERWIG

By the end of September 1914, both Austria-Hungary and Germany had suffered strategic bankruptcy, the one in the east and the other in the west. The military ramifications of the early defeats in Galicia and Serbia were immediate: the Dual Monarchy had lost fully one-third of its combat effectives; the morale of its army was never to recover fully from this initial shock; and the cohesion as well as reliability of that last remaining integrating factor in the Habsburg state—namely, the army—was now openly in question. Most indicative of the changing fortunes, the Austro-Hungarian chief of the General Staff, Franz Baron Conrad von Hötzendorf, underwent a pathetic transformation. His letters of August 1914 still lauded the eternal bond that existed between Vienna and Berlin, reaffirmed both his personal devotion to the northern ally and his unencumbered willingness to protect Germany's eastern flank while the great decision was being sought in the west, and expressed his great delight at standing "shoulder-to-shoulder" with the Germans. By early September, however, the letters had degenerated into bitter indictments of the ally at Berlin, whom Conrad now accused of selfishness, perfidy, and faithlessness.[1]

---

[1] Conrad von Hötzendorf, *Aus Meiner Dienstzeit 1906–1918,* 5 vols. (Vienna/Leipzig/Munich: Rikola, 1921–25), 4:318–743 passim; Hermann von Kuhl, *Der Weltkrieg 1914–1918,* 2 vols. (Berlin: W. Kolk, 1929), 1:60. Conrad during the Great War once received his military plenipotentiary at Berlin with the

The political ramifications of the early defeats were equally important; the last hope of gaining Italy and Rumania as active partners
in the Triple Alliance disappeared. Above all, the very tie between
Vienna and Berlin was seriously jeopardized. When Conrad on
8 September informed Foreign Minister Leopold Count von
Berchtold that Germany's failure to live up to prewar military agreements had caused the Austro-Hungarian demise in southern Poland,
Berchtold immediately instructed his envoy in Berlin, Gottfried
Prince zu Hohenlohe-Schillingsfürst, to the threaten the Germans
that the Dual Monarchy might conclude a separate peace. Moreover, Hohenlohe informed the Wilhelmstrasse that Germany "carries the responsibility for the failure of the entire military campaign"
in the east; that England's entry into the war as well as the Italian
and Rumanian neutrality declarations had come about solely due to
Germany's invasion of Belgium; and that it was Conrad's considered
opinion that Kaiser Wilhelm II cared more for his East Prussian stud
farms and hunting grounds than he did for the common cause of the
Central Powers![2]

The Germans, for their part, initially waited for the decision to
fall in the west; thereafter, they expressed barely concealed contempt
for the military prowess of their sole ally. This was perhaps most
blatantly exemplified by two letters that General Erich Ludendorff,
chief of staff of the Eighth Army in the east, wrote to the former

---

words: "Well, what are our secret enemies, the Germans, and the German
Emperor, the comedian, up to?" Cited in Josef Baron Stürgkh, *Im deutschen
Grossen Hauptquartier* (Leipzig: P. List, 1921), 116. For the wartime alliance,
which goes beyond the chronological parameters of this paper, see Gary W.
Shanafelt, *The Secret Enemy: Austria-Hungary and the German Alliance,
1914–1918* (New York: Columbia University Press, 1985).

[2] Cited in Gerhard Ritter, "Die Zusammenarbeit der Generalstabe Deutschlands
und Österreich-Ungarns vor dem ersten Weltkrieg," in *Zur Geschichte und
Problematik der Demokratie: Festgabe für Hans Herzfeld* (Berlin: Duncker
and Humblot, 1958), 547–48. Ritter used the German Army archives before
their destruction during World War II, and hence this article has served as the
basis for much of the literature in the field.

head of the General Staff, Helmuth von Moltke the Younger, in April 1915. Ludendorff accused the Austrians of "arrogance," of a "lack of resistance," of military "incompetence," and of having "constantly failed" down the line. In fact, he denied what he termed "this miserable people" any future role as a major power. For our immediate purposes, Ludendorff, recalling that he had been denied a request to attend prewar Austrian army maneuvers, levelled the "serious reproach" against Germany's military representatives at Vienna "that they had not told the plain truth before the war" with regard to the Dual Monarchy's military capabilities.[3]

Why were the ties between the two Germanic states so frail? Where was the *Nibelungentreue* of just a few years ago? Why Conrad's bitterness towards an ally that he had openly courted and with which he had conducted frequent talks and exchanged sensitive information? In short, why was the Berlin-Vienna coalition so fractious and tenuous that the initial setbacks in 1914 could cause such major recriminations?

In recent years, much has been written especially by Anglo-American scholars on the efficacy of the German military and on its ability to adapt to change at the operational and tactical levels. Unfortunately, relatively little work has been done on the performance of that institution at the grand strategic level. In 1958, Gerhard Ritter published a probing piece on the nature of the military cooperation that existed between the two Germanic allies prior to 1914, wherein he utilized the German military records that he had examined before the Second World War (and which were largely destroyed by Allied air raids during that struggle) as well as a 1934 Leipzig University dissertation by Gerhard Seyfert. What little work was done in the field thereafter by Hans Meier-Welcker in West Germany and Harold Müller as well as Helmut Otto in East Germany merely recast Ritter's findings in different lights. Rudolf Kiszling in Austria penned two essays in 1963 and 1966 that only tangentially

---

[3] Letters of 1 and 5 April 1915, Nachlass Moltke, N 78, 35: 2, 4, Bundesarchiv-Militärarchiv, Freiburg, West Germany.

touched upon the central problem of Conrad's relations with Moltke and their joint strategic planning.

On this side of the Atlantic, Gordon Craig in 1965 sought to rekindle serious discussion on the military cohesion of the Berlin-Vienna alliance prior to 1914 on the basis of several published memoirs. In England, Norman Stone the following year made available to English-language readers the main passages of the Conrad-Moltke correspondence. Neither piece evoked much reaction.

This *essai*, part of a proposed monograph on the nature of German and Austro-Hungarian diplomatic and military planning prior to 1914, is based upon the available documentary record at the Federal Military Archive (Bundesarchiv-Militärarchiv) at Freiburg, West Germany, and at the War Archive (Kriegsarchiv) at Vienna, Austria. It seeks to provide a preliminary answer to several critical questions. How well did Berlin and Vienna coordinate their joint strategies, both in the east and the west? How frank was each side in addressing common aims and problems? To what degree was either ally willing to alter its own strategy in order to accommodate the other? And how well did each understand the diplomatic, strategic, and domestic difficulties faced by the other?

It should be stated at the start that, as General Ludwig Beck noted decades later, there existed in 1914 no "systematically developed war plan" in Berlin or Vienna.[4] The reason for this was not for lack of coordinating institutions or contacts. Apart from the frequent exchanges of visits between the two monarchs—as well as between their relatives and the federated kings and archdukes, most of whom held senior military commands—informal ties between the two general staffs had been established already by 1882 at the urgings of Chancellor Otto von Bismarck. In addition, both staff chiefs frequently attended each other's annual maneuvers and, starting in 1890–91, formally sent three staff officers each to these affairs. Indeed, on one such occasion, the critical question of appointing a

---

[4] See Ludwig Beck, *Studien*, ed. Hans Speidel (Stuttgart: K. F. Koehler, 1955), 110–11.

single commander-in-chief in case of war had been raised by the Austro-Hungarian chief of the General Staff, Friedrich Count Beck-Rzikowsky, though without resolution. Moreover, Vienna had maintained permanent military attachés at Berlin since 1860, and in 1872 added the post of a more senior "military plenipotentiary." The latter, usually a flag-rank officer, acted independently of the embassy and was charged with keeping the chief of the General Staff informed of Prussian-German military and political developments by way of so called direct "private letters." Prussia-Germany likewise maintained a Militärbevollmächtigter at Vienna and, after 1911, added a naval attaché.[5]

   If not institutional, what then were the major failings of the two "Central Powers" to coordinate the military aspects of their alliance? I suggest that these were mainly due to the fundamentally differing positions concerning the nature and purpose of the alliance that evolved especially after 1888, as well as due to human peculiarities and shortcomings.

   Bismarck's position, as expressed in both the Austro-German Dual Alliance of 1879 and the Russo-German Reinsurance Treaty of 1887, was clear; he strove to preserve the Dual Monarchy against all external threats, while concurrently he sought to curb Russian ambitions in the Danubian basin. Above all, he was determined not to allow Vienna to use the new German Reich as a tool for what he

[5] See Georg Graf Waldersee, "Über die Beziehungen des deutschen zum österreich-ungarischen Generalstabe vor dem Weltkriege," *Berliner Monatshefte* 8 (1930): 105; Edmund Glaise von Horstenau, *Franz Josephs Weggefährte: Das Leben des Generalstabschefs Grafen Beck. Nach seinen Aufzeichnungen und hinterlassenen Dokumenten* (Zurich/Leipzig/Vienna: Amalthea, 1930), 348–50; Ronald Louis Ernharth, "The Tragic Alliance: Austro-German Military Cooperation, 1871–1918," dissertation, Columbia University, 1970, 60–65; Johann Christoph Allmayer-Beck, "Die Archive der k.u.k Militärbevollmächtigten und Militär-Adjutants im Kriegsarchiv Wien. Ein Beitrag zur militärge-schichtlichen Quellenkunde," in *Österreich und Europa. Festgabe fur Hugo Hantsch zum 70. Geburtstag* (Graz/ Vienna/Cologne: Institute fur Osterreichische GeschichtsForschung, 1965), 353–54; and Alfred Vagts, *The Military Attache* (Princeton: Princeton University Press, 1967), especially Chapter 2.

deemed to be Austria's expansionist policies in the Balkans. As the Iron Chancellor once put it: "Within an alliance, there is always a horse and a rider." There can be no question which Bismarck intended to be. His aide, Friedrich von Holstein, later summed up Bismarck's position as follows: "If it becomes a matter of life or death for the Austrians, we will have to intervene with or without a treaty; but as to when we feel that the psychological moment has come is our secret.[6] While some historians have deplored the absence of definite military commitments in the treaty of 1879, this "oversight" reflected perfectly Bismarck's policy of optimal diplomatic flexibility.

Moreover, having rejected any drive for European hegemony in the Bad Kissingen *Diktat* of 1877, Bismarck was content to assume a strong defensive posture in Central Europe. He feared France rather than Russia, and hence favored German concentration in the west in case of a two-front war. Both Moltke and his deputy, Alfred Count von Waldersee, on the other hand, preferred an eastern posture, albeit—as Moltke stressed—with limited operations and aims in Russian Poland. The Austrians, for their part, were not interested in war against France, and in 1879 had declined to become contractually bound in such an event. Hence, from the start, the divergent political-military aims and policies of the two Germanic powers surfaced; while the Austrians looked mainly to the east and Russia, the Germans viewed war with Russia as only the first stage in an inevitable two-front campaign.

---

[6] Holstein to Eulenburg, 9 February 1896, in Norman Rich and M. H. Fisher, eds., *The Holstein Papers,* 4 vols. (Cambridge: Cambridge University Press, 1955–63), 3:592–94. Bismarck's longer explanation of the purpose of the Dual Alliance is in a letter of 27 December 1887 to Ambassador Prince Heinrich VII Reuss, in Johannes Lepsius, et al., eds., *Die Grosse Politik der Europäischen Kabinette 1871–1914,* 40 vols. in 54 (Berlin: Deutsche Verlagsgesellschaft fur Politik und Geschichte, 1922–27), 6: 66–69. The citation concerning the "horse" and "rider" is in Keith Neilson and Roy A. Prete, eds., *Coalition Warfare: An Uneasy Accord* (Waterloo, Canada: Wilfrid Laurier Press, 1983), vii.

It is against this political panorama that General Beck's desire in 1882 to seek common understanding with regard to "war aims and, at least in outline, coordination of strategic plans" must be seen. In a word, Beck sought to get a firm military commitment from Berlin. Increasingly, bellicose Pan-Slav pressures in Russia, irredentist rhetoric in Italy, and Greater-Serbia clamor in Belgrade convinced him that a two- or even three-front war was a distinct possibility. On the other hand, Beck was aware that the Dual Monarchy was unable to exploit its manpower potential, that it was only slowly developing an industrial capacity, that it was divided by national rivalries, and that its cumbersome political apparatus constituted an effective check on the growth of Habsburg military power.

To square this circle, Beck placed his trust in the prevalent European "cult of the offensive." Wars would be brief, the argument ran, and decided by massive offensive thrusts delivered right after the outbreak of hostilities. To stand on the defensive meant defeat. Specifically, Beck sought nothing less than "to destroy the Russians" in a giant battle of envelopment in the Polish salient, and feared only that the Germans, whom he asked to commit at least one-half of their forces in the east, would mobilize first and hence take the lion's share of the anticipated spoils. Above all, he argued that Austrian forces, having been defeated recently by both Italy and Prussia, not appear as a sort of "reserve army"; rather, they needed to take the offensive at the same time and in roughly similar strength as their German counterpart. "Our army, once it is led into battle," Beck pleaded, "needs victories—indeed, decisive victories—even though these be purchased at heavy costs."[7] Thus, the "cult of the offensive" complemented Austria-Hungary's strategic needs: not only was it numerically inferior to Russia—let alone a Russian Italian-Serbian

---

[7] Eduard Heller, "Bismarck's Stellung zur Fuhrung des Zweifronten-Krieges," *Archiv für Politik und Geschichte* 12 (1926): 680–82; and Gunther E. Rothenberg, *The Army of Francis Joseph* (West Lafayette, Ind.: Purdue University Press, 1976), 113. Less useful is Harald Muller, "Zu den Anfängen der militärischen Absprachen zwischen Deutschland und Osterreich-Ungarn im Jahre 1882," *Zeitschrift für Miliärgeschichte* 7 (1968): 206–15.

combination—but a protracted war most likely would entail the breakdown of the fragile socio-political framework of the Dual Monarchy.

Bismarck undoubtedly shared Beck's concerns. While the Iron Chancellor conceded that the possibility of an Austro-Russian war was "the most important question that can confront the German Empire," in the end he refused to sanction any firm military agreements—much less a formal military convention—with the Viennese. The architect of *Realpolitik* preferred to keep his options open until a *casus foederis* actually was at hand. Determination of such would be decided not by the head of the general staff but by the chancellor.[8]

This situation was radically altered upon Wilhelm II's accession to the throne. In August 1889, he assured both Beck and Emperor Francis Joseph: "For whatever reason you mobilize . . . —the day of your mobilization is also the day of mobilization for my army, and the chancellors can say what they want." Both Waldersee, now chief of the General Staff, and General Julius Verdy du Vernois, the Prussian War Minister, assured Beck of the earnest nature of the monarch's statement. Beck, for his part, was ecstatic and informed Francis Joseph that in future the Dual Monarchy's role would likely be to "rein in" the Germans rather than, as in the past, to urge greater vigor on their part.[9] Therewith, a new era in Austro-German relations

---

[8] On 16 December 1887, the German military attaché at Vienna, Major Johann Georg von Deines, broached the question of Germany's role in an Austro-Russian war with Francis Joseph and Wilhelm I. Bismarck informed Deines that his policy was "at all costs to avoid this war," and curtly reprimanded Deines: "The foreign policy of His Majesty the Emperor is advised not by the general staff but exclusively by me." Gesandschaft Wien. 0. Dienst Instruction und Stellung des Militar-Attaches 1875–1911, vol. la, Auswartiges Amt, Politisches Archiv (hereafter AA-PA), Bonn, West Germany.

[9] Glaise von Horstenau, *Franz Josephs Weggefährte*, 337–38. In 1895 and again in 1908, Wilhelm II theatrically informed the Austro-Hungarian envoy at Berlin: "Emperor Francis Joseph is a Prussian field marshal and hence he has only to command and the entire Prussian Army will follow his command." Cited in Gerhard Ritter, *Staatskunst und Kriegshandwerk. Das Problem des "Militärismus" in Deutschland*, 4 vols. (Munich: R. Oldenbourg, 1965–68), 2: 298.

was at hand. Gone was the reserved constraint of Bismarck. Gone was the pivotal role of the chancellor in the German decision-making process. Gone were sober, rational assessments in favor of emotional (and later racial) expressions of common cause.

That the Kaiser's bold stance of 1889 in time became dogma is indisputable. In June 1908, at the height of the annexation crisis over Bosnia-Herzegovina, Chancellor Bernhard von Bülow reassured Wilhelm II that "the needs, interests and desires of Austria-Hungary are a first priority in determining our own attitude towards Balkan questions."[10] And three years later, during the second Moroccan crisis, Foreign Minister Wilhelm von Schoen minuted: "I repeat what I have allowed to reach Conrad von Hötzendorf and H.M. Emperor Francis Joseph: that in a casus foederis Austria-Hungary can count on us."[11] With this major diplomatic-political reversal of Bismarck's cautionary stance—and with the Reinsurance Treaty canceled in 1890—the way was clear for the two respective general staffs to coordinate this *Nibelungentreue*.

This, however, was not to be. In April 1891, the new German chief of the General Staff, Alfred Count von Schlieffen, met with Beck to discuss joint operational planning. The meeting was not a success. Schlieffen proved taciturn and treated Beck with reserve. While he initially agreed to the east-first strategy of Moltke and suggested that Germany might be willing temporarily (as in the days of Frederick the Great) to sacrifice East and West Prussia, Pomerania, and even Brandenburg for the joint cause, Schlieffen quickly developed skepticism concerning the Dual Monarchy's military capacities. He revised his earlier ranking of Austrian and Russian units as being equal in quality in favor of the Russians. Moreover, he questioned the ability of the Austrians to keep information secret, with the result that his correspondence with Beck lapsed after 1896—and until his

---

[10] Büllow to Wilhelm II, 23 June 1908, Beziehungen zu Deutschland, England 78 *secr.*, AA-PA.
[11] Büllow to Loebell, 19 September 1911, Nachlass Loebell, N 1, vol. 7, 62. Bundesarchiv, Koblenz, West Germany.

retirement in 1905—into formal exchanges of information, maps, and festive greetings. Schlieffen in time spoke of two separate eastern fronts, the one (German) in East Prussia, the other (Austrian) in eastern Galicia. Nor did Vienna learn of Schlieffen's general leanings by about 1892 toward a concentration in the west against France, much less of his famous treatise of December 1905.[12]

Indeed, it is interesting to note that at a time when Germany had dropped the tie with Russia, resulting in the Franco-Russian military convention of 1892, Schlieffen ignored his major ally. Not only did he refuse to convey to Vienna the fact that he now opted for a limited offensive across the Narev River designed to defend East Prussia, but he even questioned the reliability of the Dual Monarchy's armed forces. "Those characters will only desert or run over to the enemy."[13] In a private letter to the Reich's military attaché at Vienna, General Hans Count von Hülsen-Haeseler, Schlieffen avowed that he expected little from an Austrian offensive in the east, that he was no longer interested in the details of the Austrian operations plan, that he regretted past promises of aid made to the Austrians by the Elder Moltke, that he would not make any further commitments, and that it depended totally upon the German success in the west whether a single Austrian ever crossed the San River! Finally, he cautioned Hülsen-Haeseler not to speak a word of any of this to

---

[12] Von Horstenau, *Franz Josephs Weggefährte,* 344; Dennis E. Showalter, "The Eastern Front and German Military Planning, 1871–1914—Some Observations," *East European Quarterly* 15 (1981): 167–69; and Helmut Otto, "Zum strategisch-operativen Zusammmenwirken des deutschen und österreichungarischen Generalstabes bei der Vorbereitung des ersten Weltkrieges," *Zeitschrift für Miliäirgeschichte* 2 (1963): 430–31. Beck spoke openly to his military attaché at Berlin, Carl Baron von Steininger, of Schlieffen's "sensitivity," his "mistrust" of Austria, and his "taciturn" behavior. Letter of 5 February 1894, Operations Biiro Generalstab, F 59, Osterreichisches Staatsarchiv-Kriegsarchiv (hereafter OStA-K), Vienna.

[13] Cited in Hugo Rochs, *Schlieffen* (Berlin: Voss, 1921), 41. See also, Graydon A. Tunstall, "The Schlieffen Plan: The Diplomacy and Military Strategy of the Central Powers in the East, 1905–1914," dissertation, Rutgers University, 1975, passim.

Beck for fear that the Austrian might grow "more suspicious" of German intentions.[14] In 1896, Schlieffen refused even to address Beck's renewed call for a formal military convention.[15] And as far as can be gleaned from contemporary memoirs, most German general staff officers shared Schlieffen's views on the efficacy of the Austro-Hungarian military.

In fact, Schlieffen was highly skeptical of the value of alliances and of the utility of conducting alliance warfare. In October 1899, he caustically noted on a memorandum: "To count on the intercession of our ally!! What an illusion."[16] Somewhat later, he averred that "alliances produce relatively little owing to the desire of each member to pass the lion's share of the work on to the others [and] to reserve for oneself the spoils" of war.[17] In the final analysis, Schlieffen saw the Austro-German alliance become operative at the earliest after the main decision had been reached in the west, and the army shuttled to the east. Surely, this is the meaning behind his famous remark that "Austria's fate will not be decided along the Bug but along the Seine!"[18] Beck, for his part, was exasperated by Schlieffen's refusal to accede to joint military planning for the east. The correspondence between the two men ended in April 1896, as Gerhard Ritter aptly noted, with "resentment, suspicion and resignation . . . Both general staffs now drew up their operations plans without consulting each other."[19] The depth of the estrangement between Berlin

---

[14] Gerhard Ritter, *Der Schlieffenplan. Kritik eines Mythos* (Munich: R. Oldenbourg, 1956), 28-29.

[15] Max Freiherr von Pitreich, 1914. *Die militärischen Probleme unseres Kriegsbeginnes. Ideen, Grunde und Zusammenhange* (Vienna: Selbstverlag des Verfassers, 1934), 49.

[16] Cited in Otto, "Zum Zusammenwirken des deutschen und österreichungarischen Generalstabes," 432.

[17] Alfred von Schlieffen, "Der Feldherr," in *Gesammelte Schriften*, 2 vols. (Berlin: E. S. Mittler, 1913), 1:7.

[18] Cited in Ritter, *Der Schlieffenplan*, 186. General von Moltke on 10 February 1913 repeated these exact words to Conrad von Hötzendorf. B Flügeladj., vol. 3, Conrad Archiv, ÖStA-K.

[19] Ritter,"Zusammenarbeit der Generalstabe," 536.

and Vienna can perhaps best be measured by the fact that Beck's successor, Conrad von Hotzendorf, in the summer of 1908 drew up a new operations plan for a war against Russia with the full expectation that Germany would throw its major forces against the east and seek a giant battle of envelopment and annihilation east of Warsaw![20]

The final phase of the Austro-German alliance began in the wake of the Dual Monarchy's annexation of Bosnia and Herzegovina, and was highlighted by cordial exchanges—beginning in 1908-09 and lasting to the spring of 1914—between Conrad and the new German chief of the General Staff, the Younger Moltke.[21] The two soldiers could hardly have been farther apart in terms of their personalities. While Moltke was dour and pessimistic, Conrad was dynamic and energetic. While Moltke was content merely to fine-tune the Schlieffen plan, Conrad dashed off one major operations plan after another. While Moltke loyally accepted the command function of his Supreme War Lord and declined to interfere in German foreign affairs, Conrad besieged both his emperor and his foreign minister with countless position papers demanding a greater role in Austrian military and diplomatic affairs. And while Moltke basically abhorred war, Conrad reveled in urging countless preemptive strikes—against Italy, Serbia, Rumania, Montenegro, Russia, or any combination thereof—upon his monarch and government.

Of course, neither man was ignorant of the deteriorating position of the Germanic powers in Europe. The Anglo-French entente of 1904 and its expansion in 1907 to include Russia had greatly diminished the chances that Schlieffen's blueprint for victory could be realized. In addition, the growing uncertainty concerning Italy's role in any future war had further deepened the pessimism that began to set in both in Berlin and Vienna. While much has been written about the detailed operational planning contained in the Conrad-Moltke

[20] Conrad, *Aus Meiner Dienstzeit*, 1:377.
[21] Official approval for the general staff talks was conveyed to Berlin by the Austro-Hungarian foreign minister, Aehrenthal, on 8 December 1908; Bulow concurred six days later. Deutschland 128 Nr. 1 *secr.*, vol. 28, AA-PA.

letters,[22] of primary interest here is the cooperation that they engendered.

The alliance objectives of Conrad and Moltke can quickly be summarized as follows. While the Austrian actively sought to commit Moltke to deploy specific numbers of troops in the east, to offer precise dates for full-force intervention against the Russians, and to define individual military operations, the German refused tenaciously to make firm promises as to deployment strength, to set timetables for bringing the army from the west to the east, and to coordinate specific operations. Instead, Moltke sought to assuage the Austrians with emotional pledges of loyalty and common racial bonds in order to encourage them to do more in the east than merely to assume defensive positions, be it in Poland or even along the Carpathian passes.[23]

In fact, the strategic needs of both general staffs remained as diverse as they had been under Beck and the Elder Moltke. Conrad at all times had to plan against potential hostile powers on three fronts: Russia in the east (Case "R"), Serbia and Montenegro in the southeast (Case "B"), and Italy in the southwest (Case "I"). To meet this potential threat, he had divided his army into three groups. The main force, *A-Staffel*, was composed of nine corps and was to tackle

---

[22] See especially Norman Stone, "Moltke-Conrad: Relations Between the Austro-Hungarian and German General Staffs, 1909–14," *Historical Journal* 9 (1966): 201–28. Also, Gerhard Seyfert, *Die militärischen Beziehungen und Vereinbarungen zwischen dem deutschen und dem ödsterreichischen General-stab vor und bei Beginn des Weltkrieges* (Leipzig: J. Moltzen, 1934), 46ff.

[23] Ritter, "Zusammenarbeit der Generalstabe," 538. Two examples of Moltke's evasiveness should suffice. On 24 February 1909, he declined to be precise as to when German forces could be shuttled from west to east: "I am unable to give a precise answer to this most important of all questions dealt with because the enemy will play a role in this." Conrad, *Aus Meiner Dienstzeit*, 1:395. And at their last meeting at 'Carlsbad on 12 May 1914, Conrad pressed Moltke as to what the Germans intended to do in case the decision in the west was not achieved quickly and the Russians advanced upon Germany. Moltke replied: "Well, I will do what I can. We are not superior to the French." Ibid., 3: 669.

either Russia or Italy; a second force of three corps, *Minimalgruppe Balkan*, would concentrate against Serbia-Montenegro; and a strategic reserve of four corps, *B-Staffel*, could be deployed against either of the two other groups, as the situation demanded. Thus it was paramount to Conrad to acquire a firm, specific German commitment against Russia in order to attach *B-Staffel* to *Minimalgruppe Balkan* from the outset of hostilities against the adversary he most despised, Serbia. The Germans, for their part, were equally adamant not to denude the forces required for the main thrust against France through greater commitment in the east. Unfortunately, neither side was willing bluntly to spell these considerations out, with the result that for six years both heads of their respective general staffs danced a polite polonaise around the vital issue of joint military planning.

To be sure, there were occasional indications of closer cooperation. In April 1908, Conrad pondered possible German options for a two-front war and concluded that "in time" one ought to coordinate such matters between Berlin and Vienna. He estimated that it would take four months for such talks.[24] To show that generals did not possess an exclusive right to ignorance, Foreign Minister Alois Count Aehrenthal rejected Conrad's suggestion by stating "that there is no reason at this time to undertake war preparations for the immediate future."[25] Two years later, Conrad asked Francis Joseph for permission to conclude a firm military convention with Germany concerning use of connecting railroads in case of war. The emperor vetoed the initiative without giving a reason.[26] In March 1911, Conrad again pressed his monarch to conclude concrete measures with Germany in case of an Anglo-French attack on the Berlin ally. Yet again, Francis Joseph turned his request down after consulting

---

[24] Conrad's treatise of 17 April 1908, Operations Büro Generalstab 95, OStA-K.

[25] Aehrenthal to Conrad, 15 July 1908, B Flügeladj., vol. 1, Conrad Archie, OStA-K.

[26] Conrad to Francis Joseph, 3 November 1910, Operations Büro Generalstab 91, USIA-K.

with Aehrenthal.[27] And in July 1913 as well as in March 1914, the Austrian general again recommended detailed talks with the Germans concerning coordinated measures against Russia and Rumania; both German disinterest and political opposition at home to such talks assured their failure.[28]

The nature of the Berlin-Vienna alliance cohesion can perhaps best be gleaned from the following. In November 1912, Conrad's temporary successor, General Blasius Schemua, visited Berlin to undertake joint staff talks. The Berlin government found out about the visit only through local newspapers, with the result that Foreign Secretary Alfred von Kiderlen-Waechter caustically requested the Viennese government to inform Berlin of such visits in the future![29] Finally, it should be noted that no political talks had taken place concerning the future configuration of Europe after a possible war (the current concept of "war termination"). When Foreign Minister Berchtold informed Conrad on 6 July 1914 that the Germans would likely raise this question in the near future, Conrad lamely replied: "Then say that we also do not know that."[30] And while the Triple Alliance partners did manage on 1 November 1913 to hammer out a naval convention for the Mediterranean area, not only was this solidly based upon the unknown ally, Italy, but it was also devoid of any real appreciation of the actual naval situation to be encountered in a war with the Triple Entente.[31]

---

[27] Conrad to Francis Joseph, 14 March 1911, ibid.

[28] Conrad to Berchtold, 12 July 1913, and Conrad's notes on an audience with the emperor at Schönbrunn on 10 March 1914, ibid.

[29] Kiderlen-Waechter to German Embassy (Vienna), 26 November 1912, Deutschland 143 *secr.*, vol. 10, AA-PA.

[30] Conrad, *Aus Meiner Dienstzeit*, 4:40.

[31] This is the argument of Hans Meier-Welcker, "Strategische Planungen und Vereinbarungen der Mittelmächte fur den Mehrfrontenkrieg," *Österreichische Militärische Zeitschrift*, Sonderheft II (1964): 20–22. See also Paul G. Halpern, The *Mediterranean Naval Situation* 1908–1914 (Cambridge, Mass.: Harvard University Press, 1971), Chapter VIII.

The fact that Austria-Hungary and Germany failed to develop a common political-strategic war plan by 1914 is beyond dispute. The official Austrian history of the Great War concluded that Conrad and Moltke "beat around the bush concerning the heart" of the matter.[32] Theobald von Schafer, who wrote one of the volumes of the German official history, likewise noted that "neither [side] laid their cards on the table. . . . Neither Moltke nor Conrad always spoke their innermost thoughts."[33]

Four days after Austria-Hungary had commenced shelling Belgrade and on the very day that the Germans invaded Belgium, the Reich's military attache at Vienna, Karl Count von Kageneck, confirmed the deplorable lack of joint planning on the part of the two "disjointed allies" when he informed Moltke's chief aide, General Georg Count von Waldersee: "It is high time that the two general staffs consult now with absolute frankness with respect to mobilization, jump-off time, areas of assembly and precise troop strength . . . Everyone has been relying upon the belief that the two chiefs of staff had worked out these most intimate agreements between themselves."[34]

As I have suggested above, the reasons for this lack of concrete planning were neither institutional nor bred of ignorance. Rather, they were political and personal. Whereas past works on this topic have tended to stress either the fragile nature of alliance cohesion (Craig), or the incomplete exchange of information between Conrad and Moltke (Stone), or the basic military miscalculation of overestimating

---

[32] Edmund Glaise von Horstenau and Rudolf Kiszling, eds., *Österreich-Ungarns Letzter Krieg 1914–1918*, 7 vols. and 10 suppls. (Vienna: Verlag der Militärwissenschaftlichen Mitteilungen, 1931–38), 1:333.

[33] Theobald von Schäfer, "Deutsche Offensive aus Ostpreussenüiber über den Narew auf Siedlec," *Miliäarwissenschaftliche Mitteilungen* 61 (1930): 976.

[34] Kageneck's cable of 4 August 1914 is cited in Gordon A. Craig, "The World War I Alliance of the Central Powers in Retrospect: The Military Cohesion of the Alliance," *Journal of Modern History* 37 (1965): 338. Kageneck's papers have recently been deposited at the Bundesarchiv-Militirarchiv in Freiburg, West Germany, as MSg 1/1914, 2515–2517.

one's own forces (Ritter), I suggest that the failure of Berlin and Vienna to devise a coherent and coordinated strategy before 1914 lay primarily in the fact that both pursued national strategies that were not mutually beneficial. In addition, neither side was blessed with soldier-statesmen able to conduct joint strategic planning. Neither general staff comprehended the diplomatic, strategic, and domestic difficulties faced by the other. Neither Conrad nor Moltke was willing to lay his cards on the table. Both feared that such action might jeopardize their jealously guarded independent strategies. In the end, human shortcomings and vastly differing perceptions of the national interest as well as of the nature and purpose of alliances proved decisive.

In assessing the period from 1871 to 1914, it is fair to say that the cautionary approach of Bismarck, based squarely upon recognition of Germany's vital interests as a continental state wedged between France and Russia, was carelessly jettisoned by Wilhelm II at the start of his reign—without any basic reassessment having been undertaken. Once that political decision had been made, military planners in Berlin and Vienna drew up their operational and tactical studies independent of each other. Neither fully shared their plans and thoughts with the other. Vague indications of intent in case that the *casus foederis* set in proved highly inadequate in 1914. Distrust and suspicion of each other's political motives further precluded firm alliance commitments. While Conrad never fully informed the Germans of his secret desire to tackle Serbia concurrently with Russia and feared that the Germans "with greedy egoism sought to displace the [Dual] Monarchy from Serbia in particular and the Balkans in general,"[35] Moltke refused to commit himself to specifics with regard to his eastern deployment. Nor did German civilian leaders spell out clearly their Balkan policy in the wake of the abandonment of *Weltpolitik* as evidenced by Schlieffen's famous memorandum at the

---

[35] Cited in Oskar Regele, *Feldmarschall Conrad. Auftrag und Erfüllung 1906–1918* (Vienna and Munich: Herold, 1955), 72.

end of 1905. Romanticized assurances of standing "shoulder-to-shoulder" with the Austrians, of *Nibelungentreue*, and of *Bundestreue* could not in the end overcome the divergent political and military aims and polices of the two Germanic powers.[36]

Above all, Conrad never addressed the problem that his ambitious and multifaceted strategies were quite beyond the capabilities of the Austro-Hungarian state and its military.[37] Moltke, for his part, refused to face the fatal flaw in the Schlieffen Plan—namely, to gamble the Reich's future on the destruction within a few weeks of a French national army that was numerically superior to his own. Conrad as well as Moltke demanded more—both of their own forces and of their ally—than could rightfully be expected. Both sought Napoleonic battles of envelopment and annihilation *(Kesselschlachten)* in order to destroy the main enemy. Both wanted to avoid a war of attrition, which would place stress on the national cohesion of the Habsburg Monarchy and which could only favor the entente position against Germany. And, while both knew the general contours of the other's operations plan, both preferred to pursue their independent military strategies. In the end, neither managed to resolve the dichotomy between their quite separate and distinct political and strategic goals. Neither appreciated, much less addressed, the enormous political, economic, and military problems attendant to modern coalition warfare in an industrial era. Certainly, neither soldier was prepared to inform either monarch or government that the Central Powers' diplomatic and strategic difficulties probably lay beyond the realm of military resolution.

---

[36] Rudolf Kiszling, "Bündniskrieg und Koalitionskriegfuhrung am Beispiel der Mittelmächte im Ersten Weltkrieg," *Wehrwissenschaftliche Rundschau* 10 (1960): 641, claims that Moltke after the war realized that what could be expected of an alliance partner was never "the most desirable militarily, but only that which appears advantageous to both coalition partners."

[37] Rothenberg, *Army of Francis Joseph*, 178, states: "On paper Conrad's plans always had an almost Napoleonic sweep, though he often lacked the resolution to carry them out and also forgot that he did not have instruments to execute them."

In the final analysis, the task may simply have lain beyond the limited talents of Conrad and Moltke. Even a veteran of coalition warfare such as the French General Maurice Sarrail is reputed to have remarked to Premier Georges Clemenceau, himself an experienced veteran of coalition warfare during the Great War: "Since I have seen Alliances at work, I have lost something of my admiration for Napoleon."[38]

[38] Cited in Sir Charles Petrie, *The Life and Letters of the Right Hon. Sir Austen Chamberlain*, 2 vols. (London: Cassell, 1939–40), 2: 110. Comment from sometime in the spring of 1918.

5

"Freies Deutschland" *Guerrilla Warfare in East Prussia, 1944–1945: A Contribution to the History of the German Resistance*

PERRY BIDDISCOMBE

The University of Victoria

Abstract: Traditional accounts of the anti-Hitler resistance have portrayed it largely as an elite phenomenon that did not take grass-roots forms such as partisan warfare. Leftists and proponents of *Alltagsgeschichte* have challenged this thesis by noting occasional manifestations of anti-Nazi guerrilla activity, particularly along the fringes of the Third Reich. The guerrillas of *Freies Deutschland,* who parachuted into East Prussia, were one such case. However, these events also confirm the orthodox viewpoint in one respect: the forlorn guerrillas along this fringe of Nazi Germany enjoyed little local sympathy and they were politically and militarily isolated.

Most writing on the German resistance to Hitler is focused on the July 20th complex of groups and conspiracies, or to a lesser extent, on youth resistance (especially the White Rose) and underground communist opposition. An underlying theme within much of this literature has suggested, either implicitly or explicitly, that the type of out-and-out guerrilla warfare experienced in some countries occupied by the Germans was impossible within the National Socialist state itself, mainly because the instruments of repression were too intense, the opposition was atomized, adequate public support did not exist, and there was no alternate pole of loyalty (such as an exile government) that could legitimize violent resistance.[1] Partisan warfare is usually identified as a mass phenomenon and its apparent absence in Nazi Germany has contributed to the common historiographical claim that the German resistance had no popular character. It was a "resistance without people," in Hans Mommsen's memorable phrase.[2]

On the other hand, scholars have recently described instances of guerrilla warfare flickering to light in 1944/45, mostly along the fringes of the Third Reich. The most notable of these accounts describe what Detlev Peukert calls "partisans" in Cologne, as well as separatist guerrillas and Wehrmacht deserters in the Austrian Alps. There were also groups of deserters in the Harz Mountains and a small partisan band in the Lemgo-Bielefeld district, which engaged in sabotage until it was destroyed by Gestapo and Wehrmacht personnel in March 1944. As interest in regional and local history has accelerated, the historians of these movements have become more insistent about their importance and the role that they played in the anti-Nazi milieu, and they have groused about how "conventional historical representations could not take realistic account of such a rush of tangled happenings," mainly because the traditionalists were far too caught up in the crafting of a grand narrative.[3] The revisionists either talked past the issue of resistance or they perceived it in places previously unexplored or in forms hitherto unrecognized.[4]

This article will acquaint readers with yet another instance where anti-Nazi partisans functioned in a borderland region, although the sorry fate of these guerrillas also tends to reinforce the conventional wisdom about anti-Nazi resisters, i.e., that they faced an absence of popular support. This is an important point because it supports the dominant thesis about the lack of a viable base for German partisan movements. In the particular case reviewed in this work, the only extenuating factors are that our guerrillas were not spontaneously produced by local populations—rather, they were airdropped into place by the pro-Soviet National *Komitee Freies Deutschland* (NKFD)[5]—and that their sphere of operations was the conservative and politically retrograde frontier province of East Prussia. The Soviets and their German sympathizers had hoped to call to mind a tradition of Prussian-Russian friendship in East Prussia—"the spirit of Tauroggen"— but failed to muster any significant local support for their parachutist partisans. In order to understand what happened to the NKFD guerrilla contingent in East Prussia, it is necessary to first describe, in some measure of detail, how and why they were deployed. Before concluding, we will also discuss why the movement failed and how this process reflects upon the larger history of the German resistance, particularly the legacy and current image of the NKFD. Although the story of the East Prussian guerrillas suggests that the NKFD had a means of projecting its power—a realization that deflects the argument of critics who question the idea of "resistance" in a POW camp[6]—the training, treatment and deployment of the partisans shows that they were actually victims of both sides in the titanic struggle unfolding on the Eastern Front.

There is no doubt that during the last year of World War Two, considerable numbers of anti-Nazi guerrillas were set to roost in the East Prussian forests and heaths. As early as 1942, East Prussia's proximity to unoccupied portions of the USSR had made it a handy drop point for Soviet agents parachuting into Germany, a process that was continuing in 1944/45.[7] However, out-and-out guerrillas were also sighted in East Prussia during the spring of 1944, first in the Elchwald,[8] and by the summer of the same year such elements had appeared in many wilderness locations. In the Memelwalde, local authorities were alerted in July 1944 by a rising tide of written and verbal reports describing bursts of submachine-gun fire heard reverberating through the forest, as well as the sound of aircraft flying over the region from the east.[9]

In every case where partisans appeared, they were dropped by parachute. Such operations occurred throughout 1944 with heavy frequency along the eastern, northern, and southern fringes of East Prussia, particularly in the wooded terrain east of Labiau, west of

Goldap, north and south of Wehlau, south of Senseburg, and southwest of Insterburg. Individual Soviet partisans were seen parachuting into the Forst Heyderwalde (Skallischer Forst) in Kreis Angerapp,
and as noted, similar elements were encountered in the Elchwald
and the Memelwalde. The same thing happened in the Ortelsburg-
Willenberg-Neidenburg area, and in the vicinity of Lötzen, 87 parachutists had been sighted by Christmas 1944, many of whom had
been intercepted or killed during their initial descent. Another four-
man team of Russian partisans was also dropped into Kreis Rosenberg,
an area which had been in East Prussia during the interwar period,
but after 1939 had been transferred administratively to the recre-
ated jurisdiction of West Prussia. The members of this unit were
captured or killed in August 1944, although not before they had
managed to cause a handful of casualties among German soldiers
and forest rangers.

While there is no way of knowing exactly how many guerrillas
were parachuted into East Prussia, the numbers were certainly significant; the 11 Forstämter of the Elchwald reported about 100 partisans functioning in that area alone, and an *Einsatzkommando*
organized to combat guerrillas along the eastern frontier of the province counted some 200 guerrillas apprehended or neutralized before
the unit was forced to retreat on 20 January 1945. The commander
of this formation, Oberst Hans von Bredow, suggested that there
was a probably a considerably larger number of partisans facing his
unit who were never captured or who never surrendered.[10]

Guerrilla teams occasionally contained Soviet nationals, but
sabotage and harassment units were comprised almost exclusively
of German prisoners-of-war formerly held by the Soviets, often Poles
or Lorrainers who had earlier been drafted into the Wehrmacht.
Although most of these soldiers were adherents of the NKFD, the
mustering process that raised personnel to serve behind German
lines was not very selective. Von Bredow got the impression that
many of the men were not volunteers at all, but that they had been
forced to accept missions as partisans. Some, upon surrendering,
sought to rejoin the Wehrmacht or the German civil bureaucracy.[11]

Others cooperated in efforts by German military intelligence to use their radio transmitters for "playback" maneuvers, feeding useless or phony information back to their Soviet bosses. By the end of 1944 the *Reichssicherheitshauptamt* was running five of these so-called *Funkspiele* operations, codenamed "Heide," "Jutta," "Theda," "Antje," and "Kapitän II."[12] A few German POWs had probably offered themselves for NKFD guerrilla service because they had been looking from the start for a quick way to regain German lines. One *Leutnant* who was parachuted into the Elchwald waited for a favorable moment and then attacked and killed the other four members of his team. He subsequently reported to the German authorities.[13]

Partisan units were typically small, numbering up to 10 men each. They usually tried to remain in the woods and keep as low a profile as possible, at least until they were ready to engage in combat. Often they were all but invisible; one forest ranger later remembered that "naturally they stayed in the woods, where as a rule they were disturbed very little, except by the more general circumstances of unrest." They preferred to remain stationary but, when threatened with German countermeasures, they were more than willing to pick up and run; one group spotted south of Wehlau was chased for a week by German pursuers before it was finally overrun in a forest west of Insterburg.

Many of the guerrillas were still clothed in their old German uniforms. The minority who wore civilian clothes were dressed in quilted jackets and other forms of apparel that were immediately recognizable as guerrilla garb and therefore provided no more camouflage than regular military uniforms. They also carried knapsacks in which they packed their supplies, and they attempted to establish undercover identities with the aid of ration cards, identity papers, and railway passes that they carried on their person. Unfortunately for the partisans, these papers were sometimes out of date and they were quickly recognized by German authorities on the watch for people who were not who they claimed to be.

The guerrillas were typically armed with machine pistols and explosives, as well as guns equipped with silencers. Their supply situation was often acute. They were provided with little food during their initial deployment, usually only a meager quantity of hard bread and jam. They were supposed to be quickly resupplied by air but this procedure involved firing red flares at night in order to alert Soviet aircraft to the whereabouts of drop zones. Naturally, these flares were seen by German civilians and security forces who rushed to the scene and, in, many cases, found and confiscated parachuted supplies, including prodigious amounts of food, chocolate and cigarettes, as well as medicine and pep pills. Such captures of supplies left the guerrillas in a tight spot; often they had to abandon cover and wound up either surrendering to the authorities, particularly with the onset of cold weather, or plundering local German civilians. As early as June 1944, a forestry station near Kurwien was raided and looted by a group of a dozen men. Violence against the population was not intentional, but it sometimes occurred during the course of robberies. Several people were murdered; in a forest near Gauleden, for instance, a woodchopper was shot to death while laboring away at his place of work. Such incidents hardly served to win the partisans any local friends.

Guerrilla morale was also affected adversely by the fact that the personnel had been whisked through training, which usually lasted only two to three weeks and was focused mainly on narrow technical topics. As a result, the partisans were not generally sustained by much of a sense of mission. Matters were not helped by the fact that some guerrilla units had no radio contact with their headquarters behind Russian lines, which left them psychologically beached and forced them to function without the benefit of ongoing instructions.[14]

By the summer of 1944, German military and civil authorities in East Prussia had begun to react to guerrilla incursions by conducting searches of the province's extensive forests. The *Landwacht,* or countryside militia, was mobilized to track down and eliminate partisan units,[15] and it almost certainly continued to perform such functions after it was subsumed within the new levee en masse, the Volkssturm. Wilderness areas suspected of serving as guerrilla

drop zones were broken up into grids and each block methodi-
cally searched, mainly by Forest Service patrols and 100-man
Durchkämmungskommandos organized from the personnel of
Wehrmacht units in the rear. The Forest Service performed effectively and enthusiastically—it was one of the most thoroughly
Nazified elements of the German bureaucracy—although the operations of the *Durchkämmungskommandos* left something to be
desired. Unfamiliar with local terrain, their members usually wan-
dered aimlessly through the countryside, often doing more damage
to each other than to the *Freies Deutschland* guerrillas. A forest
ranger named Ehrentreich later remembered leading a group of army
medical attendants on a patrol near Gauleden; the orderlies did
not know much about chasing partisans, but they managed to save
Ehrentreich's life when he was twice hit by submachine gun fire.
After failing to make much progress, the *Durchkämmungskommandos*
were replaced by *Forstschutzkommandos*, which were small teams
comprising forest rangers and woodsmen who had been drafted into
the military. Owing to their eagerness, their familiarity with the
woods, and their adroitness in combing ground without announcing
their presence, they immediately produced good results in search
operations.[16] Army high command intelligence on the Eastern Front
(*Fremde Heere Ost*) could already report in early September 1944
that most NKFD partisan bands were being destroyed before they
could succeed in attaining their objectives.[17]

In early October, these search formations were joined by 12 com-
panies of gendarmes who had recently been forced by a Soviet offensive out of East Prussia's newly annexed frontier, the Bialystok Gebiet.
These units were reorganized into an anti-partisan strike force, or
"Einsatzkommando," which was subordinated to the Königsberg
Orpo and provided with a specific mandate to smoke out guerrillas
throughout the East Prussian borderlands. To keep them supplied
with up-to-date intelligence, units were equipped with radio receiv-
ers, and the Kommando headquarter's staff also worked closely with
the local Luftwaffe command in Konigsberg in order to get access to

radar fixes on incoming Soviet aircraft. Mobile patrols were left to their own discretion to travel to any location where their presence seemed warranted. In the early winter of 1944/45, these formations were also ordered to build barriers on frozen surfaces of the Masurian Lakes in order to prevent Soviet aircraft from using these ice fields as landing strips from which to resupply NKFD guerrillas. Like its precedecessors, the "Einsatzkommando" had considerable success in operations against partisans until it was forced by the Soviet Winter Offensive to withdraw from the frontier region.[18]

Although casualities in skirmishes were usually light, a trickle of blood began to flow almost as soon as German search units fanned out, beginning with the killing of two tracking dogs near Kurwein in June 1944. In armed engagements, the guerrillas usually came out with the short end of the stick: two were shot dead in the Memelwalde when their camp was overrun by foresters; two more were killed in Forstamt "Wischwill," near Memel, gunned down by a forest warden serving in the Wehrmacht; and another two were shot near Kurwien in early October 1944, when a team of seven men who had been dropped into the area in late July was finally pinned down and neutralized by German forest rangers. Sharp battles broke out near Frisching and Nordenburg, confrontations in which both sides lost casualities; the latter engagement, fought in early November 1944, occurred when an Einsatzkommando patrol unexpectedly bumped into strong partisan unit. The guerrillas had their greatest success with hit and run tactics. In Forstamt "Trappen," two forest wardens were ambushed while on a search operation. Shot from behind while bicycling past a clearing, one was killed instantly, while the other was wounded and then chased behind a wood pile, where he was dispatched with several shots in the nape of the neck.[19]

Guerrillas who were captured or who voluntarily surrendered—a not insignificant number were interrogated by the *Geheimfeldpolizei* (GFP), the Wehrmacht's equivalent of the Gestapo. Their identities were checked against police files in their home towns, and the circumstances of their capture by the Soviets were carefully reviewed in order to establish their bona fides. They were then pumped for extensive information about the NKFD schools and sabotage camps at which they had been trained. After this handling, the prisoners were sent to a holding camp at Lissa, the main GFP depot behind the Eastern Front, where they were again subjected to questioning at a joint Gestapo-GFP interrogation centre. Eventually, the more intractable individuals were shot or continued to be detained at Lissa; others were reposted to the Wehrmacht and dispatched mainly to Italy, the Saarland or Holland. Older men were sent to a division in Norway. The *Reichsicherheitshauptamt* also ordered local Gestapo offices in towns as far west as Cologne to keep an eye on the family and friends of Soviet-trained parachutists and "to provide increased observation of former KP [communist party] circles."[20]

After the Soviets conquered most of East Prussia in January 1945, NKFD guerrillas were deployed against the small and increasingly restricted territories still held by the Germans, particularly the Samland Peninsula. Partisans sent across the Frisches Haff tried to interfere with the evacuation of troops and civilians across the narrow neck of the Frische Nehrung. Refugees fleeing from the Samland to West Prussia in late January and early February saw many partisans lying dead along the side of the road.[21] NKFD guerrillas attacked the power station at Peyse, and agents in Pillau operated a radio transmitter through which they directed Soviet artillery fire upon the ships evacuating civilians and soldiers from the German-held beachhead.[22] Parachutists also dropped into the Känigsberg Festung itself and managed to tap a military cable running along the Arndtstraße.

In general, however, as the Germans were pushed back into districts too small and too heavily populated to provide a base for full-scale guerrilla warfare, NKFD efforts increasingly shifted to tactics that might be properly be described as commando-raiding and infiltration of the Wehrmacht chain of command. These activities included ambush attacks against German outposts by bands of *Freies Deutschland* troops presenting themselves as "stragglers," as well as the smuggling of disguised NKFD officers into German strong-points and command posts, where they issued phony orders and picked up information about Wehrmacht deployments and capabilities. Occasionally such infiltrators came without benefit of cover, openly declaring themselves as envoys delivering Soviet and NKFD appeals for surrender. Members of such NKFD "reconnaissance units" were told by the Soviets that only in case of dispersal by enemy action should they retreat to wooded districts and carry on guerrilla warfare.[23]

One might rightly wonder exactly what the NKFD and the Soviets were trying to accomplish with operations pursued at such risk and cost to the participants. To the limited extent that military and political goals are separable, it is clear that the partisans had a political aim in addition to being assigned military goals such as sabotage and reconnaissance. Obviously, this political objective involved demonstrating a measure of popular support for the anti-Hitler movement.

Shortly after the NKFD was organized in the summer of 1943, its *Frontorganisation* began to set up armed *Kampfgruppen* whose mission was to penetrate Wehrmacht rear areas, which were unexposed to Soviet loudspeaker propaganda or leaflet shelling. Once behind German lines, these *Kampfgruppen* were supposed to contact Soviet partisan formations and get busy subverting Wehrmacht service troops. Soon after the first of these units parachuted behind German lines in December 1943, northeast of Pskov, the Red Army weighed in with its considerable influence and began requesting that the *Kampfgruppen* also concern themselves with collecting intelligence and performing military reconnaissance.[24] Such units were commanded operationally by the front and territorial staffs of the Red Army, which gained sole control of guerrilla activities in early 1944, after the dissolution of the Central Staff for Partisan Warfare. In his memoirs, NKFD member Jesco von Puttkamer argues that *Freies Deutschland* commandos and guerrillas were trained and deployed by the Red Army "wholly independent of the work of the National Committee," although the latter was obviously aware of their existence.[25]

The partisan formations deployed in East Prussia were almost certainly an extension of the Kampfgruppen program, suitably tweaked to allow for the fact that the units were now operating on

German soil. The tactics of the Kampfgruppen and the East Prussian guerrillas were identical: they parachuted into place, avoided immediate combat if at all possible, and concentrated on performing reconnaissance and identifying sabotage objectives. According to von Bredow, "the main operational zones of these sabotage groups generally lay in a depth of about 100 kilometers behind the German front."[26]

It would be naive to think, however, that the deployment of NKFD guerrillas was totally military in nature, with no political aspect. The Soviets formed special partisan units primed to operate in almost every country standing in the path of the Soviet advance into Central Europe—Poland, Hungary, Czechoslovakia and Romania, as well as Germany—and the main intention was to contrive a semblance of popular support for Soviet intervention, something that the Red Army on its own could never have generated.[27] Even if not directly involved in organizing this effort, the NKFD almost certainly provided thematic direction, probably via the Political Main Office of the Red Army, which worked closely with the committee. An NKFD planning paper in 1944 quite clearly suggested the nature of the "popular" struggle that the guerrillas were supposed to embody, at least in theory—"The Kampfgruppen and Freischärlergruppen have political as well as military tasks. Through their propaganda and their deeds, they must win popular acceptance as fighters for a new, free Germany."[28]

The complicated internal politics of the NKFD was probably also a factor in launching the guerrillas. When the *Freies Deutschland* committee was formed in mid-1943, its main purpose had been a military one, namely to convince Wehrmacht officers and generals to turn against Hitler, negating the need for further combat advances by the Red Army. At the very least, the movement was supposed to increase the rate of Wehrmacht desertions and thereby make the Red Army's task easier.[29] After a year's worth of effort, not much had been accomplished: little or no contact had been made with the Beck-Goerdeler conspirators,[30] who eventually made the best attempt to eliminate Hitler, however unsuccessful; and, although the committee had scored some achievements in convincing pocketed German troops to surrender, Wehrmacht soldiers in the line were gradually becoming more resistant to NKFD appeals, particularly as the front was pushed back against the German border and the war in the east began to assume a more patriotic hue.[31]

As a result of this development, the secondary purposes of the NKFD, which had also been apparent since the movements's foundation, gradually became more important. This task was to rouse the German civilian population into opposition to the Nazi regime, something which had originally been left to the devices of Radio *Freies Deutschland,* which in 1943 began advising listeners on the requisite procedures necessary to organize a resistance movement, and which hoped to encourage partisan warfare by reporting on how guerrillas outside Germany had risen up against Hitler.[32] Even in its manifesto in 1943, the NKFD had called upon Germans at home to organize for armed action, and by 1944 committee member Wilhelm Pieck, who in July 1943 had described the Wehrmacht as the only practical tool for cleansing Germany, was talking about *Freies Deutschland* personnel serving "as the advance guard for the domestic liberation struggle inside Germany."[33] The official change of policy was proclaimed at the committee's plenary meeting in early January 1944. Committee president Erich Weinert announced the beginning of the "second stage" of the movement, which was to be organized "on the broadest possible basis," while Pieck noted: "It is senseless to expect a military or industrial leader to emerge in Germany to foil Hitler at this ultimate stage of his criminal career ... We must therefore create the forces that are to save Germany out of the German people—out of the workers, the peasants, the intellectuals. We must mobilise and organise the struggle on the part of the German people."[34] Anyone unsure about the moral and functional rectitude of guerrilla warfare, such as German soldiers and POWs, were reminded that historic Prussian patriots, such as Schill and Lützow, had actually been partisan leaders.[35]

This adjustment in strategy also reflected deeper, tectonic shifts within the structure of the NKFD. As efforts at the front proved ineffectual and officer POWs were unable to fully justify their worth as propaganda mouthpieces, real power in the committee began to flow toward German Communist Party (KPD) emigres like Pieck, who since 1943 had been forced to play second fiddle to the POW activists and their tactic of courting the Wehrmacht. In keeping with their essentially ideological perspective, the communist cadres had never entirely given up on the hope that "popular forces" could be rallied to Hitler's disadvantage, perhaps through mass uprisings, perhaps through the more slow-burn technique of guerrilla warfare.[36] A few of them had direct experience of such tactics through their service with Spanish or Soviet partisan bands. Naturally, the parts of Germany closest to the ever-advancing Red Army were chosen as the initial points where the waters of German public opinion could be tested. By April 1944, East Prussia and Upper Silesia had already been picked as "centres for the German liberation movement,"[37] and soon after, around the time that the first guerrilla parachutists were deployed, the NKFD launched an open appeal to East Prussians to aid in the province's "liberation" and foil Nazi defence efforts.[38]

Yet another complication was caused by rumours that began swirling around NKFD offices in the spring and summer of 1944 to the effect that the Soviets were preparing to detach all of Germany's provinces east of the Oder-Neiße line, transferring most of these regions to Polish control. This was disconcerting news even to German communists and it seemed like an almost unfathomable betrayal to the soldiers and officers who had aligned themselves with the NKFD and who continued to imagine themselves as solid German patriots. It is not hard to believe that with such plans circulating, German nationalists in the NKFD concluded that it was essential to make some effort to rouse eastern Germans into action against the Nazis and thereby give the Soviets some reason to reconsider their intentions. The NKFD's vice president, Major Karl Hetz, a native East Prussian and one of three POWs assigned responsibility for *Aufklärungstatigkeit* behind German lines, was on record in 1944 insisting that "something be done" vis-a-vis East Prussia.[39]

Evidence from the East Prussian partisans themselves certainly suggests that they had political goals and that they were supposed to cultivate a measure of public support. Isolating themselves in the woods in order to dodge the enemy admittedly served as a means of keeping the units intact until they could perform their military functions, but it was probably also intended as a way of avoiding the bloodshed sure to hinder any chance of cultivating a sense of common cause with the locals. Even more telling was the fact the guerrillas referred to themselves as "partisans" and that their Nazi pursuers adopted the same terminology, almost despite themselves. Two guerrillas captured in Forstamt "Elchwald"—one a young Panzergrenadier and the other the former chief of a Wehrmacht propaganda company—freely admitted that while behind Soviet lines they "had been schooled as partisans."[40] This self-conception and the type of training that induced it are important indicators of what the NKFD and the Soviets were trying to accomplish. The Soviets distinguished quite sharply between "partisans" and "diversionists": the former represented a "mass movement" operating along broad stretches of territory, while the later were less significant personnel who were sent into enemy territory for a limited time and with specific assignments.[41] Therefore the use of the expression "partisan" was significant, especially in contradistinction to "diversionist."

It goes without saying that while there may have been some pressing reasons for the Soviets and NKFD to launch guerrilla warfare in East Prussia, the actual conditions in the province offered little chance of success. Still, in the battle for the hearts and minds of East Prussians, the *Freies Deutschland* movement was not entirely bereft of potential selling points for its propaganda. Since 1943, the NKFD had been talking ceaselessly about the "spirit of Tauroggen,"[42] with the implicit message for East Prussians that they should repeat the experience of 1812/13: revolt, join hands with the Russians, and mobilize to defeat a megalomaniac tyrant. Also available for exploitation was an old feeling of common cause between East Prussian and Russian elites, who for centuries had agreed about the rights and obligations that ought to be borne by a landowning, warrior class in an autocratic society. The city of Königsberg also had a significant working class that might have harboured some secret pro-Soviet sympathies, the only such base of its kind in East Prussia, although NKFD partisans sent in to the city were sure to encounter the sort of urban environment that made guerrilla operations difficult.[43]

On the other hand, the Nazis easily succeeded in outflanking the *Freies Deutschland* movement by calling to mind other East Prussian traditions, particularly a "marchland mentality" built around an image of East Prussia as the eastern outpost of Germandom, supposedly in constant conflict with Poles, Russians, and Baits. Although this feeling was a hereditary part of the East Prussian makeup, there is no doubt that it had accelerated with the development of modern nationalism and racism in the nineteenth century and with the backlash against the Bolshevik Revolution in 1917. In addition, the Nazis could exploit sour memories of the first Russian invasion in 1914, during which towns such as Goldap, Ortelsburg, and Neidenburg had been heavily damaged; not coincidentally, the pro-Russian partisans of 1944/45 attempted to operate in all these same districts, without much luck. The embattled mien of the population had also been made worse by the consequences of the Versailles settlement, especially the borderland plebiscites of 1920 and the province's detachment from the remainder of Germany, which aggravated the weaknesses of its agrarian economy.[44] These circumstances were in turn related to the fact that the province's traditional conservatism had in recent decades begun to assume an increasingly right-radical hue; the Nazis had scored some early electoral breakthroughs in the province, once again in borderland areas that later served as drop zones for hapless NKFD guerrillas.[45] Even the Masurians of the southeast, some of whom spoke a language related to Polish, had been swept along by the prevailing winds; the huge majority of them had voted for Germany in the 1920 plebiscites. Unlike the Slovenes in southern Austria, there is no record of these semi-assimilated Masurians offering any support to the anti-Hitler guerrillas who functioned in their areas. Finally, Nazi state and party agencies were extremely successful in disseminating anti-Soviet "terror propaganda," particularly after the Red Army engaged in the widespread abuse of civilians during a brief incursion into East Prussia in October 1944.

Thus, although the deep forests of East Prussia offered natural advantages for guerrillas, the mood, psychology and culture of the population made it perhaps the worst area in Germany in which to attempt the development of an anti-Nazi partisan movement. Quite unlike the situation in the Soviet Union and in many other parts of German-occupied Europe, there were no guerrilla bands in the area which had generated spontaneously and only required coordination by parachutists.[46] Everything had to be launched from scratch. In addition, most of the guerrillas dropped into the province were not native East Prussians. Neither was there any heartening advice from interrogated German prisoners about the existence of favorable conditions in the region; in fact, those familiar with the area were largely negative in their assessments of the NKFD's local appeal. "These idiots," said one, "call to the East Prussian population to come over to the Russians with the black-white-red flag, [but] they won't know what hit them."[47] At least one prominent East Prussian Junker and anti-Hitler plotter, Count Heinrich von Lehndorf-Steinort, mulled over the possibility of guerrilla warfare "after the catastrophe," but the animus in such considerations seems to have been the Soviets rather than the Nazis.[48]

The chiefs of the NKFD were surely aware of these unfavourable factors, but they roared ahead with their plan anyway. The results were predictable: German army and gendarmerie officers reported that the partisans found no public support, but rather that they generated the opposite effect: the population was worried by their presence. The local appearance of guerrillas was immediately reported to the authorities by concerned civilians, which aided immeasurably in the apprehension or destruction of such elements. The effect, in turn, was that the partisans quickly became demoralized and their operations were crippled. For the most part, they caused little damage and were unable to aid the Soviet advance in any appreciable fashion.[49] This unhappy development almost certainly paved the way for the new emphasis in 1945 on tactics like commando assaults, operations which required no assumptions about public support or made no claim to such, but which still served Red Army purposes by harassing and diverting the Wehrmacht. Neither the communists nor the soldiers in the NKFD were enthusiastic about such forms of combat, but as Schoenhals notes, the influence of either of these groups upon the Soviets was minimal by the spring of 1945.[50] On the other hand, such operations did have an impact that earlier guerrilla activity had failed to bring to bear; Hitler himself warned about these tactics in his final address to the *Ostheer*, dated 15 April 1945.[51]

With the failure of the NKFD's one major effort at launching guerrilla warfare and the committee's continuing inability to turn the Wehrmacht against Hitler, a pervasive feeling of gloom descended upon the movement during the fall of 1944. There was talk of a "crisis" in the committee and much gnashing of teeth among KPD activists over the lack of "operative agitation" in Germany and at the front. "The German people " complained Pieck, "have done nothing."[52] Although there were attempts to make hay from the Nazi declaration of a levée en masse, with committee members encouraging the Volkssturm to use its weapons against Hitler,[53] much of the focus increasingly turned toward the standard Marxist tactic of mobilizing the working class, even at the expense of appeals toward a broader constituency. By the turn of 1944/45, Radio *Freies Deutschland* propagandists were focusing much of their effort toward the proletariat, not only in big cities like Breslau and Berlin, but also toward workers in the towns and countryside, who were instructed to form Kampfgruppen or to head for the hills and forests of eastern Germany and form Freischärler-Truppen. Waldenburg and Senftenberg miners, Silesian weavers and Lausitz glass workers were all specifically targeted in such appeals. Interestingly, however, NKFD cadres either would no longer or could no longer devote large numbers of parachutists to encouraging the achievement of these goals. Instead, they and their Soviet patrons reverted to the old tactic of depending on radio propaganda to accomplish significant results.[54] The parachutist teams dropped in the last several months of the war—some so far west that they were in territory eventually overrun

by American troops—seem to have been limited strictly to reconnaissance missions.

By late March 1945, when even this last-minute strategy had
failed, there were open discussions within the NKFD about whether
it was time to admit defeat and dissolve the committee. Walter
Ulbricht noted in a speech to KPD intimates on 13 May: "The goal
was to turn the Wehrmacht against Hitler and to inspire people to
overthrow Hitler. The NK did not bring this about; it has failed."[55]
After a brief second life as a training mechanism for cadres destined
for work in the Russian zone of occupation, the committee was dis-
solved in November 1945, although some of its antifascist schools
were still operating as late as 1947/48.

The sad ending to this story leads one to conclude that the effort
to launch a NKFD guerrilla movement never stood a chance of success, at least in areas of eastern Germany being approached by the
Red Army.[56] Thus while considerable numbers of guerrillas—hundreds, perhaps thousands—were deployed, this development does
not say much about the potential sympathy of Germans for anti-
Nazi activism, at least in East Prussia, nor does it imply any credible
opportunities for mass resistance, even when "seeded" by outside
forces. It also casts in a poor light the NKFD, the reputation of which
has recently been resuscitated thanks to the end of the Cold War and
the limited fusion of conceptions of resistance that had developed
separately in the Bundesrepublik and the DDR.[57] Our chronicle suggests, however, that the leaders of the NKFD were willing to act in
an expedient—one might almost say cynical—fashion. Many of the
men deployed as NKFD guerrillas do not seem to have made the sort
of lonely, existential decision usually associated with resistance
against Hitler. It must be conceded, of course, that wartime military
and political leaders often had to make that fundamental choice
from above, opting to sacrifice men for the purpose of battling
enemy aggression or fighting an obvious evil, even if all of the men
mobilized were not always eager to participate in this struggle. However, the sending of captured POWs against their own countrymen,
many of them under duress, without benefit of local support, and in

circumstances likely to invite abuse or death in case of capture, seems a practice hardly covered even by the raw doctrine of Realpolitik, and is certainly no reason to award accolades. Does the end justify the means? Perhaps. But from any humanist, utilitarian or even realist perspective, this calculation can only be effective if it saves more lives than it costs.

Thanks to my colleague Peter Golz for proofreading a draft of this paper.

Notes

1 Henri Michel, *Les Mouvements Clandestins en Europe* (1938–1945) (Paris: Presses Universitaires de France, 1974), 50; Franciszek Ryszka, "Formen des Widerstandes gegen den Nationalsozialismus," in *Gegner des Nationalsozialismus,* Christoph Kleßmann and Falk Pingel, eds. (Frankfurt: Campus, 1980), 24–25; Ger van Roon, *Widerstand im Dritten Reich* (Munich: C.H. Beck, 1979), 25–26; Allan Merson, *Communist Resistance in Nazi Germany* (London: Lawrence and Wishart, 1985), 289–92; and Charles Maier, "The German Resistance in Comparative Perspective," in *Contending with Hitler: Varieties of German Resistance in the Third Reich,* David Clay Large, ed. (Cambridge: Cambridge UP, 1991), 146–47. Conservative historians of the German Resistance contend that only an elite-based strategy of eliminating Hitler in a single stroke was valid because such a strategy avoided weakening Germany's war effort and, had the goal been achieved, would not have cost the lives of Germans at the front. Fabian von Schlabrendorff, *The Secret War against Hitler* (New York: Pitman, 1965), 203. For a detailed discussion about whether it was desirable or necessary for the Honoratioren controlling the Resistance Movement to provide it with a mass base, see Christoph Kleßmann, "Das Problem der 'Volksbewegung' im deutschen Widerstand," *in Der Widerstand gegen den National-Sozialismus* (Munich: Piper, 1986), 822–37.

2 Hans Mommsen, "Die Opposition gegen Hitler und die deutsche Gesellschaft 1933–1945," in *Der deutsche_Widerstand 1933–1945,* Klaus-Jürgen Müller, ed. (Paderborn: F. Schoningh, 1986), 24–26; Allen Dulles, *Germany's Underground* (New York: Macmillan, 1947), 22; Hans Bernd Gisevius, *Bis zum bittern Ende* (Hamburg: Rutten und Loening, 1947), 171; Peter Hoffmann, "Internal Resistance in Germany," in *Contending with Hitler,* Large, ed., 124–25; Anton Gill, An *Honourable Defeat: The*

Fight against National Socialism in Germany, 1933–1945 (London: BPC, 1994), 1–2; van Roon, *Widerstand im Dritten Reich,* 15–16; Michael Balfour, *Withstanding Hitler in Germany, 1933–45* (London: Routledge, 1988), 77–78; and Robert Conot, *Justice at Nuremberg* (New York: Harper and Row, 1983), 515.

3 Detlev Peukert, *Die Edelweißpiraten* (Cologne: Bund, 1988), chapter 9; Bernd-A. Rusinek, "Desintegration und gesteigerter Zwang: Die Chaotisierung der Lebensverhaltnisse in den Großstädten 1944/45 und der Mythos der Ehrenfelder Gruppe," in *Piraten, Swings und Junge Garde: Jugendwiderstand im Nationalsozialismus,* Wilfred Breyvogel, ed. (Bonn: J.H.W. Dietz, 1991), 271–94; Karl Balzer, *Sabotage gegen Deutschland* (Preußisch Oldendorf: K.W. Schuetz, 1974), 281,284; Rodomir Luza, *The Resistance in Austria, 1939–1945* (Minneapolis: University of Minnesota Press, 1984), 199–206, 245–45; Walter Maass, *Country without a Name: Austria under Nazi Rule 1938—1945* (New York: F. Ungar, 1979), 67–68, 123–25; Wolfgang Neugebauer "Widerstand und Opposition," in *NS-Herrschaft in Österreich 1938–1945,* Emmerich Talos, Ernst Hanisch, Wolfgang Neugebauer, eds. (Wien: Verlag für Gesellschaftskritik, 1988), 546; Ernst Hanisch, "Gab es einen spezifisch österreichischen Widerstand?" in *Widerstand: Ein Problem zwischen Theorie und Geschichte,* Peter Steinbach, ed. (Köln: Wissenschaft und Politik, 1987), 172; van Roon, *Widerstand im Dritten Reich,* 25; and Heinz Kühnrich, *Der Partisanenkrieg in Europa 1939–1945* (Berlin: Dietz, 1968), 403–5. For the quote, see Rusinek, "Desintegration und gesteigerter Zwang," 291.

4 Hans Rothfels, *The German Opposition to Hitler: An Assessment* (London: Oswald Wolff, 1962), 153; and Theodore Hamerow, *On the Road to the Wolfs Lair: German Resistance to Hitler* (Cambridge: Harvard UP, 1999), 3–4.

5 Wolfgang Neugebauer admits that a few of the partisan groups in the Austrian Alps were actually parachuted into place by Germany's enemies, and that these, in marked contrast to locally recruited bands, got little support from a population still influenced by Nazi propaganda. Neugebauer, "Widerstand und Opposition," 546.

6 For a discussion of this issue, see Alexander Fischer, "Die Bewegung 'Freies Deutschland' in der Sowjetunion: Widerstand hinter Stacheldraht?" in *Aufstand des Gewissens: Der militärische Widerstand gegen Hitler und das NS-Regime 1933–1945* (Herford, Verlag E.S. Mittler & Sohn), 439–54.

7 Horst Duhnke, *Die KPD von 1933 bis 1945* (Köln: Kieperheuer und Witsch, 1972), 485; Vinzent Porombaka, "Als Fallschirmspringer im illegalen Einsatz," in *Im Kampfbewahrt,* Heinz Voßke, ed. (Berlin: Dietz,

1969), 106–13; Donald Cameron Watt, "Research Notes," *Intelligence and National Security* 11 (1996): 152; H.L. von Bredow, "Partisanenbekämpfung in Ostpreußen," Bundesarchiv-Lastenausgleichsarchiv (BA-LA) Ost Dokumente 8/519; 21st Army Group "Report on the Further Interrogation of PW DO/189, Oberst Notzny, Eginhard, Abwehroffizier AGp Vistula," 10 June 1945, National Archives (NA) Record Group (RG) 226, Entry 119A,Box 28.

[8] H. Kramer "Partisanenbewegung in Ostpreußen 1944/45," BA-LA Ost Dokumente 8/556.

[9] Forstmstr. Hartwig "Aufzeichnungen über die Partisanentätigkeit im Forstamt Memelwalde uud in der Umgebung von Insterburg 1944–45," BA-LA Ost Dokumente 8/540.

[10] H.L. von Bredow "Partisanenbekämpfung in Ostpreußen 1944–1945," BA-LA Ost Dokumente 8/519; H. Kramer "Partisanenbewegung in Ostpreußen 1944/45," BA-LA Ost Dokumente 8/556; G. Konig "Bericht," BA-LA Ost Dokumente 8/216; and Major Dieckert and General Großmann, *Der Kampfum Ostpreußen* (Munchen: Grafe und Unzer, 1960), 78.

[11] H.L. von Bredow "Partisanenbekämpfung in Ostpreußen," BA-LA Ost Dokumente 8/519. E.g., Leo Krystofiak, a Pole dragooned into the German Armed Forces and then captured by the Soviets in June 1944; see 12th Army Group to War Room, 10 May 1945, NA RG 226, Entry 119A, Box 29. After being won over by the Soviets, Krystofiak was trained at Kovno and then air-dropped into East Prussia in January 1945.

[12] Summaries for these operations, dated 31 Dec. 1944, are in Bundesmilitärarchiv (BMA) RH 19 II/300.

[13] H. Kramer "Partisanenbewegung in Ostpreußen 1944/45," BA-LA Ost Dokumente 8/556.

[14] H.L. von Bredow "Partisanenbekämpfung m Ostpreußen," BA-LA Ost Dokumente 8/519; Forstmstr. Hartwig "Aufzeichnungen über die Partisanentätigkeit im Forstamt Memelwalde und in der Umgebung von Insterburg," BA-LA Ost Dokumente 8/540; H. Kramer and Forstmstr. Wallmann "Partisanenbewegung in Ostpreußen 1944/45," BA-LA Ost Dokumente 8/556; and Hans Meier-Welcker, *Abwehrkärnpfe am Nordflügel der Ostfront 1944–1945* (Stuttgart: Deutsche Verlags-Anstalt, 1963), 378.

[15] Dr. C. Brenke to Landrat v.d. Groeben, Landkreistag Kiel, 7 March 1953, BA-LA Ost Dokumente 8/518.

[16] Forstmstr. Hartwig "Aufzeichnungen über die Partisanentätigkeit im Forstamt Memelwalde und in der Umgebung von Insterburg," BA-LA Ost Dokumente 8/540; and H. Kramer "Partisanenbewegung in Ostpreußen 1944/45," BA-LA Ost Dokumente 8/556.

[17] OKH/Abt. FHO "Übersicht über die Bandenlage in der Zeit vom 21.7–31.8.1944," 7 Sept. 1944, BMA RH 2/2130.

[18] Hellwig to von Herff, 15 Oct. 1944, NA RG 242, Berlin Document Center Microfilm, A 3343 SSO-083A, frame 84; and HL. von Bredow "Partisanenbekämpfung in Ostpreußen," BA-LA Ost Dokumente 8/519.

[19] H.L. von Bredow "Partisanenbekämpfung in Ostpreußen," BA-LA Ost Dokumente 8/519; Forstmstr. Wallmann "Partisanenbewegung in Ostpreußen 1944/45," BA-LA Ost Dokumente 8/556; and Forstmstr. Hartwig "Aufzeichnungen iiber die Partisanentätigkeit im Forstamt Memelwalde und in der Umgebung von Insterburg," BA-LA Ost Dokumente 8/540.

[20] CSDIC (UK) SIR 1675 "Notes on the GFP and other Security Services in the Area of Army Group Nord (later Kurland)—1942–1 Jan 45," 24 May 1945, Annex 2, Public Record Office (PRO) War Office (WO) 208/3617; Kirsch to Sprinz, "Fahndung nach sowjet. Fallschirmagenten Peter Pleusch aus Koln," 21 November 1944, NA RG 226, Entry 119A, Box 25.

[21] "Abschrift aus Brief vom Dr. Ostermeyer von Hamburg 22.2.45 an L.O.," BA-LA Ost Dokumente 2/20.

[22] H.L. von Bredow "Partisanenbekämpfung in Ostpreußen," BA-LA Ost Dokumente 8/519.

[23] Otto Lasch, *So fiel Königsberg* (Stuttgart: Motorbuch, 1976), 85-86; Meier-Welcker, *Abwehrkämpfe am Nordfügel der Ostfrvnt 1944–1945*, 378; Kai Schoenhals, *The Free Germany Movement: A Case of Patriotism or Treason* (New York: Greenwood, 1989), 120; Obstlt. B. Kerwin "Der letzte Tag von Königsberg (Pr.)," BA-LA Ost Dokumente 2/20; Martini to the bwehroffrzier, Wehrkreiskommando XI, Hildesheim, 8 March 1945, NARG 226, Entry 119A, Box 25.

[24] Schoenhals, *The Free Germany Movement*, 67–68, 83; Max Emendörfer, *Rückkehr an die Front* (Berlin: Militärverlag der DDR, 1984), 199–205; Kühnrich, *Der Partisanenkrieg in Europa*, 39767–401; and CSDIC (UK) SIR 1675 "Notes on the GFP and other Security Services in the Area of Army Group Nord (later Kurland)—1942–1 Jan 45," 24 May 1945, Annex 2, PRO WO 208/3617. NKFD infiltration programs cannot be rated a success. One GFP officer with Army Group North later estimated that of 700 *Freies Deutschland* agents dropped into his region from late 1943 to January 1945, 75 percent gave themselves up voluntarily and most of the remainder were betrayed to the Germans by local populations.

[25] Jesco von Puttkamer, *Von Stalingrad zur Volkspolizei* (Wiesbaden: Michael, 1951), 81—82. See also Alexander Fischer, "Die Bewegung 'Freies

Deutschland' in der Sowjetunion: Widerstand hinter Stacheldraht" in *Der Widerstand gegen Nationalsozialismus,* Jürgen Schmadke and Peter Steinbach, eds. (Munich: Piper, 1986), 962.

26 H.L. von Bredow "Partisanenbekämpfung in Ostpreußen," BA-LA Ost Dokumente 8/519.

27 Matthew Cooper, *The Phantom War: The German Struggle against Soviet Partisans, 1941–1944* (London: MacDonald and Jane's, 1979), 70; and Vojtech Mastny, *Russia's Road to the Cold War* (New York: Columbia UP, 1979), 166.

28 Untitled strategic plans, Stiftung Archiv der Parteien und Maßenorganisationen der DDR im Bundersarchiv (SAPMO) NY 4182/829.

29 Schoenhals, *The Free Germany Movement,* 64.

30 The "Kreisau Circle" apparently had some contacts with NKFD agents, although Adam von Trott zu Solz, one of the main foreign emissaries of the underground, claimed in June 1944 that no link had yet been established with NKFD parachutists because it was feared that the movement was penetrated by the Gestapo. Peter Hoffmann, *The History of the German Resistance, 1933–1945* (Montreal: McGill-Queens UP, 1996), 233, 363.

31 "Handschriftliche Notizen von Wilhelm Pieck," 12 April 1944, SAPMO NY 4036/575. By February 1944, more than six months after the NKFD's founding, nine out of ten German POWs interrogated by the Soviets had never heard of the movement; too few flyers and NKFD newspapers had been distributed at the front, and not enough Germans listened to its radio propaganda. "Handschriftliche Notizen von Wilhelm Pieck," 3 Feb. 1944, SAPMO NY 4036/575.

32 Schoenhals, *The Free Germany Movement,* 70–71.

33 "Manifesto des Nationalkomitees 'Freies Deutschland'"; "Handschriftliche Notizen von Wilhelm Pieck," both in SAPMO NY 4036/575; and Schoenhals, *The Free Germany Movement,* 37.

34 Wolfgang Leonhard, *Child of the Revolution* (London: Ink Links, 1979), 259–60.

35 "Als antifaschistischen Offizier im belagerten und befreiten Leningrad," SAPMO NY 4109/81.

36 The elite antifascist courses taught by KPD functionaries, which were being run even before the organization of the NKFD, featured interpretations of German history, politics and economic affairs structured much more closely along Marxist-Leninist lines than anything closely associated with the *Freies Deutschland* movement. Significantly, these courses covered partisan warfare, sabotage, demonstrations, strikes and "antifaschistische

Aufklärungsarbeit . . . an die Front und in der Heimat." "Programm für den Kriegsgefangenenkursus," SAPMO NY 4182/830.

[37] "Handschriftliche Notizen von Wilhelm Pieck," 12 April 1944, SAPMO NY 4036/575.

[38] There is no direct record of this appeal, but German POWs were surveyed in July 1944 in order to assess its likely impact. Their comments provide some idea of the nature of the announcement. "Einzeläußerungen im Monat Juli (lg. 97/6)," SAPMO NY 4036/572.

[39] *Freies Deutschland*, 28 Nov. 1943; and "Handschriftliche Notizen von Wilhelm Pieck," 23 Oct. 1944, SAPMO NY 4036/575. Pieck cynically saw Hetz's concern arising from his "unsatisfied need for admiration" and his desire to play a future role in governing East Prussia. The communists regarded Hetz, with his constant complaints about lack of democratic procedure, as a disruptive force in the movement.

[40] Forstmstr. Hartwig "Aufzeichnungen über die Partisanentätigkeit im Forstamt Memelwalde und in der Umgebung von Insterburg," BA-LA Ost Dokumente 8/540.

[41] John Armstrong, ed., *Soviet Partisans in World War Two* (Madison: University of Wisconsin Press, 1964), 12.

[42] Leonhard, *Child of the Revolution*, 255.

[43] Dr. C. Brenke to Landrat v.d. Groeben, Landkreistag Kiel, 7 March 1953, BA-LA Ost Dokumente 8/518. Dr. Brenke recalled that NKFD guerrillas never appeared in Königsberg, although he later heard a report of their activities in the surrounding countryside.

[44] Dietrich Orlow, *Weimar Prussia, 1918–1925: The Unlikely Rock of Democracy* (Pittsburgh; University of Pittsburgh Press, 1986), 130, 241; and Giles MacDonogh, *Prussia: The Perversion of an Idea* (London: Sinclair-Stevenson, 1994), 242.

[45] John O'Loughlin, Colin Flint and Luc Anselin, "The Geography of the Nazi Vote: Context, Confession, and Class in the Reichstag Election of 1930," *Annals of the Association of American Geographers* 84/3 (1994): 360, 362; and Peter Merkl, *Political Violence under the Swastika* (Princeton: Princeton UP, 1975), 78–83.

[46] There were some guerrilla bands that had taken shape during the spring of 1944 in areas of West Prussia that had been annexed from Poland in 1939. These were comprised of Poles and members of Volksgruppe III, nominal "Germans" who were becoming subject to Wehrmacht conscription and were only too eager to dodge the draft by fleeing into the woods. Some of these bands were armed by the Soviets and were supplied by local Polish civilians. However, the only partisan groups operating along

the East Prussia borderlands before the arrival of the NKFD parachut-
ists had been comprised of Polish raiders who were well-hated locally. In
August 1943, a band of 60–70 Poles had conducted a series of attacks in
Forstamt "Mittenheide," killing eight people and wounding five others.
H.E. Lange, untitled report in BA-LA Ost Dokumente 8/71; and Forstmstr.
Wallmann "Partisanenbewegung in Ostpreußen 1944/45," BA-LA Ost
Dokumente 8/556. According to East German historian Heinz Kühnrich,
there were half a dozen Germans in Bialystok who joined an antifascist
committee and later attached themselves to the partisan group of General
Kapusto. Kühnrich, *Der Partisanenkrieg in Europa*, 390.

[47] "Einzeläußerungen im Monat Juli (Lg. 97/6)," SAPMO NY 4036/572.

[48] Count Hans von Lehndorff, *East Prussian Diary* (London: Oswald
Wolff, 1963), 74.

[49] Dieckert and Großmann, *Der Kampf um Ostpreußen*, 78; and H.L. von
Bredow, "Partisanenbekämpfung in Ostpreußen," BA-LA Ost Dokumente
8/519.

[50] Schoenhals, *The Free Germany Movement*, 83.

[51] Max Domarus, *Hitler: Reden und Proklamationen 1932–1945* (München:
Süddeutscher Verlag, 1965), ii, 2223.

[52] "Handschrifte Notizen von Wilhelm Pieck," 20 Nov. 1944, SAPMO NY
4036/575.

[53] E. Weinert "Volkssturm—gegen Hitler!" 22 Oct. 1944, SAPMO NY
4036/577.

[54] "Handschriftliche Notizen von Wilhelm Pieck," 29 Jan. 1945, SAPMO
NY 4036/575; and untitled strategic plans, SAPMO NY 4182/829; For
the information provided by members of NKFD reconnaissance squads
who eventually fell into the hands of the Western Allies, see 12th Army
Group to X-2 Paris and War Room London, 23 April 1945, NA RG 226,
Entry 119A, Box 14; 12th Army Group to War Room and X-2 Paris
(339), 30 April 1945, NA RG 226, Entry 119A, Box 9; 12th Army Group
to War Room, 10 May 1945, NA RG 226, Entry 119A, Box 2; CSDIC
(UK), "The Activities of a Russian Agent in Germany," 14 June 1945,
NA RG 226, Entry 119A, Box 28.

[55] Mastny, *Russia's Road to the Cold War*, 254; "Handschriftliche Notizen
von Wilhelm Pieck," 29 March 1945, SAPMO NY 4036/575; and 13 May
1945 speech, SAPMO NY 4182/851a.

[56] An independent NKFD group in Cologne was involved in some of the
underground activity in that city over the fall and winter of 1944/45.
A few hundred German POWs in the United States and Britain, some
of whom had joined the "*Freies Deutschland*" movement, helped the

Western Allies organize several guerrilla and counter-guerrilla bands trained for parachute deployment in the Alps. One such operation, code-named "Homespun," was broken up by the Sicherheitspolizei in April 1945. Presumably, however, NKFD-aligned partisans found more favourable environments in western and southern Germany than their confreres operating in East Prussia. See Dirk Gerhard, *Antifaschisten: Proletarischer Widerstand 1933–1945* (Berlin: Wagenbach, 1976), 141; Joseph Persico, *Piericing the Reich* (New York; Viking, 1979), 217–23, 232–37, 255–59, 270–71, 281–87, 290–95; and Karl Heinz Pech, "Deutsche Antifaschisten in Frankreich während des zweiten Weltkrieges," *Revue Internationale d'Histoire Militaire* 43 (1979): 128.

[57] Note, for instance, the arguments in Peter Steinbach, "Der Widerstand in seiner ganzen Breite und Vielfalt," *Geschichte in Wissenschaft und Unterricht* 41 (1990), 302–7.

6

Revolutions in Warfare: Theoretical Paradigms and Historical Evidence— The Napoleonic and First World War Revolutions in Military Affairs

ANDREW N. LIAROPOULOS[*]

Abstract: This article provides an alternative view for examining Revolutions in Military Affairs (RMAs), perceiving them both as sociopolitical institutions and as war-fighting models. The weaknesses in the ways in which the RMA theory has been approached are analyzed, resulting in the formation of three different, but parallel, paradigms of the RMA phenomenon (the Social Wave, the Radical Transformation, and the Continuity and Evolution). Two historical case studies, the Napoleonic RMA and the First World War RMA, are used in order to draw

---

[*] The author wishes to thank the anonymous *JMH* readers for their comments and recommendations regarding this paper. Particular thanks to Bruce Vandervort for his insightful suggestions. The author is also indebted to Professor Michael Sheehan, University of Wales, Swansea, for his assistance and encouragement.

Andrew Liaropoulos holds a Master's Degree in Intelligence and Strategic Studies from University of Wales, Aberystwyth, and is currently a doctorate candidate at the University of Wales, Swansea, Department of Politics and International Relations, and a Research Associate in the Callaghan Centre for Conflict Studies. Previously he was a Research Analyst for the Scientific Committee of the Hellenic Ministry of Defence, and the Naval War Academy in Athens, Greece.

out the lessons learned regarding past revolutions and to examine the validity of the paradigms.

As the literature on the Revolution in Military Affairs (RMA) has expanded rapidly in the last decade, RMA has turned out to be a hugely contestable concept. The rationale behind the RMA was originally a grand strategy developed during the Cold War.[1] In the early 1970s, Andrew W. Marshall was appointed as the head of the U.S. Department of Defense's Office of Assessment and Strategic Planning. Marshall's work involved efforts to measure the military balance between the superpowers and plan a strategy that would shift the balance in favor of the United States. For Marshall the centre of change in warfare lay in sensors and information systems. By utilizing the benefits of information technology, the United States could gain an operational advantage on the future battlefield. In 1976, U.S. Secretary of Defense Harold Brown and Undersecretary William J. Perry initiated a program by which the United States and its North Atlantic Treaty Organization (NATO) allies would be able to use Western technological superiority to neutralize the overwhelming advantage in size that the Soviet Union and the Warsaw Pact armies had over NATO forces in Europe. This "offset strategy," a precursor to the U.S. Revolution in Military Affairs, was pursued by five administrations during the 1970s and 1980s and consisted of the following elements:[2] the design of a "stealth aircraft" that would

---

[1] For a review of the military-technological developments that took place in the post-World War II period and led to the current Revolution in Military Affairs, see selectively Bruce D. Berkowitz, *The New Face of War: How War Will Be Fought in the 21st Century* (New York: Free Press, 2003), 23–58; and Bill Owens, *Lifting the Fog of War* (Baltimore, Md.: Johns Hopkins University Press, 2001), 80–96.

[2] By the early 1980s, the idea of transformation was incorporated in U.S military planning, and his led to ambitious strategic scenarios like Air-Land Battle, Follow on Forces Attack (FOFA), and The Maritime Strategy.

be nearly invisible to Soviet radar systems; and a program called "assault breaker," an effort to defeat Soviet armored forces with a variety of command, control, and intelligence systems, as well as advanced communications and precision-guided munitions.[3]

The "offset strategy" was carefully observed by the Soviet Union. In the early 1980s, Soviet officials first referred to a "military technical revolution" that would fully exploit the benefits of computers, space surveillance, and long-range missiles. Chiefs of the Soviet General Staff Nikolai Ogarkov (1977–84) and Sergei Akhromeyev (1984–88) argued that not only was the pace of technological change becoming more significant in itself, but also new conventional weapons were becoming as effective as small nuclear devices against armored assaults. Soviet plans for a potential war in Europe rested on a massive and organized armored offensive. Yet, the new conventional technologies provided NATO with reconnaissance strike abilities that would easily identify and destroy armored columns.[4]

Although the core technologies that are associated with the current revolution, like precision guidance, remote guidance and control, munitions improvements, target identification and acquisition, and command and control, existed from the late 1970s, the revolution took more than a decade to fully mature and overcome the political constraints operating against it. Not until the Gulf War in 1991 did U.S. military thinkers come to understand the remarkable increase that had occurred in military capability. The appointments of William Perry as Secretary of Defense and Admiral William A. Owens as vice chairman of the Joint Chiefs of Staff in 1994 allowed RMA proponents to materialize their vision of an information-intensive military force.

Before making detailed reference to past RMAs, it is important to identify the difficulties in describing and analyzing such a

---

[3] Owens, *Lifting the Fog of War*, 80–82.
[4] Colin McInnes, *Spectator-Sport War: The West and Contemporary Conflict* (London: Lynne Reinner, 2002), 118–19.

complex phenomenon.[5] To begin with, the precise meaning of the
term remains problematic. After the Gulf War, the RMA debate
attracted scholars with a wide range of expertise. On the one hand,
this has offered inspiration to the debate, but on the other hand, no
common intellectual approach has emerged about certain issues.[6]
Lawrence Freedman points out the confusion over whether the RMA
represents a stage in the historical process, or a vision that cannot be
realized unless the visionaries seize the initiative. Should the RMA
be viewed as a single step change, a movement to a new paradigm,
or a continuous process that demands constant change?[7] According
to Andrew Latham, three key conceptual weaknesses characterize
the existing literature.[8]

First, part of the scholarship reflects an ahistorical understanding
of military revolutions. A historical approach to the study of war
(and therefore to the study of Revolutions in Military Affairs) would
treat war as a social phenomenon, focusing on periodical transformations in the social, political, and cultural forces. According to
Latham, despite the fact that many scholars cite historical examples
to prove their arguments, they use them quite often to explore the
technological and tactical innovations that took place in the past

---

[5] For a brief introduction to the literature on military revolutions, see selec-
tively Williamson Murray, "Thinking about Revolutions in Military Affairs,"
Joint Force Quarterly, Summer 1997, 69–76; and Andrew F Krepinevich,
"Cavalry to Computer: The Pattern of Military Revolutions," *National Inter-
est* 37 (1994): 30–42. For a more detailed record, see MacGregor Knox and
Williamson Murray, eds., *The Dynamics of Military Revolution: 1300–2050*
(Cambridge: Cambridge University Press, 2001); and Geoffrey Parker, *The
Military Revolution: Military Innovation and the Rise of the West, 1500–1800*
(Cambridge: Cambridge University Press, 1988).

[6] See Colin S. Gray, *Strategy for Chaos: Revolutions in Military Affairs and the
Evidence of History,* (London: Frank Cass, 2002), 13–20, 31–35.

[7] Lawrence Freedman, *The Revolution in Strategic Affairs,* Adelphi Paper
no. 318 (London: International Institute for Strategic Studies, May 1998), 7–8.

[8] Andrew Latham, "Warfare Transformed: A Braudelian Perspective on the
Revolution in Military Affairs," *European Journal of International Relations*
8 (2002): 231–34.

and not to examine the broader changes in the social, political, and cultural structures.[9] The emphasis on technical and tactical aspects of the past offers a profoundly one-dimensional and misleading understanding of what is a complex phenomenon. In fact, the historical record suggests that technological change per se represents a relatively small part of the equation.[10] The crucial element in most RMAs is conceptual in nature and not technological.[11]

A second weakness is that there is no common understanding of what constitutes a Revolution in Military Affairs.[12] Although analysts agree that an RMA involves a radical change or some form of discontinuity in the history of warfare, there is no consensus regarding how and when these changes or discontinuities take place, or what causes them.[13] Therefore, some scholars analyze RMAs on the basis of battlefield technologies, such as gunpowder, or on war-fighting techniques, such as the Blitzkrieg doctrine.[14] Others, however, look beyond battlefield technologies and techniques, arguing that since war is diachronically a complex social, political, and cultural phenomenon, more emphasis should be given to the broader sociopolitical changes that a revolution involves.[15] From this point

---

[9] Ibid., 232.

[10] For a critical view of technology's role in warfare and military transformation, see George Raudzens, "War-winning Weapons: The Measurement of Technological Determinism in Military History," *Journal of Military History* 54 (October 1990): 403–33; and Colin S. Gray, *Weapons for Strategic Effect: How Important Is Technology?* Occasional Paper no. 21 (Maxwell AFB, Ala.: Center for Strategy and Technology, Air War College, January 2001).

[11] Murray, "Thinking about Revolutions in Military Affairs," 70.

[12] Even the definition of the term seems problematic, especially since various terms (Revolution in Military Affairs, Military Revolution, Military Technical Revolution, and Military Transformation) are used to describe similar notions.

[13] Michael O'Hanlon, *Technological Change and the Future of War* (Washington: Brookings Institution Press, 2000), 22; and Latham, "Warfare Transformed," 233.

[14] Krepinevich, "Cavalry to Computer," 30–42.

[15] Latham, "Warfare Transformed," 233.

of view, Revolutions in Warfare are seen as a process from the Age of Tools to the Age of Automation.[16] Likewise, they can be seen through the prism of major shifts in social structures, from Second Wave to Third Wave,[17] or from modernity to postmodernity.[18]

The third shortcoming is the tendency to categorize the history of revolutions in warfare in certain temporal periods, each of which has a distinctive character and is triggered by a revolution. Latham argues that this periodisation, although helpful for organizing the history of warfare, entails the danger that war-related phenomena will be conflated in order to fit certain eras. Organized political violence in any period of history is not a single-dimensional phenomenon, but a multidimensional one. Each dimension of warfare, whether it concerns a war-fighting technique or the political and cultural aspects of war, evolves at a separate historical speed and under a separate set of rules and logic.[19]

To sum up, there is little agreement regarding the definition of the RMA, the periodisation of relevant military history, and the causes of military innovation. Nevertheless, the RMA literature raises a number of important questions. Can there be radical change in the conduct of war without the application of new technologies? Even if new technologies are present, how important are they compared to other factors, such as societal structures, organizing principles, and military culture? Even if such revolutions take place, to what degree do they actually affect warfare? What is their importance, given the complexity of warfare?

---

[16] Martin Van Creveld, *Technology and War: From 2000 B.C. to the Present* (New York: Free Press, 1991)

[17] Alvin Toffler and Heidi Toffler, *War and Anti-war: Survival at the Dawn of the 21st Century* (Boston: Little, Brown and Co., 1993).

[18] Chris Gray, *Postmodern War: The New Politics of Conflict* (London: Routledge, 1997); and James Der Derian, *Virtuous War: Mapping the Military-Industrial-Media-Entertainment-Network* (Boulder, Colo.: Westview Press, 2001).

[19] Latham, "Warfare Transformed," 234.

Constructing the RMA Paradigms

In order to answer the above questions, a two-phase process will be adopted. The first phase involves an alternative way of approaching the RMA theory, based on three different, but at the same time parallel, paradigms. The term paradigm is used here to describe a theoretical framework, a set of hypotheses that will serve as an organizing principle for the research. Note that there is no widely accepted school of thought regarding the RMA phenomenon, but the attempt here is to categorize the most influential approaches into three working groups that sufficiently cover the literature. The appropriate way to use these paradigms is to treat them as arguments. They are not valid as prescriptions; rather, they describe categories of thinking. They instruct the scholar in what to think about, but not what to conclude. The second phase involves the implementation of these paradigms in past cases of military transformation. The demonstration of the theoretical framework and the evaluation of the historical record will be important to the credibility of the paradigms. Therefore, based on the existing literature, three main approaches can be identified.

The Social Wave Paradigm

The first approach, the *Social Wave* Paradigm, explores the broader social, political, and economic changes that affect military transformation, i.e., the way in which a society organizes for and conducts war.[20] The Social Wave paradigm examines the changes brought about by events like the French Revolution, or the Industrial and the Information Revolutions, as well as the shift from one type of warfare to another, like the shift from modern war to postmodern war. Alvin and Heidi Toffler argue in terms of the relationship between

---

[20] For this approach, see mainly the works of Alvin Toffler, *Third Wave* (New York: Bantam Books, 1990), and *Future Shock* (New York: Bantam Books, 1990).

the three waves of civilization (the Agrarian, the Industrial, and the Information Waves) and warfare, and the shift from one wave to another. They argue that the socioeconomic waves are boosted by productivity and by the resources of wealth creation and power (agriculture, industry, and, most recently, knowledge), which also in turn affect warfare.[21] The way a society makes war reflects the way it makes wealth. Starting with the very invention of agriculture, every revolution in the system for creating wealth triggered a corresponding revolution in the system for making war.

According to this approach, military revolutions are perceived as the inevitable outgrowth of basic changes in the form of economic production, a military-focused variant of the explanation of political change in history presented by Karl Marx.[22] The Industrial Revolution, for example, is regarded as the driver behind a mid-nineteenth-century transformation of warfare, which was induced by the substitution of machine for animal power and the introduction of mass production to war. By 1914, industrialized total warfare had emerged out of a long-term process of transformation. Just as mass production was becoming the defining principle of industrial economies, mass destruction was emerging as the defining principle of industrialized total warfare.[23] Mass production corresponded in military affairs to the *levée en masse,* the conscription of mass armies paid by the modern nation-state.

The thesis that military revolutions are the product of deep social, political, and economic changes and have profound implications for

[21] For an analysis of Toffler's arguments, see Thomas J. Gzerwinski, *Third Wave: What the Tofflers Never Told You* (Washington: Institute for National Strategic Studies, National Defense University, April 1996); and Robert J. Bunker, "The Tof-flerian Paradox," *Military Review* 75 (May-June 1995): 199–202.

[22] For a detailed analysis and criticism of the economic deterministic school, see Stephen Biddle, "The Past as Prologue: Assessing Theories of Future Warfare," *Security Studies* 8 (Autumn 1998): 32–44.

[23] Andrew Latham, "Re-imagining Warfare: The Revolution in Military Affairs," in *Contemporary Security and Strategy,* ed. Craig A. Snyder (London: Macmillan Press, 1999), 213–14.

the conduct of war is widely cited in the RMA literature. Despite that, certain drawbacks are apparent. In particular, cause and effect are not always distinguishable in the history of military innovations. Whether the military revolution is the outcome or the agent of complex economic, political, and social changes is not always clear.[24] The proposition that military revolutions are dependent on socio-economic changes succeeds in connecting organized political violence and society. On the other hand, the three-wave theory of the Tofflers and other similar views risk overemphasizing certain dimensions that affect the conduct of warfare. In particular, apart from the economic, there are also other factors that affect the way a nation perceives threats and wages war. History, military culture, time, geography, alliances, and technology are just some of the elements that shape a nation's decision to conduct war. Axiomatic beliefs regarding the images of them and us, as well as institutionalized perceptions of the nature of the enemy's military forces, should also be taken into consideration.

The Radical Transformation Paradigm

The second approach, the *Radical Transformation* paradigm, puts emphasis on issues like military technology, doctrines, and organizational forms and the impact they have on the war-fighting model.[25] Therefore, this paradigm views military revolutions as a series of radical transitions from the Blitzkrieg doctrine to Network Centric

[24] Linking military transformation to the state formation of modern Europe proves the above point. Did political change lead to military revolution or was it the other way around? See Clifford Rogers, ed., *The Military Revolution Debate: Readings on the Military Transformation of Early Modern Europe* (Boulder, Colo.: Westview Press, 1995), 340–41.

[25] For this approach, see mainly Krepinevich, "Cavalry to Computer"; Daniel Goure, "Is there a Military-Technical Revolution in America's Future?" *Washington Quarterly* 16 (Autumn 1993): 175–92; James R. Fitzsimonds and Jan Van Tol, "Revolutions in Military Affairs," *Joint Force Quarterly*, Spring 1994, 24–31; and Eliot A. Cohen, "A Revolution in Warfare," *Foreign Affairs* 75 (March-April 1996): 37–54.

Warfare and from the artillery revolution to the stealth revolution. The radical innovation proponents argue that only when far-sighted innovators see unrecognized potential in new technologies and create new doctrines, will revolutions take place. Change is not enough; revolutions demand innovation of extraordinary scope and speed. A characteristic example that is used to support the above argument is the development of Blitzkrieg by Nazi Germany.[26] The tank, the airplane, and the radio were available to all the great powers prior to World War II, but only the Germans understood their full potential and introduced a new doctrine in order to fully exploit it.

Regarding radical innovation, certain points should be taken into consideration. Military organizations usually tend to be conservative in their approach to technological innovation. Most of the time, their unwillingness to adapt to a new situation reflects fears concerning the impact that new technology will have on the structure of the organization, its military effectiveness, and the way it will affect the personnel involved. A decision to go for a novel technology that will prove its handiness (if indeed it ever does) in the future and may then be ready for the wrong kind of war, might actually be a risky and wrong decision.[27] In addition, RMAs often take a long time to come to fruition. The U.S. Navy began experimenting with aircraft in 1910 and then took almost three decades to fully develop carrier warfare. Similarly, the German Army began experimenting with tanks in the early 1920s and took almost two decades to develop Blitzkrieg. Therefore, the "revolution" in Revolution in Military Affairs should not be taken to mean the change will necessarily

see
use of
tank!

---

[26] Contrary to the conventional wisdom about the emergence of the Blitzkrieg doctrine, Biddle argues that the doctrine that the Germans took into the Second World War was an incremental adaptation of the methods they had used at the end of the First World War; Biddle, "The Past as Prologue," 44–55.

[27] Van Creveld, *Technology and War,* 223.

[28] Richard O'Hundley, *Past Revolutions, Future Transformations: What Can the History of Revolutions in Military Affairs Tell Us about Transforming the U.S. Military?* (Santa Monica, Calif.: RAND, 1999), 16.

occur rapidly, but just that the change will be profound.[28] Finally, military organizations can rarely replicate in times of peace the actual conditions of war. The absence of the complexity, ambiguity, and friction of war predetermine military institutions to develop concepts and doctrines that meet the standards of peacetime efficiency rather than wartime effectiveness. On the contrary, transformation efforts conducted in wartime enjoy a pace and pragmatism in field-testing which eliminates much of the debate that peacetime innovation brings about.[29]

The Continuity and Evolution Paradigm

In contrast, the *Continuity and Evolution paradigm* views military innovation and transformation as a continuous process intended to deal with the chaotic nature of war. The *Continuity and Evolution paradigm* argues that superior technology and new organizational concepts are always important, but are just parts of a complex equation that rules strategy and warfare, an equation where friction and the human element are always present.[30]

This more balanced approach towards the phenomenon of military revolutions recognizes the importance of military innovation and change, but at the same time encourages a healthy skepticism towards the irregularly paced process of innovation. The proponents of this view do not reject the idea that transformations in war occur, nor that the pace can vary, but rather view military innovations as a continuous process of coping with the challenges of warfare.[31]

---

[29] Williamson Murray, "Thinking about Innovation," *Naval War College Review* 54, no. 2 (2001): 122.

[30] For this approach, see mainly Jeremy Black, *A Military Revolution? Military Change and European Society, 1550–1800* (London: Macmillan, 1991), and "Eighteenth-Century Warfare Reconsidered," *War in History* 1 (July 1994): 215–32; Rogers, *Military Revolution Debate;* and Gray, *Strategy for Chaos.*

[31] Regarding the issue of complexity in war and strategy, see Barry D. Watts, *Clausewitzian Friction and Chaos: Friction in War and Military Policy* (Westport, Conn.: Praeger, 2001).

The argument is that there are no revolutionary discontinuities, but instead, a continuous evolution of military innovation and change. In this process of continuous change, the ability to cope with an increasingly complex battlefield has been a more important determinant of success or failure than radical innovation.[32] Revolutions of any type, whether great or small, tend to overlay rather than literally succeed each other. For example, the aviation revolution, either as a Military Revolution or even a Military Technical Revolution, is still going on, alongside the nuclear and information-led revolutions.[33] The rationale behind the *Continuity and Evolution* paradigm is that military transformation is the end result of an evolution in military innovation and that history proves that there are several paths to military success.[34]

An obvious problem with this paradigm is that there is no clear difference between innovation that is just innovation and innovation that leads (or might lead) to revolution. By attributing every attempt at innovation and change to a continuous process that deals with complexity and the chaotic nature of war, there is the danger of oversimplifying the history of military revolutions. Continuity is not the only value in military affairs. Sometimes it is necessary to implement widespread change in doctrine, training, education, and technology. Facing up to the inevitability of change and appreciating the benefits of change is often required if a military institution is aiming to prevail in a new era.

The Napoleonic Revolution in Military Affairs

During the Revolutionary and Napoleonic wars, the small professional armies of the eighteenth century quickly gave way to large

---

[32] Biddle, "The Past as Prologue," 5.

[33] It has been argued that the full maturing of airpower during the 1980s and 1990s is the real revolution of today. See Benjamin S. Lambeth, "The Technology Revolution in Air Warfare," *Survival* 39 (Spring 1997): 65–83.

[34] For a similar approach, see the Essential Continuity Theory in Biddle, "The Past as Prologue," 11–32.

national armies composed of conscripts. This same period saw artillery transformed from a specialized profession overseen by mechanics into a major service branch capable of dominating battlefields. The wars Napoleon waged were wars of conquest on a grand scale and were fought by huge armies, which consisted of professional soldiers, mercenaries, and patriotic French conscripts. The *levée en masse* adopted in France enabled Napoleon to keep under arms hundreds of thousands of soldiers, with his opponents following closely.[35]

At the end of the eighteenth century the rise of nationalism, the institution of universal conscription, the comprehensive economic mobilization of society, and the creation of the "nation in arms" combined to constitute a Revolution in Military Affairs. Napoleon's contribution was to bring together these elements in order to achieve his policy goals.[36] It was a revolution driven more by politics than by technology. Neither Napoleon's conquests nor his subsequent defeat can be explained in terms of technological factors. The *Grande Armée* and its opponents possessed very similar arsenals, and given the character of war in this period, it is not surprising that all armies imitated technical advances that were made by the others.[37]

The revolutionary system of command employed by Napoleon was not the result of any radical technological advances, but of superior organization and doctrine. Napoleon's enemies sought to maintain control by keeping their forces closely concentrated, whereas Napoleon chose the opposite path, reorganizing and decentralizing his army. In order to achieve that he had to organize the army in self-contained, mission-oriented units, the corps; to institute a system of regular reports from the corps to the General Headquarters,

---

[35] On the Napoleonic Wars, see selectively Vincent J. Esposito and John R. Elting, *A Military History and Atlas of the Napoleonic Wars* (London: Greenhill Books, 1999); and Gunther Rothenberg, *The Napoleonic Wars* (London: Cassell, 2001).

[36] Gray, *Strategy for Chaos*, 146–47.

[37] Van Creveld, *Technology and War*, 167.

and of orders from the latter to the corps; and to organize a headquarters staff capable of dealing with the bureaucratic traffic generated.[38] This enabled the various parts of the army to operate independently for a limited period of time and consequently tolerate a higher degree of uncertainty.[39] The system of *corps de armee* was a major innovation and enabled Napoleon to conduct operational maneuver with a very large force. An army organized on the corps system had an organizational framework that resisted collapse and provided a structure for quick reorganization after a defeat.[40]

The Napoleonic revolution might be limited to a period of two decades, but a long period of preparation reaching back to the 1740s can be identified. The demographic and economic expansion that occurred during that period provided nations with the necessary resources for protracted warfare. Adding to that, the emphasis of the Enlightenment on rationality and novelty, as well as the extensive military experience acquired, helped to prepare the ground for radical transformation.[41] A number of reforming efforts occurred after the Seven Years' War (1756–63)[42] and prepared the ground for the Napoleonic RMA. Marshal Maurice de Saxe, Jean-Charles Folard, Jean de Mesnil-Durand, and Jean-Pierre du Teil, just to name a few, developed ideas to enhance battlefield performance and stressed the importance of logistics.[43] The modernity and organizational flexibility

---

[38] Martin van Creveld, *Command in War* (Cambridge, Mass.: Harvard University Press, 1985), 96–97.

[39] Ibid., 100–102.

[40] Robert M. Epstein, "Patterns of Change and Continuity in Nineteenth-Century Warfare," *Journal of Military History* 56 (July 1992): 377.

[41] Jeremy Black, *Warfare in the Eighteenth Century* (London: Cassell, 1999), 192.

[42] See Williamson Murray's argument that the Seven Years' War acted as a preshock to the Napoleonic Revolution. Murray, "Thinking about Revolutions in Military Affairs," 72–76.

[43] For an analysis of the reforming efforts prior to Napoleon, see John A. Lynn, *The Bayonets of the Republic: Motivation and Tactics in the Army of Revolutionary France, 1791–94* (Urbana: University of Illinois Press, 1984); and Spenser Wilkinson, *The French Army before Napoleon* (Aldershot: Gregg Revivals, 1991).

of the French Army of the 1790s was not the result of a rapid transformation, but of more than thirty years of inspired and systematic reform and improvement. At the end of the Seven Years' War, the French realized that their armies did not perform well and therefore were open to reformist proposals. It would be fair to argue that most of the preparatory work that later enabled Napoleonic France to conduct a number of successful campaigns was undertaken by the Old Regime during the period from the 1740s to the 1780s.[44] Coming back to the paradigms, the above point would apply more to the *Continuity and Evolution* than to the *Radical Transformation* paradigm. In tactical and strategic matters the Revolution built on the achievements of the eighteenth century, most notably by Guibert in infantry tactics and Gribeauval in the deployment of the artillery. But the work of the pre-revolutionary reformers could not implement a revolution on its own. Two vital elements were required, the dynamism of the French Revolution and the leadership of Napoleon.

French efforts to reform the army did not stop with doctrines, organization, and tactics. There was a sociopolitical change, triggered by the French Revolution. The monopolizing of the commissioned ranks by the aristocracy in Bourbon France and the inability of the crown to pay for the needs of the army were threatening the political survival of the military institution. By successfully marrying professional competence to political enthusiasm, the Revolution allowed the emergence of a new military elite and succeeded in raising large armies on the claim that the French nation was in danger.[45] The French Revolution invested in ideology and nationalism. Even though the existence of a sociopolitical revolution is not considered a precondition for any RMA, in the case of Revolutionary France, it is reasonable to argue that the Napoleonic RMA developed within a sociopolitical context. Therefore, the Napoleonic RMA can be interpreted under the *Social Wave* paradigm, meaning that the political turbulence of the French Revolution was the driving force for the

---

[44] Rothenberg, *Napoleonic Wars*, 24–28.
[45] Ibid., 30–31.

military revolution. Faced with foreign invasion, the leaders of 1793 declared a *levée en masse,* which placed citizens and their property at the disposal of the state. The result was that the French tripled the size of their army in less than a year, and although they remained less effective in battle than their opponents on a unit-to-unit basis, they could accept casualties and fight on a scale like no other military formation.[46]

The above factors were essential, but not adequate for transforming French military power. Napoleon's charismatic leadership, operational brilliance, and vision were the missing ingredients.[47] In particular, the development of a more mobile artillery park and the assembling of divisions into *corps d'armée* are his major contributions to the art of war. Napoleon made use of the work of early reformers that had not been completely understood or that had not been exploited fully. Napoleon was not just a part of the equation; he recognized the full potential of the transformation in war and saw how its components could be made to work together. As far as his strategic vision is concerned, he did not regard war (major war in his case) as a last resort, but as the central element of his foreign policy.[48]

After 1789 the French artillery service was state-of-the-art for its time. The end result was more aggressive battlefield tactics that ushered artillery away from a supporting position into a decisive and highly destructive role of its own. By 1805, the corps system had matured, and Napoleon was strong enough politically to insure the execution of his operational plans. The army corps system made

[46] Murray, "Thinking about Revolutions in Military Affairs," 71.

[47] The Napoleonic RMA is probably the only military revolution where the leader played such an important role. See Peter Paret, "Napoleon and the Revolution in War," in *Makers of Modem Strategy: From Machiavelli to the Nuclear Age,* ed. Peter Paret (Princeton, N.J.: Princeton University Press, 1986), 127.

[48] Regarding Napoleon's foreign policy, see Paul W. Schroeder, "Napoleon's Foreign Policy: A Criminal Enterprise," *Journal of Military History* 54 (April 1990): 147–62.

large forces easier to command and control and ensured the flexible execution of combined army tactics.[49] The victories at Austerlitz (1805), Jena (1806), and Friedland (1807) were achieved by a modern nineteenth-century French Army, against the archaic armies of the Austrians, Prussians, and Russians.[50]

Napoleon dominated the European continent for more than a decade because his opponents were initially hesitant in adjusting to the new style of warfare. This stemmed from the fact that some of the aspects of the revolution were not products of a sudden innovation, but of the utilization of institutions and methods that had existed for decades, and therefore would not demand radical adjustment. In addition, there was the belief that adoption of reforms like universal conscription and open access to commissions would mean changing one's social and political system.[51] Prussia, for example, adopted these changes in order to defeat Napoleonic France, but after 1815 abandoned them as subversive. The reason that the Austrian Empire failed to copy the French methods early on was the sociopolitical implications of the *levée en masse*. The Hapsburgs feared providing military training to various ethnic groups within their borders.

Nevertheless, the French victories between 1805 and 1807, victories of flexible tactics and superior command and control, triggered a reaction to the Napoleonic revolution.[52] When the Allies raised modern nineteenth-century armies and used them against Napoleon, warfare changed again. The Austrians and Prussians exploited German nationalism and developed an expandable army, relying on the mobilization of trained reserves and *Landwehr*. In contrast to

---

[49] Regarding the organization of the infantry and cavalry, see Rory Muir, *Tactics and the Experience of Battle in the Age of Napoleon* (New Haven, Conn.: Yale University Press, 2000), 68–76 and 105–13.

[50] Epstein, "Patterns of Change and Continuity," 377.

[51] Paret, "Napoleon and the Revolution in War," 134–36.

[52] See MacGregor Knox, "The French Revolution and After," in Knox and Murray, *Dynamics of Military Revolution*, 66–72.

the French case, modernization in Austria and Prussia did not require support by a sociopolitical revolution. The authoritarian regimes of both Austria and Prussia were able to impose radical innovations. The different responses to the Napoleonic revolution derive from different needs and capabilities. For example, Prussia was a continental power with extensive land combat experience, whereas Britain was a naval power that chose not to reform and was therefore constrained to conduct land warfare on the eighteenth-century model.[53] By 1809 and despite the French victory of Wagram in that year, it was obvious that Napoleon's enemies had learned the art of modern warfare. The period of Austerlitz, where Napoleon was fighting obsolete armies of the eighteenth century, and defeating his opponent in decisive battles, was long gone. The war became protracted, the battles lasted for days, and the Allies proved able to mobilize greater resources.

Seen under a holistic prism, the Napoleonic RMA was the result of a combination of many factors. First of all, the ground was prepared by the reforming efforts of the Old Regime. By the 1790s, the French artillery park was the most modern, French tactics were superior, and their military equipment was as good as any in Europe. Second, the French Revolution provided the context within which social and political changes could coexist synergistically with military reforms. Human and material masses, mobilized by nationalism and the emergence of a new military elite, allowed the *Grande Armée* to wage wars where mass was the decisive element for victory. Third, brilliant leadership seized the opportunity and carried out the military revolution.

But paradoxically enough, it was these factors that led to Waterloo (1815) and the failure of Napoleon's strategy. His opponents sooner or

[53] Regarding the Austrian, British, and Prussian responses to the Napoleonic Revolution in Warfare, see Epstein, "Patterns of Change and Continuity," 378–86; Raymond E. Franck, "Innovation and the Technology of Conflict during the Napoleonic Revolution in Military Affairs," *Conflict Management and Peace Science* 21 (2004): 69–84; and Rothenberg, *Napoleonic Wars,* 116–17 and 173–77.

later adopted the military tactics, ideas, and weapons that Napoleon had used to materialize his revolution. After all, evolutionary developments like the corps and divisions had their roots in eighteenth-century warfare and were not exclusive products of Revolutionary France. The Austrians and Prussians learned their lessons and reacted successfully.[54] The Revolution allowed Napoleon to mobilize the necessary human and material resources, but at the same time its aggressive nationalism triggered countervailing nationalisms. In particular, the Austrians and Prussians appealed to German nationalism within their German-speaking territories, with the hope of creating a rival movement. The result was the creation of a German-speaking *Landwehr.*[55]

In addition, the early political gains of the Revolution outside France were soon broken down by Napoleon's foreign policy. Napoleon's campaigns for conquest and loot nullified the sympathy produced by the ideals of the French Revolution. In contrast to Frederick II of Prussia and Catherine II of Russia, whose actions were compatible with some sort of European order, Napoleon's insistence on waging major wars proved a strategic mistake, since he did not use military success to achieve peace and political survival. In certain cases (like the decision to invade Russia), his policy was unrealistic and driven by his psychological need for conquest and absolute domination.[56] Even in a period where war was accepted as a legitimate instrument of policy, Napoleon's campaigns were judged illegitimate and intolerable.[57] The enterprises of Napoleonic France were too many and too vast. As the size of the armies increased and operated in several theatres, even Napoleon's genius was not enough to cope with the clamor and confusion of battle.[58]

---

[54] Black, "Eighteenth-Century Warfare Reconsidered."
[55] Epstein, "Patterns of Change and Continuity," 378–82.
[56] Harold T. Parker, "Why Did Napoleon Invade Russia? A Study in Motivation and the Interrelations of Personality and Social Structure," *Journal of Military History* 54 (April 1990): 131–46.
[57] Schroeder, "Napoleon's Foreign Policy," 158.
[58] Rothenberg, *Napoleonic Wars,* 216–17.

The First World War Revolution in Military Affairs

Warfare at the beginning of the First World War (1914–16) differed little from that practiced in the eighteenth century. Warfare in 1914 was a linear affair, and its doctrines emphasized flank attack, envelopment, and annihilation.[59] By 1917 the industrial version of the Napoleonic War paradigm had been shown to be the wrong one. A new way of warfare was developed, where industrial mobilization, technological improvements in military methods, and the emergence of new weapons played a crucial role in changing the character of war.[60] Machine guns, trenches, and barbed wire brought maneuver to a halt, and the European armies were unable to achieve decisive victories.[61] From 1917 on, indirect artillery fire enabled decentralized combined-arms combat teams of infantry to seize and hold bite-sized chunks of the enemy's defended zone. Tanks were used to crush barbed wire and eliminate machine guns. Aircraft proved useful for collecting information and providing tactical support.[62] Light machine guns were one of the key weapons to emerge from the First World War. While heavy machine guns were a major cause of trench warfare, making dug-in troops very difficult to defeat, light machine guns helped to restore mobility to the battlefield.[63]

The revolution was technical, tactical, and conceptual, but many of the components that led to the artillery-led revolution were not new.

---

[59] Jonathan Bailey, "The First World War and the Birth of Modern Warfare," in Knox and Murray, *Dynamics of Military Revolution*, 135.

[60] Gary Sheffield, *Forgotten Victory. The First World War: Myths and Realities* (London: Headline, 2001), 105–33.

[61] Regarding the unsuccessful efforts of both Central Powers and Allies to break the Great War's stalemate, see D. E. Showalter, "Manoeuvre Warfare: The Eastern and Western Fronts, 1914–1915," in The *Oxford Illustrated History of the First World War*, ed. Hew Strachan (Oxford: Oxford University Press, 1998), 39–53.

[62] Gray, *Strategy for Chaos*, 175.

[63] Regarding the rebirth of mobility, see J. F. C. Fuller, *The Conduct of War, 1789-1961* (London: University Paperback, 1979), 172–77.

Elements of indirect fire appeared in the nineteenth century, but the armies of that era failed to realize its full potential. In particular, early signs of the effectiveness of indirect fire appeared in the Franco-Prussian War (1870–71) and the Russo-Japanese War (1904–5), but the commanders failed to realize the tactical and operational necessity of adopting it. All armies before the Great War planned to conduct fast-moving operations in which artillery would be unable to keep up. There was no concept of field artillery being used at the operational level to aid in breaking through enemy lines.[64] After all, longer-range guns would have been heavier, less mobile, and thus less relevant to the prevailing concept in which range was sacrificed for mobility. Deficiencies in mapping, ballistic calculation, and communication postponed innovation in the use of artillery at the beginning of the Great War.[65] But the prime reason for failing to exploit indirect fire was lack of imagination and doctrinal laziness. According to Jonathan Bailey, once the brutal necessity of adopting the new method presented itself, technical and tactical problems stemming from the conservative military culture were soon overcome.[66]

The German model, which dominated the second half of the nineteenth century and had been adopted by every army in Europe, was based on excellence in staff work, short-range logistics, and envelopment. Victory would go to the side with the best-trained and most-disciplined army. As a result, the opening battles were closer in conception and execution to those of the Napoleonic era than to the battles from 1916 onwards.[67] Prior to 1914 the generals in Europe were under the illusion that a war would be short and were willing

---

[64] Jonathan Bailey, *The First World War and the Birth of the Modern Style of Warfare,* Occasional Paper no. 22 (Camberley, U.K.: Strategic & Combat Studies Institute, Staff College, 1996), 8.

[65] Ibid., 9.

[66] Ibid., 10.

[67] John Bourne, "Total War I: The Great War" in *The Oxford Illustrated History of Modern War,* ed. Charles Townshend (Oxford: Oxford University Press, 1997), 107–12.

to offer a human solution to the technological problems of the battlefield.[68] The military institutions believed that a prolonged war would cause massive social upheaval and therefore rejected fighting such a war, despite the inapplicability of their doctrines.[69] The military professionals were not blind to the changes that had taken place in command and control, firepower, and logistics. They correctly anticipated the increased lethality of the battlefield and therefore adopted doctrines and tactics that would bring war closer to an end, because they feared that society would collapse under the massive and continuous demands of the modern battlefield.[70] But, while the military professionals succeeded in understanding the new warfighting model, they misunderstood the sociopolitical context of warfare. Their error at the beginning of the war was not to fail to understand the outcomes on the battlefield, but to underestimate the ability of the state to mobilize and maintain control over society during a prolonged war. Industrialization permitted advanced nations to engage in protracted and hugely costly conflicts.

In contrast to the Napoleonic RMA, no long period of preparation and evolution existed. In a way, the experience of 1914–16 was a short but efficient period of education for all the parties involved. These three years of trial and error provided both sides with new tactics for combined arms warfare and the type and quantity of machines and munitions needed to apply the new tactics. Mass was again a significant factor for victory. Modern war led to a demand for more men, more weapons, and more ammunition. The material solution to the problems of the First World War battlefield favored the Allies. The Entente Powers were in a position to mobilize more

[68] Regarding the illusion of a short war, see Ian Beckett, *The Great War, 1914–1918* (London: Pearson Education Limited, 2001), 42–66.

[69] Colin McInnes, *Men, Machines and the Emergence of Modern Warfare, 1914–1945,* Occasional Paper no. 2 (Camberley: Strategic and Combat Studies Institute, British Army Staff College, 1992), 3–5.

[70] Michael Howard, "Men against Fire: The Doctrine of the Offensive in 1914," in Paret, *Makers of Modern Strategy,* 510–26.

national resources. This had to do with the effectiveness of the liberal political institutions of France and Britain and the quality of their civilian morale.[71] Also, both France and Britain could draw on the human and material resources of their colonies. The First World War RMA lacked a central figure (like Napoleon) who could trigger or push the military revolution. This revolution thus was never pursued according to a clearly articulated, unified vision. Instead, despite a number of leading artillery colonels and generals who played an important role, it would be fair to argue that the tactical reeducation of the armies was driven from below. As a result, the RMA of the First World War showed extreme institutional and doctrinal adaptation. The military institutions had to adapt to a style of war for which they were not prepared. Moreover, the executors of the revolution had only three years to test their ideas and doctrines, which had to be proved in action on the battlefield and under the pressure of unprecedented casualties.[72]

Artillery was the tool that, more that any other element, contributed to the First World War RMA.[73] But it would be misleading to argue that artillery was the decisive weapon. It was the means by

---

[71] Regarding the issue of national mobilization as a factor in determining the outcome of the war, see John Horne, ed., *State, Society and Mobilization in Europe during the First World War* (Cambridge: Cambridge University Press, 1997).

[72] For the process of mutual adjustment, see Dennis Showalter, "Mass Warfare and the Impact of Technology" *in Great War, Total War: Combat and Mobilization on the Western Front, 1914–1918,* ed. Roger Chickering and Stig Forster (Cambridge: Cambridge University Press, 2000).

[73] Note that the First World War RMA is synonymous to a certain degree with the Artillery Revolution. According to Trevor Wilson and Robin Prior, the revolution involves mainly land warfare. Despite new technological developments, the war at sea was not strikingly different from the naval war of the Napoleonic era, and the air war, even though a new phenomenon, had not reached a state of development where it could fundamentally alter the face of battle. See Wilson and Prior, "Conflict, Technology, and the Impact of Industrialization: The Great War 1914–18," *Journal of Strategic Studies* 24 (September 2001): 128–57.

which Allied competence (in resources and overall strategy) was translated into military effectiveness. The artillery revolution of 1917–18 (among both the Central Powers and the Allies) was the result of an effort by the army, the society, and the government. The balance in these factors favored the Allies. The artillery-led revolution could not guarantee victory alone. After all, none of the combatants established a superior technique to defeat their opponent in a decisive way.

The turning point for the revolution was the battle of Cambrai in November 1917. By then, both parties had learned how to use machine guns in large numbers, to conduct trench warfare, to use gas cylinders and gas shells, to lay indirect artillery fire, and to wage air warfare. However, the way the two parties responded to the new challenges was different. In particular, the German Army developed an infantry-artillery, less-mechanized response to the needs of the battlefield,[74] and the British Expeditionary Force (BEF), a more-mechanized one.[75] The reason was that the Germans lacked adequate resources to produce a mechanized alternative.

Each national army (the BEF and the German Army) produced a reaction that was compatible with its technical, material, economic, and military-cultural elements. The fact that Germany and Britain, employing the same military technology, produced two different responses (because of different military cultures, available means,

---

[74] Regarding the German version, see Bruce Gudmundsson, *Stormtroop Tactics: Innovation in the German Army, 1914–1918* (New York: Praeger, 1989); and Timothy Lupfer, *The Dynamics of Doctrine: The Changes in German Tactical Doctrine during the First World War,* Leavenworth Papers no. 4 (Fort Leavenworth, Kans.: Combat Studies Institute, U.S. Army Command and General Staff College, July 1981).

[75] For an analysis of the British version, see Paddy Griffith, *Battle Tactics of the Western Front: The British Army's Art of Attack, 1916–18* (New Haven, Conn.: Yale University Press, 1994); and Timothy Travers, *How the War Was Won: Command and Technology in the British Army on the Western Front, 1917–1918* (London: Rout-ledge, 1992). For a shorter account, Timothy Travers, "The Evolution of British Strategy and Tactics on the Western Front in 1918: GHQ, Manpower and Technology," *Journal of Military History* 54 (April 1990): 173–200.

and needs) seems to confirm the criticism of the *Continuity and Evolution* paradigm (about the complexity of war) and weaken the dominant role of military technology that the *Radical Transformation* paradigm supports. Each side had to adjust in two directions, to the problems that its own army faced and the domestic context, and to the behavior of the enemy. The BEF adjusted to its growing manpower crisis in 1917–18 by adopting a style of firepower and mechanized warfare that rationally played to its industrial strengths. On the other hand, Germany adjusted by adopting a style of elite infantry-led warfare, which lacked the quantity of firepower that the adversary possessed. The German Army did not despise firepower, but the combination of relative disadvantage in material resources and a great tradition in victory through operational maneuver in combined-arms combat, led to a style of warfare less dependent upon firepower than that of the BEF.[76]

Regarding the changes in command, the Germans' choice was devolution, whereas the British preferred to keep a firm control from above. Taking into account the doctrinal development, the intense training, and the tough selection for troop leadership positions that characterized the German Army, it is clear that a decentralized style of command offered a significant advantage to the Germans. The weakness of the BEF in battlefield command was counterbalanced by its material strength. At the end of the day, the difference was that the BEF better matched available means to ends than the German Army did.

Many scholars believe that the German Army waged the better war technically, even though it lost in the end. A closer look at doctrine, military operations, and command proves that the performance of Wilhelmine Germany in certain areas was superior. But coming back to our point about a holistic understanding of the RMA phenomenon, the First World War was not exclusively won (or lost) on the battlefield. Both German and British societies had to adjust to the unprecedented demands of a total war. Even though both sides

[76] Gray, *Strategy for Chaos*, 208.

proved able to adjust to the massive technological needs of the modern style of warfare, the relative advantage was in favor of the Allies by the end of the war. There is no doubt who won the competition in mobilization in terms of quality, quantity, and appropriate choices.[77] German superiority in logistical planning, organization, and mobilization could not overcome the demands of a two-front war. In common with the Napoleonic case in its latter phase, the Germans in the First World War took on too many commitments; they tried to do too much with too little and were unable or unwilling to adapt policy to military reality. In addition, the Central Powers had to fight against a global sea power that dominated the sea-lanes and had access to the resources of its colonies. Britain, even though lacking the experience of conducting continental warfare on a large scale, proved capable of mobilizing its resources for the war effort.

The outcome of the conflict was not determined technologically, since technology, even though a vital element, could not produce tactical success on its own. The First World War is not a case where extremely radical ideas were applied, since most of the elements for the change already existed, but a case where battles demonstrated the necessity of combining the available means under a novel concept.[78] In this case the feedback and the everyday lessons from the battlefield proved to be the driving force of the revolution. Bearing in mind that during the First World War no side possessed decisively superior technology, it seems that this particular RMA fits more the *Continuity and Evolution* paradigm and the *Social Wave* paradigm, than the *Radical Transformation* one. The novel use of the artillery in the last two years of the war stemmed from practical and technological problems faced on the battlefield and it was this that caused the concept of indirect fire to be implemented, rather than a radical technological innovation. The war was decided by mass and attrition; therefore, the side that was more willing and capable of providing its armies with ever more resources would eventually win.

[77] Wilson, "Conflict, Technology and the Impact of Industrialization," 153–54.
[78] Bailey, *First World War and the Birth of Modern Style of Warfare*, 20.

Concluding Remarks

The above analysis of past Revolutions in Military Affairs illustrates the complexity of the issue and the difficulty faced in examining a phenomenon with social, military, and technological dimensions. Both the Napoleonic and First World War RMAs succeeded in creating a new style of warfare and therefore bringing about a change in warmaking, but neither succeeded in overcoming the complexities of warfare. The analysis given here enables us to reach certain conclusions about the nature of revolutions in warfare and the credibility of the paradigms.

First of all, the cases under examination (both as military-technical enterprises and as tools for military effectiveness) needed a sociopolitical context. Whether it is a sociopolitical revolution (like the French Revolution in the Napoleonic case and the Industrial Revolution prior to the First World War), or the perception (or even misperception) of who the enemy is to be, a complex process such as the Revolution in Military Affairs cannot succeed unless it is translated into politically defined goals.

Second, the concept of radical innovation proved not to be that radical after all. Many elements of the revolutions were already present and long known in principle, and many of the techniques and tactics had actually been employed in the past. Even in the situation where the military transformation profited from strong leadership (as in the Napoleonic case), the other side soon proved capable of adapting in some way, and as the First World War teaches us, that can be done in a short period of time by a process of parallel discovery and re-education. The BEF transformed itself from an army ill-equipped for large-scale continental warfare in 1914–15, into the most effective instrument of land warfare in 1918. In addition, the time when victory could be achieved in a decisive battle was long gone and had given way to attrition warfare, where any initial advantage would sooner or later be counterbalanced. Clausewitz's dictum that "war does not consist of a single short blow" applied in both cases examined.

Thirdly, technology is just one dimension of the RMA phenomenon. In both cases, technology was an important factor, but it did not decide the outcome of the war. In the Napoleonic case, aspects like road building, map-making, and printing technologies helped the revolution take place and mature, but did not translate into military effectiveness. Similarly, during the First World War novel technologies (U-boats, torpedoes, floating mines, poison gas, tanks, light machine guns, aircraft, and aerial photography) altered the way war was waged, but none of these technologies could produce a decisive strategic advantage on its own. The Allies achieved victory not because they possessed superior technology by the end of the Great War, but because they managed to perform better in putting together all the necessary elements: industrial mobilization, national resources, morale, and operational art.

Regarding the paradigms, both cases clearly demonstrate that the *Radical Transformation* paradigm lacks certain credibility. Military technology played an important, but not a dominant, role in the Napoleonic Wars and the First World War. The unfolding of the RMAs under examination seems to confirm the main arguments of the Social Wave and *Continuity and Evolution* paradigms. The French and the Industrial Revolutions influenced or even shaped the sociopolitical context under which the military revolutions took place, but the most valuable insights derive from the *Continuity and Evolution* paradigm. The intention of Napoleon and his enemies, as well as of the German and the British armies, was to make the best of the available military technology and doctrines in order to counter the complexity of war. In their efforts, technology was one of many tools, only an element of the art of war, one of many.

Finally, anyone trying to understand a past military revolution (or even plan for a future military transformation) should realize that it is a complex phenomenon and not a linear (technological) undertaking. The fact that almost every actor responded in a different way to the same sociopolitical and military-technical challenges makes this clear. The human, the political, the ethical, the geopolitical, and the temporal should also be included in any analysis of a military revolution. Therefore, a holistic approach that takes into account the complexity of war and uses historical evidence has more to offer than an uncritical technology-led partition of military history.[79] Getting back to the current information-technology-driven revolution, such an approach might engender some healthy skepticism regarding the uses and limits of optical and infrared sensors, stealth aircraft, and precision-guided munitions.

---

[79] See Knox and Murray, "Conclusion: The Future Behind Us," in Knox and Murray, *Dynamics of Military Revolution;* and Gray, *Strategy for Chaos,* 270–91.

7

Atrocity, War Crime, and Treason in the English Civil War

BARBARA DONAGAN

THE REPUTATION OF THE ENGLISH CIVIL WAR is unusually benign. Its literature of atrocity is minor and low key compared with the horrifying accounts and repellent illustrations of events of the Thirty Years' War and the Irish Rebellion of 1641. Yet England knew atrocities, as well as marginally permissible cruelties, and not only those committed against the Irish. They also occurred on home ground against the home-grown. These atrocities have attracted slight attention, other than for anecdotal purposes, although they raise the question of what kind of war England's was, as wars go. The question has only recently begun to engage historians.[1] Past inattention may perhaps be explained by the belief that, as all wars are bad, discrimination is irrelevant; or that the war was English and moderate,

I am grateful to the Henry E. Huntington Library and the British Academy for an exchange fellowship in 1990 that supported research in England. I am also grateful to Geoffrey Parker, Blair Worden, the editor of the *AHR* and its anonymous readers for helpful criticism of an earlier version of this article.

[1] See Ian Roy's pioneering article, "England Turned Germany? The Aftermath of the Civil War in Its European Context," *Transactions of the Royal Historical Society,* 5th ser., 28 (1978): 127–44. The question is explored in Charles Carton, *Going to the Wars: The Experience of the British Civil Wars 1638–1651* (London, 1992). See also Ronan Bennett, "War and Disorder: Policing the Soldiery in Civil War Yorkshire," in *War and Government in Britain, 1598–1650,* Mark Charles Fissel, ed. (Manchester, 1991), 254 –55, 264–65; Barbara Donagan," Codes and Conduct in the English Civil War," *Past and Present,*118(February 1988): 65–95.

and besides served virtuous historicist ends of democracy, liberalism, and toleration; or that military history is a matter of marches and battles, dramatic but marginal to mainstream historical studies.

Seventeenth-century English men and women saw things more comparatively, and they were less sanguine that a fortunate exceptionalism would protect them from war's worst excesses. They were acutely conscious of war in contemporary Europe and as aware of its rules, practice, and theories as of its social dangers and atrocities. They believed that preservation from the "sea of blood . . . [and] fury of fire" that they perceived in Germany required careful observance of the norms of war.[2]

Wars may differ in ways that greatly affect the speed or slowness with which postwar reconciliation or acceptance of status quo is achieved. One factor is the degree to which the enemy is believed to have observed or transgressed the codes of war and to have been guilty of atrocities and war crimes: not merely the unorganized, random outrages committed in all wars by troops out of control but, more important, institutionalized, officially sanctioned acts of policy. In our own day, the Geneva Conventions prohibit such acts, and the Nuremberg trials wrestled with the legal and moral difficulties of defining offenses and condemned offenders.[3] Recent proposals for a permanent international body to try war crimes, stemming

---

[2] J. Philolaus, *A Serious Aviso to the Good People of this Nation, Concerning that Sort of Men, called Levellers* (London, 1649), 3. I owe this quotation to Steven Zwicker.

[3] For continuing debate on the legitimacy and effectiveness of international tribunals and on definitions of war crimes, see the responses to Telford Taylor, *The Anatomy of the Nuremberg Trials: A Personal Memoir* (New York, 1992), in, for example, Geoffrey Best, "Between Hot and Cold War," *Times Literary Supplement* (August 27, 1993); Istvan Dedk, "Misjudgment at Nuremberg," *New York Review of Books* (October 7, 1993), and subsequent correspondence (November 4, 1993); see also Alan Donagan, "Victors' Justice," *London Review of Books* (February 16–29, 1984); Robert Conot, "In a World Beset by Violence, Who Should Face War-Crimes Charges?" *Los Angeles Times* (March 7, 1993).

from the civil war in Bosnia, are only the latest recognition that rules are broken and the latest attempt to find a way to enforce them.

What follows is neither a comparative study of conduct in the wars of early modern Europe nor a study of evolution from Lieber's Code and "General Orders No. 100" of the American Civil War to the Hague Conventions of 1899 and 1907 and the Geneva Conventions. It is instead a study of the conduct of Englishmen toward each other in their wars during the 1640s. Although theirs was a narrow and local conflict, it must also be seen in the context of European theory and practice of war, for England was not insular in its military culture. Like the rest of Europe, it struggled to observe and enforce uncodified, unwritten rules and conventions that would set limits to personal and property damage (although the limits do not always appear particularly humane). Soldiers and civilians alike sought to contain the forces of social disruption and chaos that seemed always to menace the thin skin of ordered society and in war threatened to burst free. The degree of success in maintaining the standards of conduct to which both sides subscribed, the severity of punishment or reprisal for failure, these, like the social, personal, and economic factors that modified behavior in war and encouraged selective amnesia in peace, helped to shape the politics of Interregnum and Restoration. After the war ended, the way in which former enemies perceived each other's past conduct had much to do with the ease or discomfort with which they were able to live as neighbors and to act as members of the same polity.

Englishmen of the mid-seventeenth century confronted difficulties with which we are still familiar: allocation of war guilt, the nature of charges, proper jurisdiction and constitution of courts, and appropriate punishments. Long before Nuremberg, English theorists tackled the "Nuremberg defense" of acting under orders, for they saw the need to act according to conscience on the one hand and the social and military imperatives of obedience on the other. They, too, knew the value of a scapegoat "other" who could be demonized and made responsible for the worst cruelties (and by implication mitigate the guilt of more useful or attractive enemies).

Despite historians' recent arguments that we should reject an Anglocentric perspective and instead consider British wars that encompassed three kingdoms and a principality,[4] I shall confine my discussion to war in England in the 1640s. To assimilate conflicts of different kinds to a single category impedes understanding of the wars being conducted in the British Isles. For the English were conducting three kinds of war, of which only one was unequivocally civil. Despite the union of the two crowns in 1603, Scotland remained a separate kingdom, and its soldiers normally merited the treatment due to foreign foes. The complicated struggles in Ireland can best be described as colonial wars that engaged fluctuating forces of liberation and faction. Such distinctions cannot be neat or exclusive, but neither are they purely scholastic, for codes of conduct differed according to the kind of war being fought. Against a Christian foreign enemy, the laws of war, posited on hostilities between sovereign states, were straightforwardly applicable. In a colonial war, especially one with strong racist, religious, and retributive elements, many argued that the laws of war were abrogated, since barbarian or heretic "others" or outsiders did not merit the protections due to the civilized and Christian.[5] In a civil war, laws of war came into conflict with

---

[4] See Conrad Russell, *The Fall of the British Monarchies 1637–1642* (Oxford, 1991), vii, on "genuinely British history"; J. S. Morrill, *The Nature of the English Revolution* (London, 1993), 246, 259–65.

[5] Compare the evolution of Spanish views on treatment of denizens of the New World as described in Silvio Zavala, *The Political Philosophy of the Conquest of America*, Teener Hall, trans. (Mexico City, 1953), chaps. 2–3; and see *The Rights and Obligations of Indians and Spaniards in the New World according to Francisco de Vitoria*, reconstructed by Luciano Pereña Vicente (Salamanca, 1992), for a useful abstract of Francisco de Vitoria's formulation of Indian rights and his view that war against barbarian and pagan Indians should meet the criteria for just wars and observe normal rules of conduct. Contrast the alternative tradition: for example, Gines de Sepulveda in 1547 on "fitting and . . . salutary" dominion over "barbarians . . . savages who hardly merit the name of human creatures"; and Benito de Peñalosa y Mondragón in 1629. Zavala, *Political Philosophy,* 53, 57. Seventeenth-century English attitudes to the Irish largely belong in the latter tradition. I am grateful to Michael Perceval Maxwell and Mary Gregor for leading me to Zavala and the Vicente redaction of Vitoria respectively.

laws of peace that punished taking arms against authority as treason. When fighting began in 1642, the status of the conflict as war was not self-evident. The history of the English civil war is in part a history of why it was fought as a foreign war and of lapses from that mode.

Four issues will be addressed here. The first is how the rules of foreign war came to be accepted as applicable, the second, the nature of those rules, with special attention, as illustration, to those for surrender. Third, the problem of failure to observe codes will be approached through some of the conflict's more unsettling events, which raise issues of atrocity and war crime. Finally, I will argue that a change between the first and second civil wars marked a decline from the mutually observed professional codes that moderated relations between enemies before 1648. Certain subsidiary themes that cannot be explored here underlie this discussion. One is the extent of pre-war military education among Englishmen, which has been greatly underestimated. When the war began, many soldiers on both sides were already educated in the theory and practice of modern war; their codes of conduct were assimilated by new recruits.[6] Another is English legalism and sensitivity to challenges to traditional jurisdiction, which informed anxious attention to the questions of who should decide what constituted an offense in war, who should punish, and what the relation of military to civil power should be. And a third is the overwhelming importance—not only in military affairs—of keeping faith, of the reliability of the given word, which derived from the utilitarian value of dependable promises as well as from the religious quality of the oath.[7]

WHY, IN A CIVIL WAR, were the rules of foreign war observed? The obvious answer, of course, is utilitarian: it did not pay to do otherwise,

[6] I have discussed these points in the papers "Halcyon Days and the Literature of War: England's Military Education before 1642" (forthcoming, *Past and Present*) and "Learning War: The Profession of Arms and Pre-Civil War England."

[7] See, for example, Richard Zouche, *Iuris et iudicii fecialis, sive, iuris inter gentes, et quaestionum de eodem explicatio*, Thomas Erskine Holland, ed., James Leslie Brierly, trans., 2 vols. (Washington, D.C., 1911), 2: 174.

to set the stage for a war of reprisal, of *lex talionis*. If the resolution to the problem seems obvious now, it was less so in 1642.[8] In the early messy months of the war, both sides exercised restraint; but, late in the year, the Royalists indicted three captured Parliamentarian captains, one of them the future Leveller John Lilburne, for treason. Instead of granting the protections due to prisoners of war, the Royalists proposed to try them at Oxford by the processes of civilian law before Sir Robert Heath, justice of the King's Bench; conviction would be speedily followed by execution. Only Lilburne's dramatic last-ditch appeal to Parliament saved them. The House of Commons mustered all its legal talent, and within two days a joint declaration by Lords and Commons confronted the charge of treason and, more to the immediate point, warned of consequences. If the Royalists proceeded from indictment to trial, or if these officers or any other agents of Parliament were harmed, not only would judge and officials be held liable but exact reprisal would follow: "the like Punishment shall be inflicted, by Death or otherwise, upon such Prisoners as have been, or shall be, taken by the Forces raised by Authority of both Houses of Parliament."[9]

Meanwhile, at some time early in the war, the king's secretary recorded "a serious Debate in Council" in which it was argued that exchange of prisoners— that is, countenancing a practice governed by conventions of war between nations—"tacitly impl[ied] the Justice of the War," thus granting it the status of war rather than rebellion.

---

[8] See *A Catalogue of the Names of the Dukes, Marquesses, Earles and Lords, that have absented themselves from the Parliament, and are now with His Maiesty* (n.p., 1642), 16, on on "those who have been declared Traytors" by Parliament; and compare *Military Orders and Articles, Established by his Majesty* (Oxford, 1642), 1, on the Royalist designation of Parliment's troops as "disloyall and Rebellious Subjects." (This rare early edition of Royalist articles is in the library of Lincoln College, Oxford.)

[9] *Journals of the House of Lords* (hereafter, LJ), 5: 497; *Journals of the House of Commons* (hereafter, CJ), 2: 891-92; Pauline Gregg, *Free-born John: A Biography of John Lilburne* (London, 1961), 101–03; Edward Hyde, Earl of Clarendon, *The History of the Rebellion and Civil Wars in England*, 3 vols. (Oxford, 1702–04), 3: 391.

The king, out of concern for his imprisoned followers, agreed to exchanges, but his secretary observed, "He might by the known and ancient Laws of the Kingdom have executed such as He took in Arms as Traytors and Rebels."[10] The principle of beneficial mutual restraint was clearly at work; and, by December 1642, Parliament, in what Lilburne later called "that declaration of Lex Talionis," had spelled out the consequences of abandoning it.[11] Restraint had prevailed, but both sides had established a reserve claim to the legal right to regard the enemy as traitors to a civil state, even as they refrained from implementing treason's penalties.

Many found this restraint onerous and misguided. Furthermore, what constituted treason and therefore merited punishment was a matter of partisan judgment. Sir Edward Walker, the king's secretary, argued that Parliament could only execute those taken in arms as traitors "by an arbitrary power" or by an intrinsically ridiculous claim to prosecute for statutory treason. Parliamentarians for their part argued that the king's soldiers were engaged "in the Act of War against the Parliament, which, by the Laws and Statutes of this Realm, is Rebellion and High treason against the King and Kingdom."[12] The distinction between civil and military guilt also presented problems that were to dog future debates over pardon, indemnity, and oblivion.[13] Despite difficulties, however, the principle

---

[10] Sir Edward Walker, *Historical Discourses* (London, 1705), 247–48. Walker's dating is vague; he refers to "good Subjects . . . barbarously clapt on Shipboard," but although Royalist prisoners still languished on hulks in the summer of 1643, his account seems to predate that time. Bodleian Library, Oxford (hereafter, Bodl. Libr.), MS Tanner, 62/1B, fol. 248.

[11] Thomas Bayley Howell, *A Complete Collection of State Trials and Proceedings for High Treason,* 33 vols. (London, 1811–26), 4: cols. 1303–04.

[12] Walker, *Historical Discourses,* 248; *LJ,* 5: 497. On the adaptable nature of treason charges, see Conrad Russell, "The Theory of Treason in the Trial of Strafford," *English Historical Review,* 80 (January 1965): 32–33; and John Bellamy, *The Tudor Law of Treason: An Introduction* (London, 1979), 228–35.

[13] For mingling of soldiers and civilians, see, for example, the propositions of Uxbridge and Newcastle (1644 and 1646), which excluded officials, clergy,

had been made explicit: the laws of war rather than the laws of the civil state were applicable, and Englishmen confronted each other as "lawful enemies."[14] In the first civil war and its aftermath, the codes of war on the whole prevailed over the law of treason. Yet warning had been given of the inherent danger of civil war; each side had defined the other as traitorous, and a shadow of the state's more ruthless law hovered over relations between victor and defeated. Its presence was acknowledged in 1642; it grew darker in 1648.

THE CODES OF WAR OFFERED POSITIVE PROTECTIONS of persons and property, both civilian and soldier, and negative prohibitions against certain kinds of conduct. They comprehended both crimes against humanity and crimes that infringed the laws of war. The present argument begins with the conduct of soldiers, for although the codes of war and just war theory were not unrelated, they impinged little on each other, and we are here concerned with *ius in bello,* not *ius ad bellum.* Then as now, it was agreed that war should not be undertaken except for a just cause; but, then as now, it was rarely difficult to prove that one's cause was just. Further, the legitimacy of the institution of war was rarely challenged; pacifism was a marginal issue in mid-seventeenth-century England, although neutralism was widespread. William Gouge, an influential Puritan minister, in part anticipated Carl von Clausewitz when he wrote, "Warre is a kind of execution of publique justice; and a means of maintaining right." The "iniquity of men," he added, "causeth a necessity of warre," and although it was often "abused," yet there was a "just and right use

---

and soldiers from pardon. These indiscriminate categories reflect a groping toward a political concept of war guilt. *The Constitutional Documents of the Puritan Revolution 1628–1660,* Samuel Rawson Gardiner, ed. (Oxford, 1889), 197, 215–16.

[14] Zouche, *Iuris et iudicifecialis,* 2: 37–38: "lawful enemies are those to whom are due all the rights of war" (unlike traitors, including rebels and deserters, and unlike robbers, including brigands and pirates). See also Alberico Gentili, *De iure belli libri tres,* J. C. Rolfe, trans., Coleman Phillipson, intro., 2 vols. (1612; Oxford, 1933), 2: 15, 22–26.

of warre."[15] The codes of war addressed the tension between its just and right use and its abuse.

Norms of conduct in war derived authority from three different sources: from standards of religion and morality, sometimes described as the law of nature; from the laws of war, internationally recognized professional conventions; and from army regulations. The resulting complex of rules was familiar in seventeenth-century England.[16] First, religion and morality alike—and Protestant England recognized both the teaching of the church fathers and of more recent Catholic authorities such as Francisco Suarez—forbade cruelty for its own sake, deplored blood lust, and decreed that certain categories of persons—the weak, the defenseless, and the holy—should be protected. Hence the outrage at breaches of the protections (which were admittedly not absolute) due to women, children, ministers, the old, the sick, and the dead.[17] Second, the laws of war formalized

---

[15] William Gouge, *The Churches Conquest over the Sword, in Gods Three Arrowes: Plague, Famine, Sword*, 2d edn. (London, 1631), 214; and see Barbara Donagan, "Did Ministers Matter? War and Religion in England, 1642–1649," *Journal of British Studies*, 33 (April 1994): 129–33. See Gentili, *De iure belli*, 2: chap. 5; and Zouche, *Iuris et iudicii fecialis*, 2: 112.

[16] See, for example, Theodor Meron, "Shakespeare's Henry the Fifth and the Law of War," *American Journal of International Law*, 86 (January 1992): 1-45; Donagan, "Codes and Conduct." For the authoritative account of the preceding period, from which the rules of the seventeenth century directly descended, see Maurice H. Keen, *The Laws of War in the Late Middle Ages* (London, 1965).

[17] For the evolution of the idea of protection, see Julius Goebel, Jr., *Felony and Misdemeanor: A Study in the History of Criminal Law* (1937; Philadelphia, 1976), chap. 5. Also see Gouge, *Churches Conquest*, 295. To the objection that the Israelites had on occasion killed all their enemies, including women and the old, Gouge replied, "Extraordinary cases are not exemplary." The people so dealt with "were by God devoted to utter destruction," either because his chosen people were destined to inherit their land or because they implacably hated and wronged his children. Exceptional cases did not invalidate rules, although they justified the failure to apply them. Such arguments of instrumentality in God's cause, of "implacability" or intransigent defiance, and of *lex talionis*, were prevalent in the civil war but hardly confined to it.

these protections along with much else in military conduct, covering such matters as conventions of surrender, plunder, and parole. They remained as yet unwritten, with the exception of occasional protocols between opponents on particular matters, but they were nonetheless internationally recognized and widely if not infallibly observed.[18] They relied on assurance that faith would be mutually kept, and they provided a comprehensive contractual etiquette of conduct between enemies whose personal and professional honor was impugned by any accusation of breach of their rules. In the absence of other sanctions, honor, morality, and not least reciprocal utility supported them.[19] Third, and more mundanely, articles or ordinances of war, the disciplinary regulations that governed each army, were largely concerned with practical matters—no sleeping on watch, no running away—but they also incorporated moral rules and "laws of war," as in prohibitions of rape and killing prisoners. This category of written army ordinances was the only one with formal legal and punitive machinery, for offenders against articles of war could be tried by court-martial.

One class of guide to the perplexed is notably absent from this list. This was, after all, a great age in the history of international law and the related law of war and peace. Yet, although Juan de Ayala and Hugo Grotius were known in England, and although their views were reflected and developed there by the Italian Protestant Alberico Gentili and the English Richard Zouche, both of whom held the chair of civil law at Oxford, it is difficult to perceive the influence of their academic teaching on practice or normative theory in the civil war. It was not that those with pre-war military education or the newly minted soldiers of the 1640s lacked a theoretical and literate

---

[18] For example, the Dutch-Spanish protocol on prisoners of 1602, renewed in 1622. Henry Hexham, *The Principles of the Art Militarie* (London, 1637), containing *An Appendix* (Delft, 1637), 3–8.

[19] See Meron, "Shakespeare's Henry the Fifth," 38, on prisoners' "right to life" and the contractual element in this law of war; and Gentili on the "implied contract . . . between the captor and the captive": the prisoner "seems in person to make a bargain with the enemy for his life." *De iure belli*, 2: 216.

interest in war, for early seventeenth-century England produced and consumed a large military literature. Comprehensive in subject matter and catholic in authority, it covered the minutiae of infantry drill and the large campaigns of Gustavus Adolphus; its exemplars ranged from King David and Caesar to Maurice of Nassau, and its authorities from Augustine and Xenophon to Francesco Guicciardini and the duc de Rohan.[20] Though hardly parochial, this was a vernacular literature. It was designed for those with a present professional interest in war, for citizen-soldiers at home, for potential soldiers or curious civilians, and for a population deeply interested in the fortunes of Protestantism in continental Europe. It told them how war was conducted, practically and morally, and in so doing prepared them for their own war. The English in fact did not need the new high theory, set out in Latin treatises, of Gentili and Grotius for guidance. The precepts and distinctions offered by the modern theorists on grounds for a just war, or treatment of prisoners, or division of spoils did not differ substantively from those of traditional and religious mentors such as the ministers William Gouge or Richard Bernard or from the rules culled from military manuals and popular narratives. Despite the prestige of the new theorists, their impact on the popular educated audience was as yet limited. Zouche's Latin synthesis of Grotius and Gentili, published in 1650, probably reflected views already familiar to his Oxford pupils, but they did not shape conduct in Oxford's years as Royalist capital and garrison. Grotius was much admired, but his fame was religious as well as legal, and his work on war and peace was not published in English until 1654.[21]

---

[20] For the longstanding cosmopolitanism of English writers on war, see Matthew Sutcliffe, *The Practice, Proceedings and Lawes of armes* (London, 1593).

[21] The new theorists' Latin works appeared in some of the more omnivorous libraries, and they were sought after by members of court, legal and religious elites. See Sutcliffe, *Practice, Proceedings and Lawes of armes*, 11, 14, for a somewhat grudging recognition of Ayala as "a great man among the Spaniards." Sir Robert Harley owned a copy of Ayala in Latin (title unspecified), British Library (hereafter, BL) Additional MS (hereafter, Add. MS)

Gustavus Adolphus is said to have carried a copy of Grotius in his saddlebag; we should perhaps look for the influence of the new theorists of international law in attempts to model practice on that of the "New Starr of the North," the great Protestant hero of the age, rather than in direct impact of their teaching and writing.[22]

Traditional sources of the codes of war sufficed to provide impressive regulation of cruelty and violence designed to protect civilians and soldiers alike. Yet the rules also incorporated careful distinctions, notably on the differing degrees of culpability assigned to actions in hot and cold blood. And their permissive dark side doubtless contributed to survival of the system. For nearly every military "crime" against enemies or civilians, there was a situation in which otherwise prohibited behavior became permissible or excesses became excusable. If a besieged town refused to surrender, was stormed, and fell, it was legitimate if not admirable to sack and plunder the town and

---

70,001, fol. 16; and see Zouche, *Iuris et iudicii fecialis*, 11: v, 2: viii. On Grotius's reputation and English connections, see, for example, Matthew Gibson, A *View of the Ancient and Present State of the Churches of Door, Home-Lacy, and Hempsted; Endowed by . . . Viscount Scudamore* (London, 1727), 77–94, 98–105; *Chirk Castle Accounts, A.D. 1605–1666,* W. M. Myddelton, comp. (St. Albans, 1908), 54 (for Sir Thomas Myddelton's purchases of political and religious works by Grotius in 1655). Interestingly, Grotius, Gentili, and other theorists are absent (unless in untitled manuscripts) from the large library of the earls of Huntingdon, although military works and accounts of European affairs are amply represented. I am very grateful to James Knowles for allowing me to see his reconstruction of this library from the Hastings MSS in the Huntington Library; see Henry E. Huntington (hereafter, HEH) Hastings (hereafter, HA) Inventories Box 1, item 13; HAF[inancial] 12, items 10, 19; HAF 13, items 38, 46.

[22] On Gustavus Adolphus and Grotius's influence on him, see Alexander] Gil, *The New Starr of the North, Shining upon the Victorious King of Sweden* (London, 1632); Michael Roberts, *Gustavus Adolphus,* 2d edn. (London, 1992), 68, 154; Hedley Bull, "The Importance of Grotius in the Study of International Relations," and Georg Schwarzenberger, "The Grotius Factor in International Law and Relations: A Functional Approach," in *Hugo Grotius and International Relations,* Hedley Bull, *et al.,* eds. (1990; Oxford, 1992), 75, 301.

even kill its civilians.[23] Reprisal offered a particularly useful justification for appalling actions, matching atrocity for atrocity. And it was characteristic to blame the victims for the cruelties their enemies were forced to commit against them. Towns that refused to surrender brought their fate on themselves. As one commander wrote, "[L]et the blame of that cruelty on both sides lie upon those that force it to be done."[24]

Despite such useful and flexible exceptions to protective rules, there was a strong sense of when actions that might in theory be allowable were in practice cruel and excessive.[25] So actions that might be condoned if committed in hot blood became inexcusable in cold blood, a distinction that survives in law and war. Protection extended even to "vile [and] . . . wretched" enemies. Edward Symmons, a Royalist preacher, told Prince Rupert's troops that conscience and reputation required that they

> neither do, nor . . . suffer to be done, in coole blood, to the most impious Rebells, any thing that savours of immodesty, Barbarousnesse, or inhumanity . . . To be an houre or 2 in hacking and

---

[23] For such an exception, see *The Essential Portions of Nicholas Upton's De Studio Militari, Before 1446, Translated by John Blount, Fellow of All Souls (c. 1500)*, F. P. Barnard, ed. (Oxford, 1931), 28: "a man must kepe his promys also wyth hys enmy; but that ys to be understonde when hys enmy doth so lykewyse wyth hym, or els nott." See also Gouge, *Churches Conquest*, 278–79, on duties of courtesy, humanity, charity, mercy, and kindness; but note pp. 295–96: "common *Humanity*" also recognized occasions for killing and torture.

[24] William Salt Library, Stafford, Salt MS 493, Lewis Chadwick to Sir Francis Ottley, April 18 [1644]; Ioshua Sprigge, *Anglia Rediviva* (London, 1647), 11. Sir Thomas Fairfax warned that God sometimes hardened "hearts . . . to their own destruction." John Rushworth, *Historical Collections of Private Passages of State* . . ., 8 vols. (London, 1659–1701), 6: 105. The "blame the victim" argument remains creatively useful: compare reports during the Gulf War that cruise missiles hit a non-military site in Baghdad and killed civilians only because they were diverted from their intended target by defenders' anti-aircraft fire (Baghdad, January 1993).

[25] Gentili quoted Justinian: "Not everything which is lawful is honourable." Gentili, *De iure belli*, 2: 211.

torturing a woefull wretch, or in takeing away that miserable life, which might be concluded in a moment, or to wreake ones fury upon a dead Carkasse, is a most barbarous, cowardly and impious thing . . . 'tis plainly Diabolicall to insult over men in misery.[26]

Laws and exhortation were one thing, practice another. Everyone knew that troops were often beyond the control of their officers and that soldiers, like civilians, engaged in mob actions that exceeded official policy. Henry V's warning to Harfleur foreshadowed the civil war:

We may as bootless spend our vain command
Upon th'enraged soldiers in their spoil
As send precepts to the leviathan
To come ashore.[27]

In the 1640s, commanders of both sides beat and slashed at their men in unavailing attempts to enforce proper conduct toward defeated enemies.[28]

The civil wars saw notorious atrocities that went beyond such "hot-blooded" breaches of the rules. By world standards, admittedly,

---

[26] Edw[ard] Symmons, *A Military Sermon* (Oxford, 1644), 35.

[27] William Shakespeare, *Henry V*, III: 3.24–27; and see 1–43, for Henry's use of the "blame the victim" argument. For civil war echoes, see, for example, surrender negotiations at Chester when both sides invoked "the fury of . . . enraged soldiers," or the call to Wimborne to surrender before "the enraged soldiers . . . be in blood." BL Add. MS 11,332, fol. 92v; Bodl. Libr. MS Tanner 62/1B, fol. 171.

[28] Rushworth, *Historical Collections*, 5: 267; *Diary of the Marches of the Royal Army during the Great Civil War; Kept by Richard Symonds*, Charles Edward Long, ed. (London, 1859), 66-67; Walker, *Historical Discourses*, 79–80, 247; *Calendar of State Papers Domestic 1644* (hereafter, CSPD), 502; Tho[mas] Carte, *A Collection of Original Letters and Papers, Concerning the Affairs of England, From the Year 1641 to 1660*, 2 vols. (London, 1739), 1: 32 (Royalist troops used the reprisal argument to justify non-observance of articles). See also BL Add. MS 11,810, fol. 14; C. H. Firth, *Cromwell's Army*, 4th edn. (London, 1962), 292–93.

they were small-scale horrors, but England knew atrocities nasty enough to evoke echoes of Germany. Even in the first war, less bitter than the second, massacres of soldiers who had surrendered or of women after the battle of Naseby, the hanging—with sadistic preliminaries—of civilians in Dorset, the more prolonged sadism and appalling conditions inflicted on prisoners at Oxford, the treatment of Irish men and women, all endanger any conception of a kinder, gentler war. Nevertheless, a rickety equilibrium was maintained in the conduct of enemies to each other and to civilians. War crimes did not become policy, atrocities were individual and sporadic, and reprisal was precariously contained.

To a notable degree, observance of the laws of war was self-regulated by soldiers themselves, who exhorted each other not only to be "Humane," "honest," and "Christian" but to observe "customary" and "civil and soldierly correspondence" and to maintain "the honour and reputation of gentlemen and soldiers."[29] England's prewar military education laid the foundation of knowledge of international professional norms. The fashioned self that emerged from this conditioning was a professional as well as religious, moral, and social entity. Conduct between enemies was governed by professional and personal standards without the intervention of the state.[30]

The potential for conflict between the claims of profession and state was explicitly recognized. When York fell to Parliament in July 1644, the commanders "explained" the articles of surrender: "[T]he Generals of the Armies have Treated as Generals in reference only to themselves and their Souldiers, . . . they had no Order to meddle

---

[29] BL Add. MS 11,332, fols. 86, 92v; Rushworth, *Historical Collections*, 6: 105; and see BL Stowe MS 143, fol. 119v; Devon County Record Office, Exeter, Seymour of Berry Pomeroy MSS 1392 M/L 1644/54. Mutual courtesies did not preclude hard bargaining or hard fighting; see the Fairfax-Hopton negotiations of 1646, Rushworth, *Historical Collections*, 6: 105–07.

[30] For a complaint that Parliamentarian conduct fell below international standards, see Sir John Byron (a Royalist with European military experience): "when they have an advantage, [they] think it dishonour to use those civilities practised by soldiers in foreign parts." "John Byron's Account of the Siege of Chester 1645–1646," J.B., ed., *Cheshire Sheaf*, 4th ser., 6 (1971): 23.

with any Ordinances of Parliament."[31] But if they deferred to Parliament in civil matters, there was no doubting that they claimed autonomy as generals and soldiers or that "the bounds of the Army" included terms of settlement with the enemy in particular engagements. The first civil war was characterized by military self-regulation and adherence to norms governing conduct between soldiers, which, despite variable practice, survived on the basis of mutual trust between parties to an unwritten contract. Jurisdiction over soldiers for their acts as soldiers remained in military hands. Intra-army offenses were governed by processes of trial and punishment set out in articles of war, while treatment of soldiers who fell into enemy hands was regulated by the laws of war. As we have seen, the laws of war were not purely protective; an enemy who had offended against them was liable to punishment, but his fate was determined by his professional peers.[32]

The first break in the pattern came late in 1644, when Parliament passed an ordinance forbidding grant of quarter to Irish soldiers captured in England. It raised broad new questions about punishment for conduct in war. Their development during and after the second civil war heralded a conflict between military and civil jurisdictions and subordination of the traditional codes that protected combatants to political needs of the civil state. It also relegated the Irish to the category of barbarians unworthy of the protections due to Christians, let alone Englishmen.[33]

---

[31] Rushworth, *Historical Collections,* 5: 640; the question at issue was Parliament's orders for sequestration of property of suspect civilians.

[32] Regulation of conduct between enemies must be distinguished from trials of persons of one's own side, for example of the Parliamentarian Nathaniel Fiennes and the Royalist Francis Windebank for premature surrender, or for crimes from murder to adultery; so must civilian treason cases, for example, of civilians plotting to betray a town (as at Bristol).

[33] *Acts and Ordinances of the Interregnum, 1642–1660,* C. H. Firth and R. S. Rait, eds., 3 vols. (London, 1911), 1: 554–55. Compare 1: 553–54, for an ordinance passed on the same day "for the Redemption of the Captives at Algiers," which although designed for relief of victims of non-Christians did not contain inflammatory language like that used of the Irish.

THE RESULT OF THE 1644 ORDINANCE WAS, not surprisingly, a series of retaliatory hangings. They were not the first of their kind for English or Irish.[34] In July 1644, Colonel William Sydenham had already hanged Irish prisoners with the approval of Parliament's general, the earl of Essex, and in reprisal the Royalist Sir Francis Doddington had strung up twelve civilians "upon the same tree," but this and other incidents had not led to systematic, centrally sanctioned withdrawal of protections for defeated combatants.[35] In February 1645, however, after the fall of Shrewsbury, thirteen Royalist Irish prisoners were hanged. Prince Rupert protested that the codes of war had been comprehensively breached: to kill prisoners who had surrendered to quarter was "contrary to the law of nature and nations, contrary to the rules and customs of war, in any parts of the Christian world," and in reprisal for this "provocation and . . . injustice" he hanged thirteen Protestant English. He would have been unworthy of his command, he explained, if after "soldiers of [his] . . .were barbarously murdered in cold blood, after quarter given them," he had not "let the authors of the massacre know, their own men must pay the price of such acts of inhumanity, and . . . be used as they used their brethren . . . in the same manner."[36]

---

[34] For example, executions orchestrated by the earl of Warwick, Parliament's lord admiral, and the Royalist colonel Edward Seymour in 1644. When Warwick proposed a third execution, Seymour warned, "[I]t will not rest there." Historical Manuscripts Commission (hereafter, HMC), *Fifteenth Report, Appendix, Part VII, The Manuscripts of the Duke of Somerset* . . . (London, 1898), 77–78; Rushworth, *Historical Collections,* 5: 685; see also 5: 814; CSPD 1644, 351; BL Add. MS 29,319, fol. 11.

[35] Doddington's "butcheries" were stopped by the intervention of the Royalist general Sir Ralph Hopton rather than by fear of reprisal. *The Memoirs of Edmund Ludlow . . . 1625–1672,* C. H. Firth, ed., 2 vols. (Oxford, 1894), 1: 95–96. Ludlow believed that these hangings were ordered by Parliament. See also Arthur Rutter Bayley, *The Great Civil War in Dorset 1642–1660* (Taunton, 1910), 204–05.

[36] BL Add. MS 11,331, fols. 75v–76; and see Bodl. Libr. MS Add. D.l 14, fols. 153–56 (misfoliated) for another (damaged) version of this letter; see also *The Letter Books of Sir William Brereton, Volume One, January 31st–May 29th 1645,* Robert Norman Dore, ed. (Chester, 1984), 227–29. For the terms

Contemporary Germany hovered behind the subsequent exchange between Rupert and Essex, two commanders who had served there, in their language of atrocity and their warnings of increased bloodiness now and increased irreconcilability later. Both appealed to the laws of war. Essex justified reprisal against the Irish by the atrocities of their rebellion of 1641, committed against "harmless British Protestants . . . without distinction of age or sex," and by their refusal to give or receive quarter.[37] For Rupert, the obligations of quarter were paramount. He recognized that the way in which the laws of war were observed affected both the nature of war and its aftermath. If they continued in this "rigour" of hanging prisoners, he warned, reprisal would become the norm, and the war would grow "more merciless and bloody": "[It] is like to be so managed, that the English nation is in danger of destroying one another (or . . .) of degenerating into such an animosity and cruelty that all [elements] of charity, compassion, and brotherly affection, shall be extinguished."[38] And, indeed, for a time, although reprisals rumbled on intermittently, there was no widespread collapse of the rules of quarter. Prudence as well as soldierly standards militated against it; the dangers of a war conducted according to *lex talionis* were all too clear.[39]

---

and circumstances of the Shrewsbury surrender, including the Royalists' failure to protect their Irish troops, see Eliot Warburton, *Memoirs of Prince Rupert and the Cavaliers*, 3 vols. (London, 1849), 3: 58.

[37] Bodl. Libr. MS Add. D.l 14, fols. 148–49. It hardly needs to be said that atrocities were both exaggerated and reciprocal; however, for the powerful effect of reports from Ireland, see Keith J. Lindley, "The Impact of the 1641 Rebellion upon England and Wales, 1641–5," *Irish Historical Studies*, 18 (September 1972–73): 143–76.

[38] BL Add. MS 11,331, fols. 75v, 76v.

[39] For indications that not all Parliamentarians were comfortable with the ordinance against quarter, see HMC, *13th Report, Appendix I, Manuscripts of . . . the Duke of Portland* (London, 1891), 1: 238; Edmund Staunton, *Phinehas's Zeal in Execution of Judgement . . . A Sermon Preached before the . . . House of Lords . . . October 30, 1644* (London, 1645), [A2v], 5, 13: Staunton ardently defended the ordinance against *"Politick reasonings"* but admitted "a blush of irregularitie." See also Rushworth, *Historical Collections*, 5: 814, for the soldier still unhanged six weeks after conviction. In April 1645, one

The exchange between Rupert and Essex turned on permissible action after soldiers had surrendered. Rules of surrender were, of necessity, an intrinsic part of a soldier's education. They applied to individuals in the field and to defended places, whether castles, houses, churches, or towns. In the field, the life of a soldier who laid down his arms was presumed to be safe. In sieges, there was a crucial distinction between storm and surrender. If the besiegers were forced to storm, then anything short of rape or mutilation was permissible.[40] If surrender had been negotiated, however, its terms should be binding. The rules for such surrender were elaborate, governing for example treatment of envoys and degrees of honor in the ritual of surrender itself. Terms varied according to circumstance but were drawn from a common menu. For the defeated to march out with colors flying, match lit, and bullets in mouth was a tribute to courageous resistance; confiscation of arms and colors was severe, even dishonorable. Honor, utility, and disgrace were carefully calibrated,

---

Parliamentary major wrote that he knew "of no order or ordinance that authoriseth the taking away of . . . lives" once quarter was granted; he was defending, apparently successfully, prisoners recently taken at Beeston, Cheshire. Dore, *Letter Books of Sir William Brereton*, 199–200.

[40] See Meron, "Shakespeare's Henry the Fifth," 29–31, on the tardiness with which the specific prohibition of rape was incorporated into modern international codes of war. Zouche, *Iuris et iudicii facialis*, 2: 180–81, followed Gentili and Grotius (against Jean Bodin), in concluding that prohibition of rape was, in Grotius's words, "the Law of Nations, not of all nations, but of the better among them." For its prohibition in English military law before and during the civil war, see "Ordinances for Warre, &c, at the Treate or Council of Manuce," printed in Francis Grose, *The Antiquities of England and Wales*, new edn., 8 vols. (London [1783–87]), 1: 34 (Henry V's laws); *Lawes and Ordinances of Warre, Established for the better Conduct of the Army by . . . The Earle of Essex* (London, 1642), 11, "Of Duties Morall," No. II: "Rapes, ravishments, unnaturall abuses shall be punished with death"; *Orders and Institutions of War, Made and ordained by His Maiesty, And by Him delivered to His Generall . . . The Earle of Newcastle* ([London?], 1642), 4, No. 12: "Whosoever shall force or ravish any woman within our quarters, or any other place, shall suffer death." This provision was dropped from some later Royalist articles of war.

as when defeated troops marched out with half their colors flying and half furled or were allowed to carry out their arms only to deposit them outside the town for the use of the victors; and the practical value of match and bullets at the ready against surprise attack is self-evident. Terms for civilians—such as severity of financial penalties—also varied, as did disposition of the defeated, whose main options were to go home (usually with a promise not to bear arms again), to enlist with the victors, or to become prisoners. Much depended on the length and bitterness of the siege or the victor's anxiety to move on.

For individuals, the most important distinction was that between surrender to quarter and surrender to mercy, a distinction that even raw troops and civilians learned fast, for practical reasons. Quarter and mercy were terms of art, and "mercy" was less "merciful," in the word's moral and untechnical sense, than quarter. To grant an enemy quarter was understood to guarantee that his life would not be forfeit for his actions as a soldier, although he could be held liable for civil or military crimes committed *while* a soldier(for example, rape, or robbery committed as a free agent, or breach of parole).[41] To kill a soldier who had surrendered to quarter by laying down his arms or by negotiated articles offended against the laws of arms. A surrender to mercy only, however, left a victorious commander extensive discretionary power.

---

[41] See, for example, Richard Bernard, *The Bible-Battells, or, The Sacred Art Military* (London, 1629), 247–52: it was "perfidious" to kill those who had yielded to "good quarter" with promise of life and good treatment—*unless* they were guilty of crimes: "To slay poore prisoners in cold blood is a note of a savage and implacable nature. But here is to be excepted, such prisoners taken as do deserve justice to be executed upon them." Captives who proved treacherous or posed a threat were also excepted (as at Poitiers; but contrast Gentili's condemnation of Henry V's action at Agincourt; Meron, "Shakespeare's Henry V," 38–39; Gentili, *De iure belli*, 2: 211–12). See also Sutcliffe, *Practice, Proceedings and Lawes of armes,* 338: killing prisoners led only to reprisal, and "such savage cruelty is contrary to the nature of faire warres."

Despite wide general understanding, negotiators were careful to define and elucidate. So at Arundel castle in 1644, the Parliamentary commander Sir William Waller's "explication" distinguished the "fair quarter and civil usage" he offered to Royalist officers from the "quarter for their lives" granted to their men: "By fair quarter, I understand, giving life to those that yeeld, with imprisonment of their persons, but civill usage, which is sufficient security, they shall not be plundered."[42] And Sir Thomas Fairfax, Lord General of the New Model Army, explained in 1648, "[C]ommon quarter to any Enemy, taken in a Field-Engagement, or other Action, [was] . . . always understood . . . to be an assuring of Life against the immediate execution of the military Sword, or any further execution thereby without judicial Trial." The most reassuring protection came from "Quarter . . . upon Captitulation or Agreements," that is, from a pre-surrender treaty containing specific protective clauses, whereas mere "common Quarter," by "the general sense and practice in all Wars," did not guarantee against future punishment for offenses extrinsic to the surrender. Mercy, however, was an even harsher matter. If soldiers were forced to yield to mercy, either because of circumstances of capture (such as unduly prolonged resistance) or because specifically excepted from general quarter and "rendr[ed] to Mercy," a victorious general was "free to put some immediately to the Sword, if he [saw]cause."[43] Such "causes" were often tendentious and became occasions for anxious self-justification and bitter recrimination.

Admittedly, the protections of quarter, even when not hedged about by stipulations, were less than perfect in practice. Accident, confusion, ignorance, lack of discipline, even love and grief, led to breaches of acknowledged rules.[44] Such failures stemming from hot blood, confusion, or particular cruelty, however, did not threaten the

---

[42] *Certain Propositions Made By Sir William Waller, At the Surrender of Arundell-Castle* (n.p., 1644), 6. Social status of course affected the degree of "civility" extended to prisoners, See also Bernard, *Bible-Battells*, 252.

[43] Rushworth, *Historical Collections*, 7: 1247, 1303. Fairfax defined "fair quarter" to include life, freedom from wounding or beating, warm clothes, shelter, and food.

broad context. Fairfax and his officers were noted for their care "to see Articles always kept, in which they judged their honour deeply concerned," and for their insistence to Parliament that surrender terms should be observed. On the very eve of the second civil war, an ordinance confirming the Oxford surrender terms and requiring that they should be observed "in all Things whatsoever" was before Parliament.[45] The principles of the laws of war applicable to the defeated had not been abandoned.

IF LAWS WERE ACKNOWLEDGED although practice was imperfect, what kinds of breaches of the soldierly code of conduct elicited outrage, when did they qualify as atrocity or war crime, and when were they assimilated under the law of the state rather than the law of the soldier? Four nasty cases illustrate success and failure in observation of the laws of surrender. These differ in scale, but the same rules applied. In all four, soldierly codes of conduct were breached. All, it can be argued, were atrocities. Yet they reveal ambiguities of partisan judgment and inconsistencies of response. They also reveal a progression from first to second civil war, toward the increased bloodiness of which Rupert had warned and toward supervention of political over professional jurisdiction in treatment of the defeated. The potential dangers, for soldiers and society, were immediately evident.

---

[44] See Lucy Hutchinson, *Memoirs of the Life of Colonel Hutchinson,* James Sutherland, ed. (London, 1973), 181, on the soldiers at Preston in 1648 who, "enrag'd" by the death of their colonel, "fought not that day like men of humane race. Deafe to the cries of every coward that askt mercy, they kill'd all, and would not a captive [should] live to see their Collonell die."

[45] Howell, *State Trials,* 4: col. 1159; Rushworth, *Historical Collections,* 7: 864; *LJ,* 10: 338; *CJ,* 5: 607, 622. This confirmation was intended as part of a general political settlement rather than as parliamentary intrusion into military affairs. In March 1648, Fairfax emphasized the equal obligation of Parliament and soldier to observe articles: "It much concern[s] the parliament and myself to make good that engagement for the performance of those articles [for the surrender of Portland], which I do in an especial manner recommend to your consideration." Derbyshire Record Office, Gell of Hopton MSS, D3287, C/PARL/P/ld.

To Parliamentarians, the events that took place at Hopton castle in Herefordshire and Barthomley in Cheshire during the first civil war were indisputable atrocities. The language of narration reveals how deeply ingrained were the criteria for proper conduct in war and how deep the revulsion when its "laws" were broken. In March 1644, the garrison of Hopton castle surrendered to Royalist troops commanded by Sir Michael Woodhouse. They asked for "quarter for their lives," but instead they had to agree to abandon their arms and "submit to mercy." Nevertheless, they "came out expecting mercy" (in its non-technical sense) and that they would "only be made prisoners"—a reasonable hope in view of precedents elsewhere. They had not thought, said their colonel, "of such a death as . . . was upon so many honest souls." They were bound together and "stripped naked as ever they were born, it being about the beginning of March very cold and many of them sore wounded." After an hour, "the word was given"—that is, it was an official decision, unlike those occasions when troops ran wild ignoring officers' orders—"that they should be left to the mercy of the common soldiers, who presently fell upon them, wounding them grievously, and drove them into a cellar unfinished, wherein was stinking water, the house being on fire over them, when they were every man . . . presently massacred."[46] Most of the victims were clubbed to death. Their colonel described the event as "Siege, Surrender and Butchery." Another witness wrote,

---

[46] HMC, *Manuscripts of the Marquis of Bath*, vol. 1 (London, 1904), 29, account of Captain Priamus Davies; and see 37–38, account of Colonel Samuel Moore. Hopton, small but strategic, was garrisoned by about thirty men. Compare the fate of the garrison at Wakefield, Yorkshire (1643), who "scorned" surrender and refused quarter yet survived to become prisoners. Bodl. Libr. MS Tanner 62/1 A, fol. 103. John Webb, *Memorials of the Civil War between King Charles I and the Parliament of England as It Affected Herefordshire*, 2 vols. (London, 1879), 1: 387–90, suggests that the defenders of Hopton were "ignorant of the severe rules of war," but Moore distinguished between surrender to quarter and to mercy and exonerated Woodhouse of breach of quarter. HMC, *Manuscripts of the Marquis of Bath*, 1: 39.

"This inhuman and barbarous act, wherein the laws of God, of man, of nature, of nations and of arms are violated, cries to the great Justice of heaven to revenge; and we hope that the justice of England will in due time require an account of it."[47]

Hopton was at least a real military event. In the trivial and confused affair at Barthomley the previous Christmas, Royalist forces marauding through Cheshire "set upon the Church, which had in it about 20 Neighbours, that had gone in for Safety." When Major John Connaught and his men entered the church, they took refuge in the steeple, but the Royalists smoked them out:

> being stifled in the Steeple, [they] called for Quarter; which was granted by Connought. But when they had them in their Power, they stript them all naked, & then most barbarously murthered 12 of them, contrary to the Laws of Arms, Nature, & Nations. This cruell Connought cut the Throat of one Mr. John Fowler, a hopefull yong Man, 8c Minister there. Only 3 of them miraculously escapt with Life.[48]

Barthomley was a notorious atrocity. The mayor of Royalist Chester recorded that "divers of the parliament party . . . were most barbarously used and murdered in cold blood," and he saw divine justice in the fact that these forces "prospered not after."[49] At the trial of Charles I, the blood of "those honest souls that were killed in cold

---

[47] HMC, *Manuscripts of the Marquis of Bath*, 1: 29, 36. The note of horror survived in Webb's nineteenth-century account, *Civil War . . . Herefordshire*, 1: 389–90, particularly 1: 390, n. 3; but he comforted himself: "many of [the Royalists], it is fair to state, are said to have been Irish."

[48] *Memorials of the Civil War in Cheshire and the Adjacent Counties by Thomas Malbon, . . . , and Providence Improved by Edward Burghall*, James Hall, ed. (Chester, 1889), 94–95. John Fowler was in fact the schoolmaster and son of the rector.

[49] BL Harl. MS 2125, fol. 135v.

blood ... at Barthomley in Cheshire" cried out for justice, and "their wives and their children cry[ed], Justice upon the Murderer."[50]

Both cases exhibit classic characteristics of atrocity narratives. At the center was the fact of massacre and insistence on its cold-blooded nature, on guilt by intention. Circumstantial phenomena clustered around this core. There were justificatory counter-claims that the Parliamentarians at Hopton had used poisoned bullets; aggravated individual horrors, such as the death of an eighty–year–old man, "weak and not able to stand, [whom] they were so compassionate as to put ... in a Chair to cut his throat"; and pathetic codas, such as a maidservant still "distracted" from fright in 1695.[51] Revulsion at individual cruelties mingled with dismay at abandonment of laws of war, and the mayor of Chester was not alone in believing that "the great Justice of heaven" punished those responsible.[52]

Yet those responsible did not face the "justice of England," civil or military.[53] Major Connaught, though financially penalized and

---

[50] Howell, *State Trials*, 4: col. 1043. Oral tradition suggested a more complex story—that the rector's son fired from the steeple on the Royalist troops and killed one of them, whose fellows revenged his death "by butchering many within the church." Edward Hinchcliffe, *Barthomley: In Letters from a Former Rector to His Eldest Son* (London and Newcastle-under-Lyme, 1856), 41–42. Hinchcliffe's 97-year-old informant (in 1839) heard the story from his father, the grandson of a survivor. Seeking to palliate "barbarity," Hinchcliffe suggested a military purpose behind occupation of the church; however, compare a Royalist letter: "I put them all to the sword, which I find to be the best way to proceed with these people, for mercy to them is cruelty." Quoted in "John Byron's Account," *Cheshire Sheaf*, 6 (1971): 2.

[51] Webb, *Civil War ... Herefordshire*, 1: 388–89.

[52] "After this Massacre the King's affairs never prospered," wrote one observer, "& whenever his soldiers craved quarter, the reply was we'll give you none but Hopton Quarter." Webb, *Civil War ... Herefordshire*, 1: 389, n. 2.

[53] Peter R. Newman, *Royalist Officers in England and Wales, 1642–1660* (New York, 1981), 81, believes Lieutenant-Colonel Congrave, one of Woodhouse's officers at Hopton castle, was killed in revenge for the massacre there, but he seems to have been merely one among other victims at Littledean, Gloucestershire, where Royalists who surrendered to quarter were "put to the sword" by enraged Parliamentarians in circumstances

politically marginalized, was not physically punished.[54] Sir Michael Woodhouse survived despite the claims of his "cruelties" and "base . . . murder" at Hopton, and some elements of his story suggest explanation for unexpected clemency.[55] Shortly after the massacre, he showed kindness and courtesy to the captive children of Sir Robert Harley, a leading Parliamentarian, and observed the honorable conventions of war in arrangements for their transfer to London. When he himself was finally forced to yield Ludlow after a courageous defense, he did so confident that he would receive "fair terms and performances."[56] The courtesies that survived between enemies were evidence of shared social interest and personal bonds that ameliorated the practices of war (while not significantly lessening the zeal with which it was waged). These, together with shared professionalism and respect for opponents who acted bravely, and recognition that it did not pay to allow intermittent, unsystematic breaches of codes to endanger larger mutual observance, combined to protect the defeated from widespread abandonment of the codes of war.

The sieges of Colchester and Pontefract illustrate the change brought by the second civil war. Its greater bitterness was not alleviated by its

---

ironically mirroring Barthomley (see n. 50 above). *Bibliotheca Gloucestrensis,* John Washbourn, ed. (Gloucester, 1825), 93, 328; Peter Gaunt, The *Cromwellian Gazetteer* (Gloucester, 1987), 58–59.

[54] Newman, *Royalist Officers,* 78 (under "Colnock"); *Calendar of . . . the Committee for Compounding, &c, 1643–1660* (hereafter, CCC), 5 vols. (London, 1889–92), 1: 117. See also the case of Colonel Ralph Snead, implicated at Hopton and captured soon after, who benefited from the laws of war for exchange of prisoners. Newman, *Royalist Officers,* 350; Malbon, *Civil War . . . Cheshire,* 94–95; CCC, 2: 893, 1032–34; *Calendar of . . . the Committee for Advance of Money* (hereafter, CAM), 3 vols. (London, 1888), 2: 1180; CSPD 1661–1662, 164–65.

[55] Washbourn, *Bibliotheca Gloucestrensis,* 91; HMC, *Manuscripts of the Marquis of Bath,* 1: 29; Webb, *Civil War . . . Herefordshire,* 1: 389–90. For Woodhouse's career, see Newman, *Royalist Officers,* 421; Warburton, *Memoirs of Prince Rupert,* 3: 56; Webb, *Civil War . . . Herefordshire,* 2: 359.

[56] Hmc, *Manuscripts of the Marquis of Bath,* 1: 33–35; Webb, *Civil War . . . Herefordshire,* 2: 268.

brevity and futility or by Royalist incompetence. Instead, Royalist desperation was matched by Parliamentarian shock, fear, and outrage rendered more acute by the number of former colleagues who now joined the king. It was expressed in religious terms by Oliver Cromwell and more secularly by Fairfax, in response to pleas on behalf of old Parliamentarians who had turned their coats. Former Royalists had "not apostasised," said Cromwell, but these officers "formerly served . . . in a very good cause" and had "sinned against so much light." For Fairfax, it was a matter for Parliament's justice, "not so much that they were in Hostility against them, . . . as that they have betrayed the Trust they reposed in them, to the sad engaging the Nation again in War and Blood."[57] Breach of faith, sin against the light, betrayed allegiance, and return to war and blood all embittered relations between enemies.

The second war was effectively over in five months during the spring and summer of 1648. The victors later argued selectively that Royalist participants were subject to the law of treason; but, despite Parliament's apparent dominance of the country by early 1648 and the disparity between the forces of the two sides, combatants fought the war according to the laws of war and as a conflict between "lawful enemies." The king may have been Parliament's prisoner, but Royalists argued that a commission from his son Prince Charles was fully legitimate: "The prince hath his [commission] from his father, and I have mine from the prince, which is full power, he being captain-general of his majesty's forces," said one, a view the king reportedly fostered.[58] England's constitutional condition in fact remained unresolved.

---

[57] Wilbur Cortez Abbott, *The Writings and Speeches of Oliver Cromwell*, 4 vols. (Cambridge, Mass., 1937–47), 1: 620–21; Rushworth, *Historical Collections*, 7: 1190, 1233.

[58] "An exact Relation of the Trial and Examination of John Morris, Governor of Pontefract-castle," in *A Collection of Scarce and Valuable Tracts . . . of the Late Lord Somers* (hereafter, *Somers Tracts*), Walter Scott, ed., 2d edn., 13 vols. (London, 1809–15), 7: 10. Morris argued the analogy of the legitimacy of commissions issued by Fairfax, who was himself commissioned by Parliament. See Howell, *State Trials*, 4: col. 1111, for a witness at the king's trial who deposed that Charles advised him "That he being upon a Treaty,

The king, though imprisoned, was still nominally sovereign, and it was still possible to invoke the mantra of fighting for king, lords, and commons. Not until the middle of 1649 did Parliament pass new treason ordinances reflecting abolition of "the Kingly Office."[59]

Despite shock and bitterness and occasional lapses into savagery, the usual rules governed combat relations between enemies in the field.[60] In victory, however, they could no longer be relied on—not because soldiers rejected them but because the state intervened. The status of defeated Royalists was admittedly problematic. Those who had formerly surrendered with an undertaking not to take up arms again but who now returned to the king's colors had broken faith, yet it was clearly impractical to impose en masse the dire penalties they theoretically merited: most paid with money, not life.[61] Those who had formerly served Parliament were ordered to "be sent to the Lord General Fairfax, and tried, for their Lives by a Council of War"; but in practice most of them were pardoned.[62] As with the "guilty"

---

would not dishonour himself [by issuing commissions]; but that if he, this Deponent, would take the pains to go over to the prince, his son, (who had full authority from him), he . . . should receive whatsoever commissions should be desired."

[59] The first was passed in May 1649, a second followed in July (adding counterfeiting and clipping to treasonous acts, and protecting property of heirs). Firth and Rait, *Acts and Ordinances*, 2: 120–21, 193–94. At the trial of Colonel Morris (see below), defendant and court wrangled over the applicability of statutes of Edward III or Henry VII. *Somers Tracts*, 7: 9–10, 12; and see 11: Morris made the point, "[S]ince the abolishing of regal power I have not meddled with anything against the parliament."

[60] Note the savage retribution meted out to one eminent turncoat, the former Parliamentary quartermaster-general John Dalbier, then in arms for the king, whose soldier-captors, "to express their detestation of [his] treachery, hewed him in pieces." Ludlow, *Memoirs*, 1: 198.

[61] Prisoners regarded as mere deluded countrymen were sent home. For undertakings not to bear arms again after the first civil war, see surrender articles for Oxford (1646), Rushworth, *Historical Collections*, 6: 281–84.

[62] Rushworth, *Historical Collections*, 7: 1145, 1198–99, 1250, 1272; *CJ*, 6: 245. See the characteristically "mixed" terms granted after Pembroke fell in July 1648: "5 to mercy being Leaders, 16 to 2 years banishment, the rest sent home." "Letters and Documents by or Relating to Hugh Peter," Raymond Phineas Stearns, ed., *The Essex Institute Historical Collections*, 72 (April 1936): 126.

men of Hopton and Barthomley, a modus vivendi evolved, albeit one untidy and unequal in its justice. What happened after Colchester and Pontefract, however, signaled a harsher response and a novel and dangerous erosion of soldiers' protections. In 1648 and 1649, crimes against humanity were overshadowed by crimes against the state. What happened to some Royalist officers after surrender represented a change that went beyond outrage at return to arms. Retribution was selective, but it introduced "victors'justice" to England. Although most Royalists ultimately went home or "voluntarily" enlisted for Ireland or Europe, some were tried and executed. That was new. If sin against the light was a crime against God, breach of trust was now a crime against the state rather than professional peers. Only after the war, however, did it become treason.[63]

Colchester and Pontefract were militarily serious affairs, unlike Barthomley and even Hopton. The siege of Colchester lasted for ten weeks in the summer of 1648; it engaged major leaders on both sides, Lords Goring and Capel for the king and Fairfax for Parliament. It was famous in its day for the sufferings of the besieged, whose hunger and sickness could not persuade Goring to surrender until mutinous troops forced his hand.[64] Colchester's fall signaled the effective end of the second civil war, but Pontefract held out until March 1649; by then, the king and some of the Royalist leaders of that war were already dead, the Rump Parliament sat in London, and monarchy had just been formally abolished. In both sieges, enemies were accused of atrocious conduct, from ill-treatment of prisoners to

[63] Firth and Rait, *Acts and Ordinances,* 2: 120–21, 193–94. See Richard Tuck, *Natural Rights Theories: Their Origin and Development* (Cambridge, 1979), 116–17, on problems of execution of justice and definition of treason in a state with an excluded rightful king and an established usurper.

[64] On the siege, see *A Diary of the Siege of Colchester by the Forces under the Command of his Excellency the Lord Generall Fairfax* (London, 1648), broadside; HMC, *14th Report, Appendix, Part IX* (London, 1895), 281–90; *A True and Exact Relation Of the taking of Colchester* (London, 1648); M[atthew] C[arter], *A Most True and exact Relation of That as Honourable as unfortunate Expedition of Kent, Essex, and Colchester* (n.p., 1650); Rushworth, *Historical Collections,* 7: 1155–1242.

use of poisoned bullets, but these were not counted as their notorious crimes. To Parliamentarians, the crimes were broken faith, betrayal, and return to blood, exacerbated at Pontefract by infamous murder; to Royalists, they were the martyrdom of defeated leaders.

Surrender terms at Colchester were harsh. Private soldiers and junior officers were granted "fair quarter" and became prisoners, but "the Lords, and all Superiour Officers and Gentlemen . . . [were] to render themselves to the Mercy of the Lord General."[65] Negotiations had elucidated this proviso: "it was in the Generals power to save any of those who did so submit to Mercy, or to put them to the sword."[66] On the afternoon of the surrender, three were promptly brought before Fairfax's council of war and condemned to death. Two, Sir Charles Lucas and Sir George Lisle, were summarily shot, and became instant Royalist martyrs.[67] Both saw their fate as a departure from the decencies and laws of war. At the council of war, Lucas had "urged it much, that the way taken with him was without Precedent; but this was sufficiently answered, and a Soldier told him,

---

[65] Rushworth, *Historical Collections,* 7: 1242.

[66] *True and Exact Relation Of . . . Colchester,* 2. Bulstrode Whitelocke later commented on this gloss, "[O]f this learning, I hope none of this nation will have use hereafter." Howell, *State Trials,* 4: col. 1210.

[67] Clarendon believed that Fairfax "respited" the third, the Italian Sir Bernard Gascoyne, for fear of reprisals against English travelers in Italy. Newman, *Royalist Officers,* 150; Clarendon, *History,* 3: 137–38. See the frontispiece to C[arter], *Most True and exact Relation.* Headed "The Loyall Sacrifice," it portrays the martyrs' deaths before a four-man firing squad. Lucas lies dead on the ground; Lisle defies his executioners: "Shoot Rebells./ Your Shott your shame./ Our fall our fame." The frontispiece does not appear in all copies of this work; see Barbara Donagan, "Prisoners in the English Civil War," *History Today,* 41 (March 1991): 29; see also *The Royal Martyrs; or, A List of the Lords, Knights, Commanders, and Gentlemen, that were slain in the late Wars, in defence of their King and Country, As also of those Executed by High Courts of Justice or Law-Martial* (London, 1660), broadside; reprinted and expanded 1663, 1700. The fate of Lucas and Lisle continued to elicit passionate, partisan responses; see notably J. H. Round, "The Case of Lucas and Lisle," *Transactions of the Royal Historical Society,* n.s., 8 (1894): 157–80.

how he [Lucas] had put some of ours to death in cold Blood, with his own Hand."[68]

Thus, as an afterthought, a justificatory charge of atrocity was introduced, but the situation was nonetheless tricky. Fairfax admitted that Lucas and Lisle were victims of exemplary justice—"the Persons pitched upon for this Example." But he argued that it was a "military Execution" and that "in this distribution of justice . . . I did nothing, but according to my commission."[69] They were "prisoners at mercy," and, as he reiterated, "delivering upon mercy is to be understood, that some are to suffer the rest to go free."[70] Quarter was shortly granted to the other officers previously admitted only to mercy, yet Fairfax then found it necessary to defend this action, too, and to make clear that it was no military preemption of Parliament's right to try them later: the decision on "farther Publick Justice and Mercy" was Parliament's.[71]

Fairfax was beleaguered from two sides. He not only had to defend the legitimacy under the laws of war of the deaths of Lucas

---

[68] Rushworth, *Historical Collections,* 7: 1242 (bis); and see 7: 1243 for Fairfax's justification of the action as "military Justice" and as vengeance for "innocent Blood" and "the Trouble, Damage, and Mischief, they have brought upon the Town, this Country, and the Kingdom." Lisle, however, in his dying speech recalled all those whose lives he had saved even in hot blood, only now himself to be murdered in cold blood by the beneficiaries of his clemency. BL Sloane MS 3652, fol. 112.

[69] Rushworth, *Historical Collections,* 7: 1243; BL Harl. MS 2315, fol. 11 v. The latter passage from Fairfax's "Short Memorialls of some things to be cleared during my command in the Army," written years later, shows a continuing need to vindicate his actions. When the "Memorialls" came to be printed in 1699, the legitimizing phrase "distribution of justice" was one of a small but telling group of omissions. *Short Memorials of Thomas Lord Fairfax, Written.by Himself* (London, 1699), 123. Lucas and Lisle were professional soldiers, characterized by Fairfax as "soldiers of fortune," thus demoting them morally to the status of mercenaries without principles; compare Firth and Rait, *Acts and Ordinances,* 1: 1166.

[70] BL Harl. MS 2315, fols. 10v–ll.

[71] Fairfax to the Earl of Manchester (Speaker of the House of Lords), August 29, 1648; Rushworth, *Historical Collections,* 7: 1243.

and Lisle but also to educate Parliament in the "general sense and practice in all Wars," while at the same time reassuring its members that present preservation of life did not foreclose later prosecution and was not a claim to the primacy of military over civil power.[72] Protection indeed proved limited. Goring and Capel were tried before a special High Court of Justice together with other aristocratic leaders of the second civil war, the earl of Holland and the duke of Hamilton.[73] Of the four, only Goring escaped with his life, reprieved in the House of Commons by the speaker's casting vote. His preservation was as much a function of Parliament's overriding authority as was the condemnation of Capel, Holland, and Hamilton.[74] Colchester and its ramifications raised new issues of civil and military jurisdiction and the subordination of the army to the state.

The case of Pontefract demonstrated even more acutely than Colchester the dangers for soldiers when civilian law overrode the laws of war, for its "offenders" joined common criminals at the assizes. The capture of Pontefract by the Royalists in 1648 had been a prime example of the betrayal and breach of faith that outraged Parliamentarians in the return to war, for it had fallen by "conspiracy"

[72] In October 1648, explaining that "common Quarter" assured life for the present and due process for the future, Fairfax added, "but whether it imply to protect, or exempt them from any judicial Trial or Proceeding to Life, either by the civil Sword . . . against which . . . they rebel, or by the martial Power, as to Persons and Causes subject to its cognizance, . . . his Excellency left it to their determination." Rushworth, *Historical Collections,* 7: 1247, 1303.

[73] A fifth defendant, Sir John Owen, accused of murder and of breach of faith from terms accepted after the first civil war, pleaded not guilty, was convicted, and reprieved by the House of Commons. Howell, *State Trials,* 4: cols. 1207, 1211, 1216, 1217.

[74] Social status preserved them from summary trial like that of Lucas and Lisle: "[B]eing considerable for estates and families" (and raising the specter of objections from the residual House of Lords), Fairfax "thought fit to transmit [them] over to the parliament, being the civil judicature of the kingdom, consisting then both o[f] Lords and Commons, and so most proper judges in their case." BL Harl. MS 2315, fols. 11–11v; Clarendon, *History,* 3: 205. For the families of Lucas and Lisle, see Newman, *Royalist Officers,* 235, 240.

orchestrated by the governor, Colonel John Morris, now a double turncoat—he had previously let the Parliamentarians into Royalist Liverpool.[75] Narratives of the siege reveal the sense of mixed and shifting loyalties, of inability to trust those in whom trust had been placed.[76] In its most notorious incident, however, bad faith and atrocity combined: the raid that culminated in the death of the noted radical Colonel Thomas Rainsborough originated in Pontefract. A Royalist narrator was at pains to establish that Rainsborough resisted and died with a sword in his hand, another victim guilty of his own death: "it was only his own fault that he was killed, and not [taken] prisoner." To Parliamentarians, it was murder, and the elegies published in his memory demanded revenge.[77]

When at last the siege ended, most officers and men were allowed to march out and live quietly at home. But there were six "excepted persons," headed by the treacherous Colonel Morris. Two, a lieutenant

---

[75] Morris denied responsibility for the fall of Liverpool, *Somers Tracts*, 7:14. The slapstick side of early Royalist efforts to take Pontefract did not render final success less shocking: a corporal "fell down drunk" on one crucial evening, thus failing to ensure that a complicitous sentinel was on watch; the brave attackers fled "because they begin to fire their muskets & we to run away leaving our ladder which was very heavy behind us." Bodl. Libr. Clarendon SP, vol. 34, fol. 25.

[76] See Worcester College, Oxford, Clarke MSS, vol. 114, fol. 41, for doubts entertained about one officer despite the fact that "all men judge [him] faithful." The Parliamentary officers instrumental in the "betrayal" were double turncoats who had reverted to their original Royalist allegiance. They exemplified the risks inherent in surrender terms that allowed the defeated to reenlist in the victor's ranks—as at Portland in 1646. Derbyshire Record Office, Gell of Hopton MSS, D3287, C/PARL/Plb.

[77] Bodl. Libr. Clarendon SP, vol. 34, fol. 27v; *Dictionary of National Biography* (hereafter, *DNB*), "Rainborow, Thomas." A Royalist officer claimed that the "design was honourable, not to kill a general in the midst of his army, but to take him prisoner, and thereby save the life of our own general, Sir Marmaduke Langdale, then a prisoner, and condemned to die," that is, Rainsborough was to be captured for use in an exchange of high-level prisoners. *Somers Tracts*, 7: 4. Clarendon, *History*, 3: 146–48, characterized Rainsborough as "bold and barbarous," a man whose death "no brave Enemy would have revenged in that manner," in effect as an "other" to whom the laws of war did not apply.

and a cornet, were "those that killed Rainsborough." Three more
had been Royalist "moles" in 1648. Murder and breach of trust
were the crimes that earned "exception," although John Lambert,
the Parliamentary commander, acted with professional regret, for
"they were gallant Men"; but, like Fairfax, "his hands were bound."
Although the guilty six "had liberty to make their escape if they
could," Morris and Cornet Michael Blackborne were captured ten
days later and faced civil justice.[78] In August 1649, they were tried at
the York assizes and hanged. The charge was "treason for levying
war against the late king and the parliament." Morris denied the
court's jurisdiction. "I being a martial man," he said, "I ought to be
tried by a council of war." Like Lucas before him, he saw dangerous
precedent in trial for what he claimed to be soldierly service. "[I]f
it must be so that you will make me a precedent," he added, "you
must . . .mak[e] an act for the future, that this my suffering shall not
be a precedent to any soldiers hereafter."[79]

THE PROBLEM OF SOLDIERLY IMMUNITY for acts committed in the
course of military service thus emerged more starkly in the second
war than in the first, and it foreshadowed modern accusations (as at
Nuremberg) of "victors' justice."[80] In the first civil war, as we have
seen, both sides had agreed, however grudgingly, not to treat defeated

---

[78] Clarendon, *History*, 3: 147—48; *Somers Tracts*, 7: 8; Ludlow, *Memoirs*, 1:
199. In the escape attempt, one officer was killed, Morris and Blackborne
"charged through and escaped," and three were driven back but later slipped
away to safety.

[79] *Somers Tracts*, 7: 9, 12; see also Howell, *State Trials*, 4: cols. 1249–70. See
Bodl. Libr. Clarendon SP, vol. 34, fol. 28, for emphasis on the common law
character of their trial and hanging.

[80] Another argument heard at Nuremberg might have been appealing to
Parliamentarians enraged at return to "war and blood," namely that the law
of war was not applicable to those engaged in unjust war, a view rejected by
the Nuremberg tribunal. See G. I. A. D. Draper, "Grotius' Place in the Development of Legal Ideas about War," in Bull, *Hugo Grotius and International
Relations*, 205. Draper concluded that "full and equal application to the
just' and the 'unjust' belligerent . . . is demanded by morality, the nature of
law, humanity, and sheer necessity."

opponents as traitors but as enemies meriting the protections of the laws of war between sovereign states, unless they had committed an offense beyond merely killing, wounding, plundering, and related activities—the activities of soldiers as soldiers—in hot blood and in the course of action. Even then, retribution was moderated by social and prudent considerations. The second civil war brought two new elements into play, and the military crime of breach of faith and the civil crime of treason mingled. Exemplary justice, long a staple of discipline *in terrorem* within one's own army, was extended to defeated enemies.[81] On the one hand, military justice became more dangerous to the defeated, while on the other Parliament's interpretation of the second war as treason against a settled state sanctioned the supervention of civil justice. Had the war evolved to a long-term and more equal conflict, these positions might have proved untenable, and a second "declaration of Lex Talionis" might have curtailed vengeance. Instead, in July 1649, a month before Morris's trial, Parliament's new treason act declared the Commons "the Supreme Authority of this Nation." Any plot or force against "the present Government . . . shall be . . . deemed . . . to be High Treason."[82]

In these cases after the second civil war, defendants claimed that they should be subject to military jurisdiction, but they also presented defenses based on civilian law. Morris argued that his "offense" predated the new treason act and was no offense under the old. He got short shrift. "I have received hard measure," he said,

---

[81] For example, the execution of Colonel Poyer in Covent Garden in 1649, selected by lot from three renegade colonels, Samuel Rawson Gardiner, *History of the Commonwealth and Protectorate 1649–1656*, 4 vols. (1903; rpt. edn., Adlestrop, Gloucs., 1988), 1: 41. See Phillips, *Civil War in Wales*, 2: 377–79, on designation of one of the three guilty colonels as "that shameful apostate, who indeed deserves no mercy at all, but that he should be cast into that current of the flood-gate of Justice, and be made exemplary to Posterity and to all perfidious villains." In December 1648, it was expected that all three would hang. Bodl. Libr. Clarendon SP, vol.34, fol. 19.

[82] Firth and Rait, *Acts and Ordinances*, 2: 193; and see 2: 18–20 for the "Act . . . abolishing the Kingly Office" of March 17, 1649.

"for none could have found me guilty of treason had they gone according to the letter of the law, which they did not."[83] The assize judges, for their part, had no doubt about their jurisdiction: "we have a power to try you here," they said, and found the law to which Morris appealed "void, . . . to no purpose." His defense that he had "not done any unsoldierly and base act" was irrelevant, for, they told him, "[Y]ou are not looked upon here as a soldier; we shall do what in justice belongs to us."[84] The duke of Hamilton also offered a double defense, civil and military. He argued both that he was a Scot in the service of the kingdom of Scotland and "no Englishman," a claim involving lengthy discussion of the Jacobean law of naturalization, and that he was a prisoner of war; hence a court that was both English and civil had no jurisdiction. His dual defense was as ineffectual as Morris's. He was tried, pointedly, under his English title of earl of Cambridge, and the court rejected all his claims.[85]

Soldiers and civilians alike recognized the novel hazards of this rejection of military self-regulation. At Hamilton's trial, one officer declared that in granting the duke quarter his intention had been "only to preserve him from the violence of the soldiers, and not from the justice of the Parliament."[86] To his credit, Hugh Peter, preacher to the army and publicist for Parliament, rose in court to object:

[H]e had seen many Articles of War, but never heard of such ambiguity; . . . it was clear by these Articles the Duke held his

---

[83] *Somers Tracts,* 7: 13; and see 10, 12.

[84] *Somers Tracts,* 7: 11–13. One of the two judges, Francis Thorpe, fell from favor in 1655 for refusal to try the western rebels on grounds similar to those raised in Morris's defense. *DNB,* "Thorpe, Francis."

[85] Unlike poor Morris, who was denied counsel, Hamilton had four counsel, including the eminent Matthew Hale, whose extensive notes for the defense survive. *Somers Tracts,* 6: 60, 62; Howell, *State Trials,* 4: cols. 1155–56; Lambeth Palace Library (London), MS 3479, fols. 128–206.

[86] Howell, *State Trials,* 4: cols. 1155, 1158. John Lilburne had a radical solution to Parliament's dilemma: "*they should have killed them in the heat of blood,* and not have given them quarter, or after quarter given should

life secured, as well from the Parliament as from the soldiers; and [he] wished to God, that if their Commissioners had meant otherwise, it had been so expressed in the Articles, it being most necessary that Articles in a concernment of life should be plain and certain.

The president of the court conceded his point, but it was "now too late" to help Hamilton.[87]

If mercy had always been discretionary, the protections of quarter had now become equally uncertain. Royalists like Hamilton surrendered secure in soldierly convention, only to find their feet on slippery ground.[88] Capel argued that Parliament's ordinance prohibiting quarter to the Irish "implied, that quarter given to others, should be inviolable for life"; Hamilton and Morris demanded trial by court-martial for alleged breach of laws of war.[89] All recognized that, beyond the narrow focus of their own fates, new precedents were being established: Parliament, by reneging on the sanctity of articles, was abandoning international norms and practice, and by overriding them was extending its powers in novel ways. Hamilton adjured

---

notwithstanding [have] broke it, and so . . . dispatched them by shooting or otherwise killing them in their Chambers or the like." Instead, the defendants had been "gull'd" of their lives, for "to reserve them many moneths together alive . . . , *pretending to take away their lives by the rules of Justice and Law*" constituted "a president of wrong." John Lilburn, *The Legal Fundamental Liberties of the People of England*, 2nd edn. (London, 1649), [70] (misnumbered 52)–73.

[87] Howell, *State Trials*, 4: col. 1158. For the confused circumstances of Hamilton's surrender, which affected subsequent claims regarding custody and conditions, see Stearns, "Letters . . . Relating to Hugh Peter," 128–30. Commissary-General Henry Ireton, Cromwell's son-in-law, testified that Fairfax had promised a trial by peers and that "Parliament's Authority could not be restrain'd" thereby. Clarendon, *History*, 3: 204–05.

[88] Their fellow defendant Sir John Owen also "pleaded quarter." Howell, *State Trials*, 4: cols. 1213, 1216, 1250–51, 1264.

[89] Hamilton was additionally accused of breach of faith as a prisoner. Howell, *State Trials*, 4: cols. 1158, 1213, 1216.

the court "to consider, how sacred Articles of War were reputed in all places, and among all nations, and how inviolably they were kept, . . . not only to strangers but to subjects." While he did not dispute "what the parliament had the power to do, . . . no parliament had ever done the like before."[90]

Fortunately, the threat of treason as the exemplary charge of choice against defeated enemies receded. Even at its height, its use had been selective and arbitrary, revealing yet again its quality as what Conrad Russell has called a "barometer of political panic."[91] Despite revulsion at return to war and blood, old ways were not universally abandoned. At Scarborough in December 1648, for example, generous terms allowed the defeated the full panoply of honor, and it was not long before some discretion and leniency returned.[92] In March 1649, the Lfouse of Commons ominously debated whether "any more [were] fit to be proceeded against for Life, besides those who are appointed to be tryed, or are tryable, by a Court Martial for Revolts by Land or Sea." By June, however, they were considering a general pardon.[93] The third civil war of 1651— better described as invasion with limited domestic support—admittedly saw another notable Royalist victim of treason charges who vainly claimed the status of prisoner of war. The earl of Derby was executed amid general regret and despite Cromwell's reported efforts to save him, but his case fits a traditional category of treason. Although his fate was harsh and could be seen as a return to the justice of 1648 and 1649, it was legally defensible on the basis of an

---

[90] Howell, *State Trials*, 4: cols. 1158–59, 1164.

[91] Russell, "Theory of Treason," 32; and see 46 for the evolution of the theory.

[92] Bodl. Libr. Clarendon SP, vol. 34, fols. 10–10v; CJ, 6: 128; compare Rushworth, *Historical Collections*, 7: 1271–72, for the harsher treatment ordered by the Commons for an earlier group of Scarborough prisoners in September 1648.

[93] CJ, 6: 162, 245. In June, some offenders were not yet thought fit to be received into grace and favor, a formulation clearly excluding capital punishment and offering hope for the future.

ordinance of 1651 that predated his actions; in this, it differed from the cases of Morris and Hamilton.[94]

Charges of treason did not disappear—John Lilburne's was a famous later case—but they reverted to normal; soldiers and civilians alike, victims fell into familiar categories of rebellion and revolt (scale failing to dignify events as civil war, as in the case of Penruddock's Rising), of plotting and subversion.[95] Meanwhile, old habits of obligation and civility reasserted themselves. The implacable preacher Edmund Staunton had been prescient when in 1644 he lamented the "fleshly barre" to draconian justice set up by natural and civil relations and engagements between kinsmen and old companions. The ties that in the first civil war led a Parliamentarian to intervene on behalf of a Royalist prisoner—"Sr, the truth is hee married my sister"—were not swept away in the second.[96] Social bonds, political prudence, and decline of the Royalist threat prevented long–term entrenchment of exemplary and arbitrary "justice" against defeated

[94] Derby and some fellow officers were tried and executed under a special ordinance passed in August 1651 and in force for three months only; it was directly applicable to their subsequent "offenses." (Contrast Morris's claim that the new treason law of 1649 postdated the crime he was accused of.) It mandated trial by council of war and the penalties of treason for any who aided and abetted "Enemies and Invaders" and Charles Stuart. Firth and Rait, *Acts and Ordinances*, 2: 550–51. It was directed specifically against native English. Scots taken in 1651 may have met with severe treatment, especially from English civilians, but they were not designated as traitors. See Gardiner, *Commonwealth and Protectorate*, 2: 60–66; CJ, 6: 615.

[95] Penruddock, too, pleaded that his actions did not qualify as treason and that he had surrendered to articles guaranteeing life. *DNB*, "Penruddock, John."

[96] Staunton, *Phinehas's Zeal*, 19; Jerrilyn Greene Marston, "Gentry Honor and Royalism in Early Stuart England," *Journal of British Studies*, 13 (November 1973–74): 29. Note Hutchinson's efforts on behalf of an "enemie" cousin: L. Hutchinson, *Life of Colonel Hutchinson*, 177. Compare John Clopton of Essex, who with "much ado" obtained the release of a "mutinous" cousin in May 1648; in September, Clopton refused to pay up for an uncle's freedom, but his uncle's ensuing anger reveals expectation that ties of kinship should have prevailed. Essex County Record Office, Chelmsford, D/DQ si8, fols. 37, 52v.

military enemies. Yet, although the excursion into that territory was brief, while it lasted it reversed conventional wisdom on the superiority, as defender of victims' rights, of parliamentary and civilian law over military. Armies' rule of law, within their traditional jurisdictions, had provided a safer protection for the defeated than did Parliament's.[97]

In both the first and second civil wars, the conduct of soldiers, individually and collectively, was governed by the nexus of laws of war—professional, religious, and moral—previously described. In the first war, offenses were normally punished, if at all, according to the professional code governing the conduct of military enemies with equivalent legal "standing," and opponents were constrained not only by mutually acknowledged standards but by utilitarian considerations of reciprocity. The victors' justice of the second war moved toward reduction of military enemies from professionals to whom the laws of their fellows applied to traitors subject to the penalties of civilian treason law. In the process, atrocity, while still invaluable for propaganda purposes, came to run second to "war crimes," in the broad sense of the term. The putative guilt of Lucas and Lisle for "atrocious" actions in "cold blood" was less important than the value of their deaths as deterrence, as a warning against endangering the peace of the realm. Like Lord Capel, the earl of Holland, and the duke of Hamilton, Morris and Blackborne were criminals and traitors, guilty of breach of faith and of returning the kingdom to war and blood. Atrocities were not forgotten, but the crimes for which these men suffered were essentially crimes against the state, not against fellow soldiers or civilians. Parliament's claim to embody the state and the extension of its powers weakened rather than strengthened subjects' rights. The muddled ideology of the Petition of Right of 1628, with its attempt to protect subjects from ill-defined martial law, was temporarily turned on its head, while

---

[97] On the dangers of politicization of treason through changes in the law and of "fickle" votes that would "demolish . . . your own Bulwarks," see Lilburn, *Legal Fundamental Liberties*, 79.

Lilburne's assertion that the powers of martial law were merely derivative from those of the state lost its liberating force when the state turned to treason charges to punish former military enemies.[98]

The proceedings of 1648–1649 foreshadowed those of the Restoration against regicide war criminals. Yet the parallel suggests another that was equally part of the moral economy of war and restoration and that helps to explain survival of a viable polity and society. Just as after Colchester and Pontefract, most Royalists were ultimately allowed peacefully to go home, so at the Restoration, most of those engaged under Parliament and Cromwell were granted "indemnity." The reasons were more practical than charitable. The benefits of "oblivion" overrode those of vengeance. The earl of Bristol, who supported execution of the regicides, told the House of Lords in July 1660, "I find myself set on fire, when I think that the blood of so many vertuous and meritorious . . . persons . . . so cruelly and impiously shed, should cry so loud for vengeance, and not find it from us." Yet when "the criminal and the misled . . . [made] up so numerous a part of the nation," failure to provide them with "the firmest assurances of impunity" would open the way to "new combustions." Only "security from . . . guilty fears" could ensure "still water" for the kingdom after its "past tempests." To fail to mete out justice was a mischief, but the alternative was worse: "[B]etter innumerable mischiefs

---

[98] See Paul Christianson's illuminating discussion in "Arguments on Billeting and Martial Law in the Parliament of 1628" (forthcoming). In 1628, there was no clear distinction between military law applicable within armies and martial law in the modern sense of temporary suspension of civilian law and subjection of civilians to army power. The only alternatives, it was argued, were either martial law or civilian jurisdiction over soldiers. The first attempt by articles of war to demarcate jurisdiction over civil offenses by soldiers, in ways that would maintain army autonomy but cooperate with civilian magistrates, came in 1640 in *Lowes and Ordinances of Warre, Established . . . by . . . The Earle of Northumberland* (London, 1640), D2, "Of Administration of Justice," Nos. 4, 5. The confusions of 1628 derived from failure to conceive either of war in England or of a standing army in need of military discipline—as some old military hands pointed out. I am grateful to Paul Christianson for allowing me to see this article before publication.

to particular persons and families, than one heavy inconvenience to the publick."[99] Bristol may have felt that his solution to retroactive justice for atrocity and war crimes lacked nobility, but he saw it as the only practical route to a reconciled state.

England's wars "against our selves, our brothers," were brutally intimate.[100] Yet civil war had some advantages. Alongside the atrocities and the prudence instilled by fear of reprisal or of ultimate victory by the other side lived the hope that "the sword . . . might be dipt in oyl, rather than in blood," that enemies could "live to be friends" and "win by civility [more] than by harshness."[101] The fragile survival of these ameliorating qualities depended on civil war being regulated as foreign war; they were endangered by declension from laws of war to treason.

In both wars, the relation between professional and often humane regulation of conduct in war and political agendas that threatened it remained uncomfortable. Maintenance of an uneasy balance aided postwar stability and reconciliation and England's survival, to an imperfect but remarkable degree, as a functioning society—despite factions, hardships, injustices, and limited and grudging tolerance. The country not only largely escaped contemporary Germany's physical fate as a victim of prolonged war, but its good fortune appears in comparison with long-term effects of some other civil wars, whether in Ireland, Spain, or, we can predict, Bosnia. The nature of the moral economy of the English civil war contributed to this relatively happy outcome. Yet the interlude of politicized response to "war crimes" casts a less than flattering light on the conflict's place in the history of international attempts to legislate better wars. If history offers no simple lessons, no neat recurrences, by which the present can learn from the past, it may yet, as R. G. Collingwood observed, warn of

---

[99] *Somers Tracts*, 7: 460–61.
[100] *Orders and Institutions of War . . . Newcastle*, 8.
[101] William Sedgwick, *Justice upon the Annie Remonstrance* (London, 1649), 25; *Vindication of the Character and Conduct of Sir William Waller* (London, 1793), 7–8; Bodl. Libr. MS Tanner 62/2A, fol. 423.

tigers that lurk in the grass.[102] The English civil war, if not in the first division of wars in terms of scale, destructiveness, and atrociousness, nonetheless exhibited evils in conduct of war and retribution after it that remain familiar. If tigers of cruelty and revenge have changed little since the seventeenth–century and are still at large in the twentieth, the wary traveler may yet learn something from the successes and failures of seventeenth-century Englishmen in evading, by luck or policy, their worst depredations.

---

[102] Robin George Collingwood, *An Autobiography* (Oxford, 1939), 100–01.

8

Shell-shock and the Cultural History of the Great War

JAY WINTER

The term 'shell-shock' has never before been examined in comparative historical perspective. This is a surprising omission, since the term was invented during the war, and has served as a prism through which much of the cultural history of the 1914–18 war has been viewed.

'Shell-shock' is an essential element in representations of war developed while the conflict was going on. The term, among many others, informed a language which contemporaries used to frame our sense of the war's scale, its character, its haunting legacy. Cultural history, in one sense, is the study of narratives of meaning; any cultural history of the 1914–18 war must evaluate and locate in context the various narratives, including 'shell-shock', relating to psychological injury and traumatic remembrance during and after the conflict.

'Shell-shock' was a term of mediation, but one with a quicksilver and shifting character. It stood between soldiers who saw combat and physicians behind the lines who rarely did, between pensioners and medical boards, between veterans and families often unable to comprehend the nature of the injuries that men bore with them in later years.

The following articles examine this complex phenomenon in two ways. The first is by locating it within medical discourse and medical practice. The crucial question is how did physicians, physiologists, neurologists and others come to an understanding of psychological breakdown during the first world war? How much did professional discourse determine diagnostic practice and prejudice?

This aspect of our enquiry is linked to a second interrogation, which explores the way the term 'shell-shock', and all it conveyed, managed to carry with it a specific set of attributes describing not a physical injury, but a new kind of war. My claim is that 'shell-shock' — in some places and not in others, and only under certain circumstances — turned from a diagnosis into a metaphor.

'Shell-shock' was a term which took on a notation which moved from the medical to the metaphysical. In one set of contexts, the term had a very specific location, documented in medical files, in asylum records and by pension boards. But it also had another life, one which, in its ambiguous quality, has received less attention in a comparative context. My central argument is that the term 'shell-shock' was a specifically Anglo-Saxon representation not solely of damaged soldiers, but more generally of central facets of the war itself. To compare the different terms used in different languages, developed both during and after the war to diagnose and describe psychological disabilities among soldiers, is to disclose some striking variations. Only by making such comparisons can we fully appreciate the richness of different national traditions and perceptions within the overall cultural history of the Great War.

I want, therefore, to suggest that the term 'shell-shock' has been central to some representations of the Great War, and emphatically not to others. One objective of these articles is to find out why this is so. In the English-speaking world, the term 'shell-shock' imaginatively configured a particular question, one related to how differences in degree — the size of the war, its scope, its scale, its repercussions — became differences in kind. 'Shell-shock' thereby in some places became a metaphor for the nature of industrialized warfare, a term which suggests the corrosive force of the 1914–18 conflict *tout court,* and in peculiarly compelling ways. Why did this linguistic form, this medical metaphor, take on this resonance only in parts of the world disfigured by the war?

In this comparative project, we must at all times examine and respect national differences. 'Shell-shock' as metaphor has a set of meanings in English which may simply not be translatable. Perhaps this is one area in which, as Salman Rushdie has it, a culture is defined by its untranslatable words. The precise term does not exist in the same form in French or German. Why this is so, is another question I wish to examine.

As an initial hypothesis, the following argument may serve as a point of departure for the broader comparative history that has yet to be written. I want to suggest that the relative *insignificance* of veterans' movements in British political history may help to account for the greater *significance* of 'shell-shock' as metaphor in narratives of the war experience.

It is a commonplace that British veterans' movements played no significant role in interwar political life. Some elements carried on, and tried to perpetuate in politics the 'soldierly spirit', as Wilfred Owen ironically put it. But the political space at local and national level, occupied by *anciens combattants* in France and Germany, did not exist in Britain.

While the political meaning of military service became a dominant motif in interwar political discourse in France and Germany, in Britain, the veterans' movements faded away at national level. To be sure, many ex-soldiers highlighted how deep was the imprint on their lives of their time in uniform. Harold Macmillan, Anthony Eden and Clement Attlee reminisced about the Great War at the drop of a hat. But they did so as individuals, not as part of a veterans' movement. The presence of old soldiers at the local level was more complex, but it still had few of the features of the world of sociability inhabited by their German and French counterparts.

As Antoine Prost has shown, on the Continent, in their organizational life, these men were living out the convictions forged before 1914 and deepened during the war itself. Here, too, the British case displays continuities. There were deep similarities between the language and comportment of the British Legion and pre-1914 friendly societies. Both manifested the generosity of spirit of the Protestant voluntary tradition. When others tried a different kind of mobilization, more Continental in character, as in Mosley's New Party and his British Union of Fascists, with its uniforms, parades and salutes, it found no purchase among veterans, and was quickly consigned to the political oblivion it deserved.

One hypothesis to test is, therefore, that 'shell-shock' is a term which helped people to conjure up the long-term effects of war service in a political culture unprepared to provide a special place for ex-soldiers and sailors. Everyone knew that the war was traumatic; the question is, what was the appropriate language in which to express that fact? In Britain a political discourse was unavailable for the expression of the soldiers' point of view about the damage the war had caused to many of the men in uniform, whether or not they were physically disabled. The term 'shell-shock' denoted a violent physical injury, albeit of a special kind. That injury was validated by the term, enabling many people and their families to bypass the stigma associated with terms like 'hysteria' or 'neurasthenia' connoting a condition arising out of psychological vulnerability. 'Shell-shock' was a vehicle at one and the same time of consolation and legitimation.

And those suffering from 'shell-shock' needed all the help they could get. Time and again government actuaries, civil servants and ministers applied as narrow as possible an interpretation of what constituted a war-related injury. In Britain, the responsibility of establishing that a disability was war-related rested with the soldier; in France, the burden fell on the state to prove that the injury was *not* war-related. If ex-soldiers and their families in Britain had a grievance, it was hard to know where they could turn. Their position within postwar British society was by and large non-political.

This powerful residue of early traditions in British history — in which social values derived from participation in the associative life of civil society and not primarily from dialogue with the state — must be related to the tardiness of universal suffrage, only achieved in 1929. The peculiarities of the British are also to be seen in the relatively low status of the profession of arms, tolerated, and occasionally honoured, so long as it resided primarily in naval power. Popular opinion located the navy and its weapons far away from mainland Britain. The nastiness of the military was, of course, not something that needed emphasis to anyone with Irish connections. The ugly civil war between 1918 and 1921, waged by irregulars on both sides who had fought in the British army during the war, further distanced military virtues from civic values in Britain. These special features of British historical tradition may help to account for the evolution of different linguistic forms in which a sense of the traumatic nature of the war was expressed.

And what a successful linguistic form it is. 'Shell-shock' may describe a kind of English genius of linguistic compression, in which a host of allusions are fused in two simple vertical syllables. Compare the alternatives: *Kriegs-hysterie, choc commotionnel, choc traumatique, hystérié de guerre*. None carries the dramatic, alliterative, time-specific, yet universal echoes of 'shell-shock'. I wonder how many other such additions to our vernacular vocabulary have arisen from an article published (by Myers in 1915) in *The Lancet?* Here again, medical discourse and cultural discourse, at least in Britain, form one continuum on account of the war.

Outside the political arena and the medical world, what terms and images informed the British discourse of the trauma of the war? One way to understand the significance of the discourse of shell-shock is to identify its socially-ascribed class character.

Many accounts attest to the variation in the incidence of paralysis among enlisted men and neurasthenia — or what we might describe as 'nervous breakdown' or 'combat fatigue', to use the second world war notation — among their officers. This distinction is ascriptive. But it has been used time and again to describe a real difference in reactions to the terrifying conditions of combat.

I wonder if this social distinction in symptoms of psychological stress is present in different armies? If it is not, then this argument follows. One way of understanding the significance of shell-shock within the British vocabulary of the war is to see it as the language of the officer corps, the 'Lost Generation' whose casualty rates were well above those of the men they led. 'Shell-shock' is therefore a code to describe the shock of the war to the ruling élite, whose sons and apprentices, being groomed for power, were slaughtered in France and Flanders.

This is not the place to rehearse the evidence supporting the view that in Britain the 'Lost Generation' was a palpable social phenomenon. There was a social structure of casualties such that the higher up a man was in the social structure, the greater were his chances of becoming a casualty of war. The notion of a 'Lost Generation' was therefore a demographic reality which expanded to provide a symbol to social élites of the effect of the war on both their own social formation and British society as a whole, which many of them took to be interchangeable.

Whatever their perceptions, though, it is true enough that in a host of ways Britain has never recovered from the shock of the 1914–18 war. The war poets and novelists who wrote of 'shell-shock' provided a poetic way of making that point. It is a point that has been located imaginatively in one section of British society — the middle and upper classes who provided the men of the officer corps who manifested 'shell-shock' and wrote about it in enduring prose and poetry.

Those works of literary men like Owen and Sassoon, of the poet/ musician Ivor Gurney, have lasted. They are part of the history of shell-shock because they have told later generations what it was. Individual memories fade away, but cultural representations endure. But there were others who suffered, to whose voices we must also attend. Fortunately, British society is made up of many groups beyond the élite. It is necessary to supplement this argument by pointing out how deeply engraved the notion of 'shell-shock' is in non-élite family narratives. Here I do not believe that the British experience is different from that of Continental survivors of the war. Family narratives everywhere made room for the disabled in body and mind.

But such is the stratified nature of British society, and the powerful cultural position of élites, that a language derived from the poetry and memoirs of young officers has come to stand for a much wider phenomenon. It is unclear to what extent non-élite narratives of what Samuel Hynes so eloquently calls 'The Soldiers' Tale' shared a common syntax and grammar with élite narratives. But my hunch is that while class variations exist, national forms of narrative about shell-shock persist. Since 1918, most British men and women have encoded their narratives about psychological trauma among ex-soldiers in a distinctive set of representations, amplified in poetry, prose, plays, and later on film, in school curricula, on radio and television. It is a varied body of images, but within them, the notion of the 'shell-shocked' soldier is iconic.

Relatively recently, and to her credit, the working-class novelist Pat Barker enlarged the *dramatis personae* of shell-shocked soldiers in her *Regeneration* trilogy. She added to the Owens and Sassoons the entirely mythical figure of Billy Prior. True, the 'hero', Rivers, is a Cambridge don, but Prior stands among the rest, an officer, though emphatically not a gentleman. A school-mistress from a poor area in the north-east of England has told a truth we need to bear in mind. Trauma is democratic; it chooses all kinds of people in its crippling passage. The history of shell-shock, properly configured, is not the history of the officer corps, but the history of the war itself.

Jay Winter

is Reader in Modern History at the University of Cambridge and Fellow of Pembroke College, Cambridge. He is the author of *Sites of Memory, Sites of Mourning: The Great War in European Cultural History* (Cambridge 1995).

9

War Casualties, Policy Positions, and the Fate of Legislators

SCOTT SIGMUND GARTNER

University of California, Davis

GARY M. SEGURA

University of Iowa

BETHANY A. BARRATT

Roosevelt University

Politicians appear to anticipate that the public will hold them accountable for war deaths. Yet, little is known about why some politicians openly oppose costly conflicts while others do not and the difference this makes to their electoral fortunes. Examining U.S. Senate elections from 1966–1972, we find that state-level casualties, military experience, and a variety of other factors affect candidate positions on the Vietnam War. Challenger and incumbent positions are negatively related, suggesting that strategic considerations play a role in wartime policy formation. We also find that war plays a role in elections. Incumbents from states that experience higher casualties receive a smaller percentage of the vote, an effect ameliorated when the incumbent opposes the war and his or her opponent does not. Wartime casualties, we conclude, influence both the perceived cost of the war and its salience, affecting both candidate positions and elections, suggesting that selectorate/electorate-type arguments about war and domestic politics can apply to the US system.

Nearly 30 years after the conclusion of the Vietnam War, it has become conventional wisdom that the U.S. population remains extremely

---

NOTE: This research was supported in part by grants from the National Science Foundation, SES-0079063 and SES 01-96534.

sensitive to wartime casualties, and that this sensitivity serves as a check on the behavior of decisionmakers. That casualties matter to citizens and leaders alike appears obvious, but what is less clear is the process that connects the two. Specifically, politicians act as if they might be held accountable for war deaths, yet little is known of the process that makes this possible. What evidence is there that the public is willing or capable of holding decisionmakers accountable for the human costs of war?

Virtually all analyses of war and domestic politics focus on presidents, prime ministers, or states as unitary actors. On one hand, this makes sense, as foreign policy operates primarily at the national level. Yet there are a number of reasons to explore the effects of war at sub-national levels of aggregation. First, democratic leaders with sub-national constituencies frequently influence foreign policy, and some systems, such as the U.S., have a disaggregated policy process that includes politicians with sub-national constituencies—e.g., U.S. Senators. Second, arguments about the electoral accountability of leaders to policy outcomes are not theoretically bound to operate exclusively at the national level, and testing these arguments on a population of sub-national actors helps to determine better the penetration of international affairs into domestic politics. Finally, the domestic effects of international politics, and in particular wartime casualties, dramatically vary both geographically and temporally within a single conflict. An advantage of disaggregating the political processes of nation states to explore the effects of war on politics is that it allows us to capture this variation.

We argue that wartime deaths, which vary considerably across space and over time, represent *a*, if not *the*, most visible cost of a nation's involvement in war and serve to highlight both the relative importance of the conflict to its citizenry, as well as the successfulness of the effort. As casualties increase, *ceteris paribus,* voters are less satisfied with the status quo. As approval declines, incumbents seeking reelection are more likely to pay a price if they are perceived to be responsible for, or continue to support, the current war policy. Candidates openly opposed to current policy may reap electoral benefit, particularly as costs mount. During periods of international conflict, proximate casualties and candidates' positions on the conflict augment previously established domestic political variables in predicting electoral outcomes.

Casualties also influence the wartime positions of both incumbents and challengers. Challengers might choose to differentiate themselves by articulating opposition to a status quo policy, particularly one perceived as increasingly costly. They might, however, be constrained in this strategy if they perceive that the incumbent holds the median voter's position on the war. Similarly, incumbents are somewhat constrained by previous policy positions they might have taken, but may change their position if the costs of the war become unpalatably high.

This perspective differs sharply from that of early scholars of political representation, who maintained that foreign policy issues are of low salience, do not correspond well to a unidimensional ideological classification, and are part of the 'high politics' of national unity (Miller and Stokes 1963, Converse 1964). This view was challenged by studies that demonstrate the influence of foreign policy on public opinion (Cook 1979; Markus 1979; Hurwitz and Peffley 1987; Page and Shapiro 1992; Niemi and Weisberg 1993; Zaller 1991, 1992) and new studies of representation that incorporate the impact of low information and low salience issues (Carmines and Kuklinski 1990; Gerber and Jackson 1993; Wood and Andersson 1998).

Recent analyses find that casualties play a critical role in the interaction of domestic and international politics—especially the democratic peace (DeRouen 2000; Fordham 1998; Gartzke 2001; Gelpi and Feaver 2002; Holsti 1996). Ray (1995: 203) writes that the pacifying effect of publics caused by wartime casualties represents a critical point in democratic peace arguments. Research suggests that for democracies, concerns about casualties influence the likelihood of conflict (Morgan and Campbell 1991), the cost of fighting (Siverson 1995), the likelihood of victory (Reiter and Stam 2002), and post-war leader tenure (Bueno de Mesquita and Siverson 1995).

Yet, because the U.S. political system disaggregates decision-making across two elected branches not bound by responsible party government, the public is able to assess blame across multiple decisionmakers (Nicholson and Segura 1999; Nicholson, Segura, and Woods 2002). Thus, applications of democratic peace arguments and selectorate/electorate arguments (Bueno de Mesquita et al. 1999; Bueno de Mesquita et al. 2003) to U.S. politics necessitate a research design that moves beyond a unitary actor approach and establishes this process across branches.

We estimate the role casualties played during the Vietnam War in both the policy preferences of U.S. Senators and their subsequent electoral fortunes. We find that international affairs influence subnational domestic politics, suggesting that arguments about democratic electoral accountability and war apply beyond a nation's leader.

Theory

Research suggests that proximate or "local" casualties influence the formation of attitudes towards the conflict by both individuals (Gartner and Segura 2000; Gartner, Segura and Wilkening 1997) and mass publics (Gartner and Segura 1998). Carson et al. (2001) find that a measure of likely Civil War district casualties helps to explain the mid-term House election of 1862-63. For Senate elections, the critical unit of analysis is the state. If casualty rates were spatially uniform, then analysis at the national level would capture all casualty-based effects (Mueller 1973, 1994). National casualties hold only four different values during Senate election years in the Vietnam War, 1966, 1968, 1970, and 1972 and thus provide insufficient temporal and geographic variation to be meaningful beyond simply representing year identifiers.[1]

---

[1] Recent work raises doubts about the explanatory power of logged national casualties, as used by Mueller (1973) and others, showing that when temporal auto-correlation concerns are controlled for, coefficients on this measure lose statistical significance (Gartner and Segura 1998).

There is, however, wide variance in both annual and cumulative state-level war dead per-capita. During the Vietnam War, annual per-capita casualty rates varied by over 11,000 percent in states holding Senate elections, from a low in New Jersey in 1972 of 1.116 persons killed in action per one million residents to a high in Oklahoma in 1968 of 123.877. Even within the same year, variation was quite large. For example, New Mexico's 1972 killed in action rate per one million residents (8.850) was over 793 percent higher than that of New Jersey's (1.116).

While exact estimations of per-capita casualties are not necessary for casualties to convey information, a number of mechanisms facilitate perceptions of state-wide casualties. Government figures are broken down by state and the announcement of individual casualties almost always is accompanied by a state reference. Gravestones in national and foreign military cemeteries include state identifiers and obviously are clear in state-specific military cemeteries. Local and national media, as well as anti-war protestors, provide information on state-level casualties. For example, *Life* magazine published the names, state, and pictures of 242 American soldiers who died in Vietnam between May 28 and June 3, 1969 (*Life* June 27, 1969). Anti-war protestors took out an ad in the April 12, 1970 issue of the *Des Moines Register* with crosses representing each of the 714 Iowan deaths that had accumulated to date (Bryan 1976). Newspaper stories frequently emphasize the local aspect of casualties and research suggests that local casualties positively affect a conflict's coverage by local media (Gartner 2004). These examples represent a variety of formal and informal processes that facilitate state-based casualty assessments.

Position Formation

When do candidates speak out against a conflict? While previous research largely treated political positions as exogenous, particularly those dealing with foreign policy (Murray 1996), recent research argues that candidates' positions in elections are moderated by information on policy costs and salience (Alvarez 1997; Franklin 1991).

Local casualties are the costs of war most salient to citizens in the formation of attitudes. Elites respond to these local attitudes, which for senators revolve around the state as the unit of analysis. As a result, Senate candidates will see state-level deaths as more costly than those that occurred from other states. By capturing the state-level costs of the war, per-capita casualties are likely to increase elite opposition to the war in a manner similar to their well-documented influence on individual and aggregate opinion.

H_1: *Candidates from states that experience higher levels of casualties are more likely to oppose a conflict.*

Since opinion effects are of interest to both challengers and incumbents, we need to consider circumstances under which these two similarly motivated people will choose opposite positions. Challengers are strategic (Jacobson and Kernell 1981) and need to provide voters with a reason to vote for them and, hence, have an incentive to select positions that differentiate them from incumbents. At the same time, challengers and incumbents are each more likely to be elected if they support the median policy position of the voters. An incumbent sensitive to casualties likely already occupies the median voter position. This creates what we call the *Challenger's Dilemma*: how do challengers differentiate themselves from incumbents without sacrificing the advantage of holding the median voter position?

A quick glance at the data suggests that the urge to differentiate is the stronger of the two effects. In 76 of the 127 contested Senate elections during Vietnam, the challenger and incumbent-party candidate held different positions on the war. Of course, this could have been the result of party politics or other electoral forces. And while we might be correct in conceptualizing the candidates' positions as the product of individual policy judgment or political strategy, there is an entire selection process—particularly primary campaigns—which may well have played a role in the positions held by the eventual nominees of each party. Though we believe that wartime variables including casualties are one component of this process, by no means are they the only relevant factors. For us, then, the test would be to hold these other factors constant to assess if *ceteris paribus,* candidate positions are really inversely related.

H$_2$: *Challengers will take positions contrary to that held by incumbents.*[2]

In a democracy, wars largely start with strong legislative support. Even if not formally required, legislative approval is frequently sought out. For example, in Vietnam, the 1964 Gulf of Tonkin Resolution was opposed by only two senators and unanimously approved by the House of Representatives (Karnow 1991: 391–92). For most incumbents, speaking out against the war means moving from a position of support to opposition. Reversals of position may be politically costly. Acting strategically, however, we think incumbents switch positions when a position becomes too costly or when changing circumstances legitimately change an incumbent's perception of the issue. And there is a large and well-developed literature on strategic reelection seeking behavior and shirking (Kuklinski 1978; Thomas 1984; Bernstein 1991).

Changing positions may entail political costs, but it does happen. During the Vietnam War, a number of incumbents changed positions between elections. For example, in 1966 Senators McClellan (Arkansas) and Spong (Virginia) were hawks, while in 1972 they were doves. Some incumbents even changed positions within an election. For example, in 1970 Senators Stennis (Mississippi) and Montoya (New Mexico) both changed from hawkish to dovish positions during the course of the campaign (*Congressional Quarterly Weekly Report* 1970: 945, 25-S). Looking at the data, in 46 percent of the elections we study, the incumbent party's candidate was opposed to the conflict, despite near unanimous support at the outset. Interestingly, challengers were less likely to hold dovish positions (only 34 percent of the cases).

---

[2] When we refer to incumbents, we mean both incumbent candidates and those representing the incumbent party should the seat be open, unless specified otherwise.

We predict that the costs incumbents face for altering their positions decreases the effect of casualties on policy formation when compared to challengers. We do not anticipate that these differences are sufficient to alter the directional relationship between variables, but we do anticipate that the intensity of those relationships—the size of coefficients and the degree of statistical significance—varies between incumbents and challengers.

H_3: *The magnitude and significance of the relationships between casualties and candidate position are weaker for incumbents than for challengers.*

Elections

Since earlier research has shown that costly conflicts are likely to suffer diminishing public support, we would expect to see the effects of this opinion change manifested in the electoral arena. Variations in cost and in the relative positions of the candidates seeking election should both have a bearing on the outcome. State-level casualties, we argue, best represent wartime costs to their specific audiences. Other things equal, incumbents, particularly those who hold office in institutions such as Congress, which can be seen as having responsibility for the prosecution of the war (Fiorina 1981), will fare worse in states with high state-based casualties compared with states suffering comparatively fewer losses.

H_4: *The vote share of the incumbent candidate will be negatively related to state per-capita casualties.*

We believe the influence that incumbent and challenger positions on a war have on election outcomes depend on their pair-wise interactions. Shared positions are less useful as a voting cue. When opposing candidates hold the same position, we would expect the increasing costs of the war to have less of an effect. For example, Page and Brody (1972: 982, 984) found that, "Vietnam policy preferences did not have a great effect on voting for the major party candidates in 1968," because there was, ". . . rather little difference between Nixon's and Humphrey's stated positions on Vietnam policy."

> H_5: *The vote share for those opposing the war will increase while the vote share for those not opposing the war will decrease, if the two major party candidates hold different positions.*

In Senate elections, when candidates disagree and human costs of the war are high, those openly opposing the conflict are likely to be rewarded with additional votes.

Data and Variables

The universe of analysis is *all* regularly scheduled, two-party Senate elections between 1966 and 1972 inclusive. Because of the difficulty of partisan interpretation represented by Harry Byrd (I-VA), his re-election is dropped as are five uncontested elections (N = 127).[3]

Positions

We identify challengers and incumbents as *Hawks, Administration Supporters, Doves,* or *No Position* each coded 1 or 0.[4] We create two sets of dependent variables. First, *Incumbent Dove* and *Challenger Dove* are coded 1 if the relevant candidate is a dove and 0 otherwise. Second, we generate two ordinal variables, *Challenger Position* and *Incumbent Position,* coding doves as 3, administration supporters and those with no position 2 (since both represent explicit or implicit supporters of the status quo), and hawks 1.[5]

---

[3] We think strategic choice is critical to position formation. We could include and control for unopposed cases. These outliers (percent of vote = 100) likely contaminate the other relationships while artificially increasing explained variance (R2).

[4] If multiple positions exist, we use the position that was articulated closest to the election.

Capturing the relationship between casualties and their domestic political effects is complicated by findings that demonstrate that different casualty measures are more appropriate under different circumstances (Gartner and Segura 1998). This is because of the fundamental differences between marginal casualties, which increase and decrease, cumulative casualties that monotonically increase, and opinion change—which is generally unidirectional, moving from support to opposition. When costs increase, marginal casualties better capture temporal and spatial variation and should be associated with opposition. By contrast, when marginal casualties decrease, we would not expect a concomitant decline in opposition because, of course, total casualties continue to climb, albeit at a slower rate. Mueller (1973) shows this uneven sensitivity to casualty experiences. We create casualty variables that combine three measures: marginal casualties, direction of change in marginal casualties, and cumulative casualties.

---

[5] About half of our position data came from *Congressional Quarterly*. Other sources included anthologies of congressional biographies and *Facts on File* (Cook 2000) and Nader's *Congress Project* (1972). Remaining positions were obtained from candidate and war histories and, as a last resort, the largest daily in the state's largest city or the state's capital city was examined for each of two two-week periods preceding and immediately following the election. A complete list of candidate positions and the sources from which they were obtained is available from the authors. Candidates are coded as "doves" when they endorse less aggressive policies than those in effect or espoused by the administration. These include: (1) terms such as "dove," (2) a preference for early or aggressively seeking an end to the war or (3) criticism of the president or of the candidate's opponent for being too hawkish. Candidates are coded as "hawk" when they endorse more aggressive policies than those in effect or put forward by the administration. These include: (1) terms such as "hawk," (2) support for more aggressive pursuit of the war or (3) criticism of the president or of the candidate's opponent as being too restrained in the pursuit of victory. Candidates are coded as "supports administration" when they are consistently described as echoing or following the lead of the administration or, for incumbents, if there is no textual reference to a candidate's position, and their votes conform to the administration's current preferences. For 29 challengers and 8 incumbents we found no information regarding their thoughts on the war and identify them as holding "no position."

To determine marginal casualties, we count the number of KIA from each state for one year prior to the election. Since this number will vary in part as a consequence of state population, we divide this number by the state's population (taken from the 1970 Census and measured in thousands). The result, *State Marginal Casualties,* is a per-capita measure of a state's recent sacrifices and a salient indicator of the overall costliness of the conflict. We also measure *State Cumulative Casualties,* which represent the total number of KIA from a state since the onset of hostilities in the conflict, again divided by state population in thousands. We determine *Direction of State Marginal Casualties* by comparing the marginal casualty rate for the most recent 12-month period before the election (time$_t$), with the 12-month period a year earlier (time$_{t-1}$). When the most recent year's casualties are greater—costs are getting worse—we code *Direction of State Marginal Casualties* as 1, and code it 0 when costs are deceasing.[6] We capture state casualties with *State Marginal Casualties* when costs increase (*Direction* of *State Marginal Casualties* = 1) and *State Cumulative Casualties* when marginal casualties are declining (*Direction* of *State Marginal Casualties* = 0). Values of each variable are otherwise coded to zero. *Direction* of *Marginal Casualties* itself is not directly included in the analyses. We expect that both casualty measures will be positively associated with *Incumbent Dove* and *Challenger Dove,* and *Challenger* and *Incumbent Position,* because higher casualty levels shift the opinion of the median voter towards opposition to the conflict, and provide the candidates with electoral incentives to be more dovish.

Military service also likely influences a candidate's position (Gelpi and Feaver 2002). There are two contrasting arguments. First, those who served are better able, politically, to take dovish positions (the only-Nixon-could-go-to-China claim). Second, military service socializes those who serve to be more hawkish. Candidates can also react

---

[6] This divides the Vietnam War sample almost exactly in two, with 63 elections occurring when marginal casualties are increasing or unchanging in a particular state and 64 when they decrease.

to their adversary's military experience, again in two ways. Candidates facing opponents with military experience may be more likely to take hawkish positions in order to neutralize a possible opponent advantage. Second, candidates—especially challengers—facing opponents who served in the military, and are thus perceived to be more hawkish, may distinguish themselves by being doves. We create the variables *Incumbent* and *Challenger Military Service* (coded 0 or 1).

We include seven contextual factors that we think are critical to predicting candidate choice of position. *Open Seat* indicates that the incumbent party candidate is not actually the current occupant of the seat—who has retired or been defeated in the primary. *State Partisanship* measures the Democratic Party's state strength, and is the share of the two party vote received by LBJ in the 1964 presidential election (standardized). We expect this measure to be positively associated with the probability that the candidate chooses a dove position. Because candidates who take no position give opponents greater strategic latitude, we include *Opponent No Position* (coded 1 or 0). *Party* is coded 1 for Democrats and 0 for Republicans. We include *Population* (in millions) because we adjust the casualty figures for state-population. In order to determine the source of any effect in a ratio variable, the denominator needs to be included separately. Only then, can we isolate the effect of casualties without fearing that the coefficient is driven by the effect across population size.

Presidential popularity has often been found to affect the likelihood of legislators supporting the policies of the current administration. We include *Presidential Approval*, the percent of support expressed nationally for the president in the fall immediately preceding the election.[7] When the administrations managing the War are more popular nationally, we expect support of the war effort to be higher, and opposition lower, than when those same administrations attract less overall approval. The coefficient, then, should be positive.

---

[7] Gallup Polls, quarterly percent in support of the president, fourth quarter.

Defense Personnel Per Capita represents the number of people in a state actively working in the military or defense industries divided by state population. It is reasonable to expect a higher degree of vigilance to the progress of the war among those with more at stake— especially since we control for state casualties, for which we anticipate opposite effects.

Southerners have repeatedly been found to be more supportive of military activity, "representatives from the South [are] most hawkish, followed by those of the West, with those of the North last" (Nisbett and Cohen 1996: 64). We hypothesize that in Southern states the effect that war deaths have on the likelihood of candidates opposing the conflict and the electoral effect of opposition, or will be dampened, missing, or even present in the reverse—that is, increasing support for hawks rather than doves. Though doves can be hurt outside the South as well, the distribution of hawks and doves by region suggests that the opinion dynamics in the South are different. Given the relative non-competitiveness of southern elections in this era, we also anticipate that southern incumbents will do better than other incumbents. The variable *South* is coded 1 if the election occurs in a Southern or border state and 0 otherwise.[8] Our expectation is that the *South* will have a negative effect on the probability of either candidate being a dove and a positive effect on incumbent party vote share.

Elections

We analyze the share of the two-party vote received in the general election by the incumbent senator (or the candidate of the incumbent party in open seats) which we call *Incumbent Percent*. We expect both *Marginal Casualties* and *Cumulative Casualties* to be negatively associated with *Incumbent Percent*.

Using *Challenger Dove* and *Incumbent Dove*, we include three variables to represent joint position dynamics: $Dove_I$, Not $Dove_C$;

---

[8] This includes the 11 states of the Confederacy plus Missouri and Kentucky.

Not Dove$_P$, Dove$_C$; Dove$_P$, Dove$_C$. The unexpressed category is *Not Dove$_P$, Not Dove$_C$.*[9] We think that each pair will have a different effect on election outcomes, and that these effects are moderated by the state's region. We expect an incumbent who speaks out against Vietnam is rewarded if the opponent does not follow suit, such that *Dove$_P$, Not Dove$_C$* will have a positive coefficient. Similarly, we expect that *Not Dove$_P$, Dove$_C$* will have a negative coefficient, indicating that incumbents that support the status quo policy or are openly hawkish, can be hurt if the challenger stakes out an anti-war position. In this case, challengers may select positions with some beliefs about what the effect will be at the polls. We anticipate that *Dove$_P$, Dove$_C$* will have little effect given the candidates' agreement.

Second, our expectation is that the control dummy *South* will have a positive coefficient given the dominance of the Democratic Party in that region during this period, resulting in members from the South being routinely reelected with large margins. We think that in the South, the negative effect anticipated for *Not Dove$_P$, Dove$_C$* will be weaker or perhaps reversed. We check this by including the interactive term *South × Not Dove$_P$, Dove$_C$.* A significant and positive effect would be an indication that those more supportive of the conflict were punished less or even—should the coefficient be larger in magnitude than the one on the main-effects position variable—rewarded for that position in the South.

We control for *Open Seat, South, Incumbent Party, Population* as described above. *Open Seat* indicates the absence of an actual incumbent and likely leads to lower vote shares for the incumbent party. *Incumbent Party* simply controls for the difference between Democrats and Republicans. *Population* is included for two reasons. First, as suggested above, its presence as a denominator in the per-capita

---

[9] An additional factor to consider might be whether an incumbent's position has changed. A recent change of position should dampen the hypothesized relationship between position and performance. This is untestable because it is essentially impossible to identify exactly and under what conditions the candidates change their preferences prior to an election.

casualty measure requires that we include it as a main effect. Second, some have suggested that *Population* will have a direct effect on the quality of representation and, by extension, the popularity of incumbents (Lee 1998; Oppenheimer 1996).

The literature on Senate elections suggests that we need to control for additional factors (Abramowitz 1981; Abramowitz and Segal 1986; Abramowitz and Segal 1992; Segura and Nicholson 1995; Squire 1995; Westlye 1991). *Electoral Cycle* is coded 1 if the presidential and midterm cycle favors the incumbent's party and 0 otherwise. That is, Republican incumbents receive more votes in presidential years when the GOP wins the White House and in midterm years when the White House is in Democratic hands, and vice versa (Campbell 1960; Campbell 1997). *Incumbent Party Advantage* controls for the degree of partisan dominance of the incumbent's political party in that state. To assess this, we standardized the mean Democratic vote shares in two presidential elections—1964 and 1972—in each state. For Democratic incumbents, the *Incumbent Party Advantage* is this standard score (with negative numbers indicating that Democrats do less well on average in Presidential elections). For Republicans, *Incumbent Party Advantage* represents the standard score multiplied by negative one.[10]

Finally, we include a modified measure of presidential approval, since same party candidates generally do better as approval increases. *Presidential Approval Advantage* is coded as the *Presidential Approval* variable for the president's copartisans, and recoded as 100 minus *Presidential Approval* for incumbents of the opposition party. We expect a positive coefficient here, indicating that incumbent co-partisans to better when the president is more popular, while incumbents from the opposition to better when the president's popularity is suffering.

---

[10] Campaign spending, a key variable in earlier studies, is not applicable here because those data were not available prior to the formation of the Federal Elections Commission in 1971.

Results

Positions

We analyze separately four dependent variables representing candidates' positions: *Challenger Dove and Incumbent Dove* (using logit analyses), and *Challenger Position and Incumbent Position* (using ordered logit estimations).[11] In all cases, a positive coefficient suggests that an independent variable makes a candidate more likely to hold a dovish position.

The logit results for the likelihood that candidates hold dovish positions are shown in Table 1. Models for both incumbent party candidates and challengers are both highly significant and predict between 75.6 percent and 78 percent of the cases correctly, reducing the proportional error between 35 percent and 48 percent (using Lambda-p calculation for Proportional Reduction of Error). *State Marginal Casualties* has a significant effect on both challenger and incumbent position taking, making each more likely to hold dovish positions. Challengers from states with increasing *State Cumulative Casualties* are also more likely to be doves, though the effect of this variable is zero for incumbents. These results are supportive of Hypothesis 1; higher state casualties increase the probability that candidates oppose the conflict.

For challengers and incumbents there also appears to be an inverse relationship between the positions of candidates, as opposition from one candidate lowers the probability of opposition by the other. The likelihood of taking a dovish position is decreased when faced with a dovish opponent (*Opponent Dove* has a negative and significant coefficient in both models), which supports our contention in H_2 that positiontaking includes strategic considerations.

Incumbents are also less likely to be doves when they face challengers with no stated position on the conflict. Similarly, incumbent party candidates running for open seats previously held by their

---

[11] All analyses are conducted in Stata™.

party are less likely to be doves. Democratic incumbents, incumbents from more Democratic states, and those running in periods of relatively high presidential popularity are more likely to be doves. The military service records of neither the incumbents nor their opponents appear to have an appreciable effect on incumbent position.

As we have indicated, both measures of casualties significantly shape challenger opinion, as does the position of their opponent. In addition, challengers are less likely to be doves when they have military experience. Challengers are more likely to hold positions in opposition to the war if they are Democrats and if their opponent has a record of military service. Unlike the model of incumbent party candidate position, challenger positions appear unaffected by the presence of an open seat, the popularity of the president, or state-level partisanship. The last result should not be surprising given the strategic fix presented by the challenger's dilemma, i.e., choosing a position in opposition to someone already elected by this specific electorate.

For both challengers and incumbents, being from the South does appear to have the effect we anticipated. Southern challengers are significantly more hawkish than others, while southern incumbents also appear to be more hawkish, though the coefficient is marginally insignificant.

The changes in predicted probabilities for significant variables are reported in the columns adjoining the coefficients. Changes reported represent the net change in the probability that the dependent variable equals one (Dove) given a shift in the predictor variable holding all other predictors constant at their means. The change in value for dichotomous variables is 0 to 1, while the change for continuous variables is a single standard deviation change from .5 standard deviations below the mean to .5 standard deviations above. In each case, the estimated effects of casualties are substantial. Controlling for other effects, when marginal casualties are increasing, the shift in the marginal casualty value of one standard deviation around the

≡ TABLE 1 Logit Estimates for Dichotomous Measure of Candidate Opposition to the Vietnam War in U.S. Senate Elections, 1966-1972

Variables	Incumbents		Challengers	
	Model 1 Coefficients, (Std. Errors)	Model 1 Changes in Predicted Probability y=1	Model 2 Coefficients, (Std. Errors)	Model 2 Changes in Predicted Probability y=1
State Marginal Casualties	.027* (.015)	.234	.026* (.014)	.178
State Cumulative Casualties	−.003 (.004)		.008* (.005)	.215
South	−1.071† (.657)	−.247	−2.356** (.796)	−.334
Party	2.402*** (.581)	.518	1.534** (.618)	.308
Defense Personnel Per Capita	.008 (.031)		.039 (.032)	
Population	.092† (.062)	.092	.059 (.061)	
State Partisanship	.055* (.031)	.155	.006 (.033)	
Incumbent Military Service	.837 (.589)		1.059* (.584)	.180
Challenger Military Service	−.807 (.611)		−1.095* (.553)	−.236
Presidential Approval	.308* (.153)	.076	−.066 (.158)	
Opponent Dove	−1.873** (.652)	−.412	−1.115* (.617)	−.210
Opponent No Position	−1.845** (.763)	−.378	1.394 (1.033)	
Open Seat	−1.270* (.580)	−.287	−.432 (.587)	
Constant	−20.942** (8.760)		1.847 (8.793)	
Chi-square	57.860		44.740	
Chi-Square Significance	.000		.000	
Pseudo R-Square	.330		.275	
% Predicted Correctly	75.590		77.950	
PRE Lambda-p	.475		.349	
N (Sample Size)	127		127	

One Tailed Significance: † p< = .075, * p< =.05, ** p< = .01, *** p< = .001

mean raises the likelihood of the incumbent opposing the war by .23, and among challengers by .18. Challengers also appear to be affected by the cumulative loss (when marginal casualties are declining), with a one standard deviation shift raising the probability of opposition by .22. Looking at the effects of strategic considerations, we also see a sizable impact. Incumbents facing dovish challengers have a .41 lower probability of themselves being in opposition, while challengers facing dovish incumbents have a .21 lower probability of being openly opposed to the conflict. We can fairly conclude that opposition to the Vietnam War among members of, and candidates for, the U.S. Senate is significantly driven, at least in part, by both casualty rates in their respective states and strategic considerations in their specific races.

We replicate the previous analysis, this time using an ordinal variable separating those who were hawks from those who simply articulated support for the current administration's policies, something of a middle position. Again, open opposition is coded as the highest values. Table 2 shows the results of the ordered logit analyses of *Incumbent Position* and *Challenger Position*. The results from this approach are remarkably similar to those using the dichotomous version of the dependent variable. With only minor variation on control variables, the direction and significance of predictors is the same as before. Most importantly, the effect of casualties on opposing the war remains. When marginal casualties are increasing, variation in these increases is directly related to the likelihood of challengers and incumbents opposing the conflict. Challengers from states with higher *State Cumulative Casualties* are also more likely to oppose the war. Similarly, the strategic effects remain, with the positions of two candidates in the same race consistently inversely related, and southerners remain more hawkish, with significant coefficients for both challengers and incumbents. Using dichotomous or trichotomous measures of candidate position, the effects we anticipated with our first two hypotheses are persistent.

And what of our third hypothesis? We argue that incumbents and challengers face somewhat different strategic circumstances when

≡ TABLE 2 Ordered Logit Estimates for Trichotomous Candidate Position on the Vietnam War in U.S. Senate Elections 1966-1972

Variables	Incumbents		Challengers	
	Model 1 Coefficients, (Std. Errors)	Model 1 Changes in Predicted Probability y=1	Model 2 Coefficients, (Std. Errors)	Model 2 Changes in Predicted Probability y=1
State Marginal Casualties	.026* (.013)	.231	.020* (.011)	.138
State Cumulative Casualties	−.002 (.003)		.007* (.003)	.202
South	−1.157* (.574)	−.268	−1.694** (.570)	−.266
Party	2.089*** (.456)	.467	−1.814*** (.501)	−.369
Defense Personnel Per Capita	.004 (.026)		.025 (.026)	
Population	.016 (.052)		.058 (.053)	
State Partisanship	.038* (.022)	.108	−.026 (.020)	
Incumbent Military Service	.673 (.480)		.760*(.446)	.136
Challenger Military Service	−.926* (.500)	−.227	−1.209** (.467)	−.265
Presidential Approval	.307* (.133)	.386	−.030 (.118)	
Opponent Dove	−1.599*** (.523)	−.365	−1.009* (.464)	−.194
Opponent No Position	−1.710** (.609)	−.364	1.591* (.842)	.371
Open Seat	−.673† (.458)	−.162	−.165 (.436)	
Cut Point 1	17.982 (7.389)		−4.670 (6.581)	
Cut Point 2	19.420 (7.427)		−2.448 (6.569)	
Chi-Square	60.770		59.680	
Chi-SquareProb.	.000		0.000	
Pseudo R-Square	.227		0.215	
N (Sample Size)	127		127	

One Tailed Significance: † p<=.075, * p<=.05, ** p<=.01, *** p<=.001

selecting a position. We suggest that the sensitivity of incumbent position to external forces, particularly casualties, would be circumscribed by past positions and the fear of political costs from switching sides. Similarly, in our discussion of the challenger's dilemma, we suggest that challengers are constrained in their desire to differentiate themselves from incumbents by the simultaneous urge to adopt the position of the median voter in their state, a position the incumbent may already occupy.

In both specifications, casualties appear to have a more powerful effect on the challenger position, with both variables reaching significance. By comparison, only one of the two variables reach significance for incumbents. These results support both H_3 and, more generally, our argument that incumbents face more structural constraints in choosing policy positions.

Elections

In order to assess whether these positions have meaningful political effects, we examine their impact on vote shares. We conduct an OLS regression on the incumbent party candidate's share of the two-party vote. As suggested by H_4, *State Marginal Casualties* and *State Cumulative Casualties* have significant, negative effects on incumbents share of the two-party vote. Without respect to their positions and holding other factors constant, both higher rates of marginal casualties (when casualties increase) and higher total accumulated war dead (when casualties decrease) cost incumbents votes.

Population and *Open Seat* also have significant, negative effects. Incumbent party candidates defending open seats, or incumbents from more populous states, receive a smaller percentage of the vote. As expected, incumbents are impacted from the well-recognized effects of the electoral cycle, doing well with co-partisans winning the White House, doing poorly in mid-terms if a co-partisan holds the White House, and vice versa for opposition party members. With regard to the strategic considerations we offer in H_5, the results are supportive if somewhat more mixed. Dovish incumbents facing non-dove challengers appear to benefit from the difference, whereas challenger doves do not appear to be helped in facing non-dove incumbents. As we anticipated, there is no meaningful effect when both candidates oppose the war. And again, southerners differentiate themselves. Southern non-dove incumbents facing dovish challengers

≡ TABLE 3 OLS Estimates of Casualties, Positions and Domestic Politics on Incumbent Percent of Vote, U.S. Senate Elections, 1996-1972

Variables	Coefficients (Std. Errors)	Betas
State Marginal Casualties	−.068* (.035)	−.251
State Cumulative Casualties	−.020* (.009)	−.296
South	2.649 (2.277)	.118
Incumbent Party	−.313 (2.883)	−.016
Defense Personnel Per Capita	−.064 (.102)	−.051
Population	−.454* (.200)	−.189
Electoral Cycle	2.806* (1.991)	.143
Presidential Approval Advantage	−.221 (.168)	−.160
$Dove_1$, $Dove_c$	3.795* (2.137)	.187
Not $Dove_1$, $Dove_c$	2.561 (2.488)	.111
Open Seat	−7.941*** (1.868)	−.353
South X Not $Dove_1$, $Dove_c$	11.093* (5.904)	.172
$Dove_1$, $Dove_c$	3.708 (3.089)	.115
Incumbent Party Advantage	−1.071 (.943)	−.102
Constant	70.992*** (10.256)	−
N	127	
R^2	0.3180	
Adj. R^2	0.2327	
F	3.73	
Significance	.0000	

One Tailed Significance: *$p < = .05$, ** $p < =.01$, *** $p < = .001$

receive a higher percentage of the vote, suggesting that more hawkish stands remained relatively popular in the South, controlling for other factors. Model fit statistics suggest the model does reasonably well.

Looking at the standardized coefficients reported in the second column, we see that the absence of a true incumbent has the most substantial impact on the incumbent party's vote share, and this is not surprising. After *Open Seat,* however, the two most powerful predictors of incumbent vote share are our two casualty measures.

Conclusion

War can be costly to leaders of democratic societies even when decisionmaking is divided across multiple institutions. We examine whether the costs of war had political consequences for holders of and aspirants to U.S. Senate seats during the Vietnam War. We show that state-level per-capita killed in action levels, which vary significantly across states and over time, had effects on the positions candidates chose to articulate and shaped the electoral prospects of incumbents, particularly in elections where candidates hold contrary positions.

Casualties affect elections in two ways. First, wartime variables affected position formation, where higher state casualties increased the likelihood that incumbents and challengers alike openly opposed the War. Second, casualties influence Senate elections directly. Incumbents are held responsible for the conduct of the war, and their vote share is adversely affected by higher casualty rates in their states. These results are consistent with earlier research demonstrating similar casualty-driven effects in mass publics, at both the individual and aggregate levels (Gartner and Segura 1998, 2000; Gartner, Segura, and Wilkening 1997).

Challengers face a wartime bind. If they come out against the war and the incumbent does not, they will not benefit; yet if they fail to differentiate themselves, they are unlikely, at least on the basis of this issue, to present the voters in their state with a compelling reason to elect them, a result consistent with earlier work on information, salience and strategic considerations in elections (Alvarez 1997; Franklin 1991).

Although both incumbents and challengers face constraints, our findings suggest that their behavior is endogenous to casualties. Candidates react strategically to the information provided to them by their state-level casualties, suggesting strategy is not reserved to the battlefield. Candidates behave strategically when formulating wartime positions, rightly perceiving that electorates respond to candidate position differences when voting.

What are the larger implications of these results for the relationship between international and domestic politics? War profoundly affects domestic politics through the instrument of casualties. We argue here that citizens are well informed of local costs and sensitive to the positions of locally elected leaders. If the effects of war extend beyond national executives to legislative politics, then selectorate/ electorate-type arguments about war and domestic politics, when properly operationalized, can apply to the U.S. system. Furthermore, it is not just the existence of war but its conduct that exerts a domestic political influence. In particular, the distribution of casualties across space and time provides elites and constituents with highly varied and critical information. Envisioning casualties as information begins to provide a process model for the democratic peace as it operates in the U.S. Wars and their attendant costs are directly tied to the fates of legislators, as they influence both the perceived cost of the war and its salience, affecting candidate positions, elections, and ultimately, we suspect, policy.

As a result, leaders, or those who aspire to become leaders, are correct in interpreting that the costs of international conflict—and their reactions to the same—have tremendous importance to their electoral future. The costs of their foreign policy actions will influence the political fortunes of sub-national leaders. Just as the casualties of a conflict are not uniformly distributed within the country, neither are the political consequences resulting from foreign policy actions.

References

Abramowitz, Alan I. 1981. "Choices and Echoes in the 1978 U.S. Senate Elections: A Research Note. *American Journal of Political Science* 25 (1): 112–18.

Abramowitz, Alan I., and Jeffrey A. Segal. 1986. "Determinants of the Outcomes of Senate Elections." *The Journal of Politics* 48 (2): 433–39.

—. 1992. *Senate Elections*. Ann Arbor: University of Michigan Press.

Alvarez, R. Michael. 1997. *Information and Elections*. Ann Arbor: University of Michigan Press.

Bernstein, Robert A. 1991. "Strategic Shifts: Safeguarding the Public Interest? U.S. Senators, 1971–86." *Legislative Studies Quarterly* 16 (2): 263–80.

Bryan, C. D. B. 1976. *Friendly Fire*. New York: Putnam.

Bueno de Mesquita, Bruce, James Morrow, Randolph M. Siverson, and Alastair Smith. 1999. "An Institutional Explanation of the Democratic Peace." *American Political Science Review* 93 (4): 791–807.

Bueno de Mesquita, Bruce, and Randolph M. Siverson. 1995. "War and the Survival of Political Leaders: A Comparative Study of Regime Types and Political Accountability." *American Political Science Review* 89 (4): 841–55.

Bueno de Mesquita, Bruce, Alastair Smith, Randolph Siverson, James Morrow. 2003. *The Logic of Political Survival*. Cambridge, MA: MIT Press.

Campbell, Angus. 1960. "Surge and Decline: A Study of Electoral Change." *Public Opinion Quarterly* 24 (3): 397–418.

Campbell, James E. 1997. "The Presidential Pulse and the 1994 Midterm Congressional Election." *Journal of Politics* 59 (3): 830–57.

Carmines, Edward G., and James H. Kuklinski. 1990. "Incentives, Opportunities, and the Logic of Public Opinion in American Political Representation." In John A. Ferejohn and James H. Kuklinski, eds., *Information and Democratic Processes*. Urbana: University of Illinois Press.

Carson, Jamie, Jeffery Jenkins, David Rhode, and Mark Souva. 2001. "The Impact of National Tides and District-Level Effects on Electoral Outcomes: The U.S. Congressional Elections of 1862-63." *American Journal of Political Science* 45 (4): 887–98.

Congressional Quarterly Weekly Report. 1970: 945, 25-S.

Converse, Philip E. 1964. "The Nature of Belief Systems in Mass Publics." In David Apter, ed., *Ideology and Discontent*. New York: Free Press.

Cook, Beverly. 1979. "Judicial Policy: Change Over Time." *American Journal of Political Science* 23 (1): 208–14.

DeRouen, Karl. 2000. "Presidents and the Diversionary Use of Force: A Research Note." *International Studies Quarterly* 44 (2): 317–28.

Fiorina, Morris P. 1981. *Retrospective Voting in American National Elections*. New Haven, CT: Yale University Press.

Fordham, Benjamin. 1998. "Partisanship, Macroeconomic Policy and US Use of Force, 1949–1994." *Journal of Conflict Resolution* 42 (4): 418–39.

Franklin, Charles. 1991. "Eschewing Obfuscation? Campaigns and the Perception of U.S. Senate Incumbents." *American Political Science Review* 85 (4): 1193–1214.

Gartner, Scott Sigmund. 2004. "Making the International Local: The Terrorist Attack on the USS Cole, Local Casualties, and Media Coverage." *Political Communication* 21 (2): 139–59.

Gartner, Scott Sigmund, and Gary M. Segura. 1998. "War, Casualties and Public Opinion." *Journal of Conflict Resolution*. 42 (3): 278–300.

—. 2000. "Race, Opinion, and Casualties in the Vietnam War." *The Journal of Politics* 62 (1): 115–46.

Gartner, Scott Sigmund, Gary M. Segura, and Michael Wilkening. 1997. "All Politics are Local: An Analysis of the Effects of Proximate War Losses on Individual Opinion in the Vietnam War." *The Journal of Conflict Resolution* 41 (5): 669–94.

Gartzke, Eric. 2001. "Democracy and the Preparation for War: Does Regime Type Affect States' Anticipation of Casualties?" *International Studies Quarterly* 45 (3): 467–84.

Gelpi, Christopher, and Peter D. Feaver. 2002. "Speak Softly and Carry a Big Stick? Veterans in the Political Elite and the American Use of Force." *American Political Science Review* 96 (4): 779–93.

Gerber, Elisabeth R., and John E. Jackson. 1993. "Endogenous Preferences and the Study of Institutions." *American Political Science Review* 87 (3): 639–56.

Holsti, Ole R. 1996. *Public Opinion and American Foreign Policy.* Ann Arbor: University of Michigan Press.

Hurwitz, Jon, and Mark Peffley 1987. "How Are Foreign Policy Attitudes Structured? A Hierarchical Model." *American Political Science Review* 81 (4): 1099–1120.

Jacobson, Gary C., and Samuel Kernell. 1981. *Strategy and Choice in Congressional Elections.* New Haven.CT:Yale University Press.

Karnow, Stanley. 1991. *Vietnam: A History.* New York: Penguin.

Kuklinski, James H. 1978. "Representativeness and Elections: A Policy Analysis." *American Political Science Review* 72 (1): 165–77.

Lee, Frances E. 1998. "Representation and Public Policy: The Consequences of Senate Apportionment for the Geographic Distribution of Federal Funds." *Journal of Politics* 60 (1): 34–62.

Life. June 27, 1969. 66 (25): 20–31.

Markus, Gregory B. 1979. "The Political Environment and the Dynamics of Political Attitudes: A Panel Study." *American Journal of Political Science* 23 (2): 338–59.

Miller, Warren E., and Donald E. Stokes. 1963. "Constituency Influence in Congress." *American Political Science Review* 57 (1): 45–56.

Morgan, T. Clifton, and Sally Howard Campbell. 1991. "Domestic Structure, Decisional Constraints, and War." *Journal of Conflict Resolution* 35 (2): 187–211.

Mueller, John E. 1973. *War, Presidents and Public Opinion.* New York: Wiley.

—. 1994. *Policy and Opinion in the Gulf War.* Chicago: Univer sity of Chicago Press.

Murray, Shoon Kathleen. 1996. *Anchors Against Change: American Opinion Leader's Beliefs After the Cold War.* Ann Arbor: University of Michigan Press.

Nader, Ralph. 1972. *Ralph Nader Congress Project: Citizens Look at Congress.* Washington, DC: Grossman.

Nicholson, Stephen P., and Gary M. Segura. 1999. "Midterm Elections and Divided Government: An Information Driven Theory of Electoral Volatility." *Political Research Quarterly* 52 (3): 609–30.

Nicholson, Stephen P., Gary M. Segura, and Nathan D. Woods. 2002. "The Paradox of Presidential Approval: The Mixed Blessing of Divided Government to Presidential Popularity." *Journal of Politics* 64 (3): 701–20.

Niemi, Richard G., and Herbert F. Weisberg. 1993. *Classics in Voting Behavior.* Washington, DC: Congressional Quarterly Press.

Nisbett, Richard E, and Dov Cohen. 1996. *Culture of Honor: The Psychology of Violence in the South.* Boulder, CO: Westview.

Oppenheimer, Bruce. 1996. "The Representational Experience: The Effect of State Population on Senator-Constituency Linkages." *American Journal of Political Science* 40 (4): 1280–89.

Page, Benjamin I., and Richard A. Brody. 1972. "Policy Voting and the Electoral Process: The Vietnam War Issue." *American Political Science Review* 66 (3): 979–95.

Page, Benjamin, and Robert Shapiro. 1992. *The Rational Public.* Chicago: University of Chicago Press.

Ray, James Lee. 1995. *Democracy and International Conflict: An Evaluation of the Democratic Peace Proposition.* Columbia: University of South Carolina Press.

Reiter, Dan, and Allan C. Stam. 2002. *Democracies at War.* Princeton, NJ: Princeton University Press.

Segura, Gary M., and Stephen P. Nicholson. 1995. "Sequential Choices and Partisan Transitions in U.S. Senate Delegations: 1972–1988. "*Journal of Politics* 57 (1): 86–100.

Siverson, Randolph. 1995. "Democracies and War Participation: In Defense of the Institutional Constraints Argument." *European Journal of International Relations* 1: 481–89.

Squire, Peverill. 1995. "Field Essay: Candidates, Money, and Voters— Assessing the State of Congressional Elections Research." *Political Research Quarterly* 48 (4): 891–918.

Thomas, Martin. 1984. "Election Proximity and Senatorial Roll-Call Voting." *American Journal of Political Science* 28 (1): 96–111.

United States. Department of the Census. 1966. *Statistical Abstract of the United States.* Washington, DC: United States Government Printing Office.

Westlye, Mark C. 1991. *Senate Elections and Campaign Intensity.* Baltimore, MD: The Johns Hopkins University Press.

Wood, B. Dan, and Angela Hinton Andersson. 1998. "The Dynamics of Senatorial Representation." *Journal of Politics* 60 (3): 705–36.

Zaller, John R. 1991. "Information, Values, and Opinion." *American Political Science Review* 85(4): 1215–37.

—. 1992. *The Nature and Origins of Mass Opinion.* New York: Cambridge University Press.

10

Chinese Military Power: What Vexes the United States and Why?

JONATHAN D. POLLACK

Abstract: *The enhancement of Chinese military power over the past decade is generating ample debate over its meaning and consequences for American security interests. China's characterization in larger conceptions of U.S. national security strategy has experienced repeated shifts over the decades. China is now an arrived major power according to virtually all relevant power criteria, without U.S. policy makers conclusively resolving the implications of China's military modernization for American security interests. Comparable uncertainties bedevil Chinese thinking about American military power. The latent elements of strategic rivalry (if not outright confrontation) are beyond dispute, and could readily take deeper root in the bureaucratic processes of both countries. Without leaders in both systems fully imparting and communicating to one another their respective strategic equities in Asia and the Pacific, the emergence of a reconfigured regional security order fully accepted by both states remains very uncertain.*

After an extended post-September 11 hiatus, China's military modernization and its presumed strategic objectives are again on the U.S.

Jonathan Pollack (jonathan.d.pollack@gmail.com) is Professor of Asian and Pacific Studies at the Naval War College, where he also chairs the College's Asia-Pacific Studies Group. The opinions expressed in this paper should not be attributed to the Naval War College, the U.S. Government, or the Department of Defense.

policy radar screen. China's accelerated military development and the supposed obscurity of Beijing's long-term national security goals both feature prominently in U.S. concerns. There is a clear need for analysts and policy makers to understand Chinese capabilities in a realistic light, beginning with the context, attributes, and prevailing directions of China's military modernization. Grounded, realistic explanations of Chinese military modernization are apparent among some U.S. officials, but China's military advancement is also being employed to validate and advance narrower policy and institutional agendas. Moreover, American policy makers have yet to meaningfully address an even larger long-term issue: is the U.S. prepared to move toward a future concept of international security that does not assume unambiguous U.S. strategic dominance, and (if not) what does the U.S. propose to do about it? This question pertains at present to long-term relations with China, but it will increasingly shape U.S. relations with other major powers aspiring to strategic autonomy in the 21st century, in particular, India and Russia.

Chinese policy making is also not immune to self-serving policy and institutional rationales. American defense programs are validating and sustaining increased Chinese military efforts across a diverse spectrum of programs and activities. China's anti-satellite test (ASAT) of January 2007 fits in this context.[1] The delayed Chinese acknowledgment of the test was strikingly divergent from China's repeated statements opposing the "weaponization of outer space." The test was the evident product of many years of research and experimentation within Chinese military R&D, the requisite inter-agency coordination, and without senior officials weighing fully the potential policy reverberations following the test. Though there are signs of increased awareness among some officials in Beijing about the

---

[1] "Chinese Military Messages," International Institute for Strategic Studies (IISS) *Strategic Comments*, February 2007; and Phillip C. Saunders and Charles D. Lutes, *China's ASAT Test: Motivations and Implications* (Washington, DC: Institute for National Strategic Studies, National Defense University Special Report, June 2007).

potential effects of China's growing military power on the interests and strategic calculations of external powers, narrower institutional priorities are also shaping Chinese programs, and could readily trigger larger consequences that would undermine Beijing's larger strategic objectives. There is mounting evidence of debate among informed Chinese specialists on the purposes and priorities underlying military modernization. Chinese security policy may still be formally decided atop the system, but the increasing diversity of viewpoints within the system suggests that central guidance is far less authoritative than in the past. The belief that Chinese policy making operates with control rigorously exercised at the apex of the system thus seems increasingly quaint.

Beijing's reemergence as a major power also reflects larger changes underway within China and in its relationship with the outside world. Unlike the former Soviet Union, it is a "dual capable" major power ever more integrated in global economics, politics, and security, and upon whom Washington relies to address critical regional issues, most notably efforts to inhibit and reverse North Korea's nuclear weapons development. It is a rapidly modernizing state that combines reformist policies oriented toward market-led growth, while the leadership simultaneously hopes to preserve the Party's political prerogatives, amidst societal dynamics that the leadership is increasingly less able to control. China is an ever larger magnet for trade and foreign direct investment with the U.S. and a major enabler of U.S. deficit spending through its large-scale purchases of U. S. Treasury notes, while it also seeks to ensure unequivocal strategic autonomy from the United States. Last but not least, the People's Liberation Army (PLA) is increasingly able to complicate, inhibit, or directly challenge the employment of American military power in areas contiguous to China, with contingencies related to Taiwan the clear focus of such efforts. These multiple policy considerations and the inherent contradictions in how the U.S. addresses China's political, economic, and military ascendance do not have a ready precedent or parallel in U.S. relations with any other state. A fuller understanding of U. S. policy dilemmas also needs to review some of the history that has brought both countries and both militaries to their present circumstances: Americans may have forgotten or dismissed much of this history, but Chinese have not. One conclusion seems inescapable: Chinese and American defense planning and their effects on the military strategies of both states will be pivotal factors in future bilateral ties.

This paper will explore three issues. First, I will summarize U.S. defense strategy toward China during the early decades of the Cold War, and then describe the implications of Sino-American normalization for the planning assumptions of both states. Second, I will review the primary factors that have altered the framework of defense planning between the United States and China over the past decade and a half. Third, I will highlight some of the dominant characteristics of contemporary defense thinking in both systems, and how they could shape longer-term outcomes in Sino-American relations.

U.S. Assessments of Chinese Strategy: The Cold War and Beyond

Throughout the 1950s and 1960s, the United States deemed China its primary political-military adversary in East Asia. This led the United States to adopt (at least in broad conceptual terms) a "two and a half war" defense strategy. This was judged appropriate when Beijing was allied with the Soviet Union in the 1950s, and it was redefined only marginally after the shattering of the Sino-Soviet alliance at the end of the decade. However, the conflict in Korea (1950–1953) sobered both leaderships on the risks and implications of renewed warfare. There were indisputable strategic and operational constraints imposed on both leaderships in the Taiwan Strait during the 1950s and in the subsequent U.S. escalation in Vietnam.[2]

---

[2] For insightful examinations by two senior Chinese and American scholars, consult Zhang Baijia, "'Resist America': China's Role in The Korean and Vietnam Wars," and Allen S. Whiting, "U.S. Crisis Management Vis-à-vis China: Korea and Vietnam," in Michael D. Swaine and Zhang Tuosheng (eds.) with Danielle F.S. Cohen, *Managing Sino-American Crises: Case Studies and Analysis* (Washington, DC: Carnegie Endowment for International Peace, 2006), pp. 179–213 and 215–249 respectively.

But China's presumed revolutionary ambitions in Asia were a primary justification for U.S. "pactomania" across the region and for the large scale deployment of U. S. forces on air, land, and sea around the periphery of China. This was well understood in Chinese strategic assessments, as these issues dominated Chinese security planning throughout the 1950s and much of the 1960s. It was only with the militarization of the Sino-Soviet dispute in the mid and late 1960s that American planners began to ponder seriously the implications of the political-military confrontation between Moscow and Beijing for U.S. security interests. (China's nascent nuclear weapons capabilities were a separate concern of American strategic planners, but space limitations preclude consideration of this issue.)

Once the Sino-American rapprochement began in earnest during the early 1970s, the Nixon Administration wasted little time in adjusting its defense strategies toward China. With U.S. military involvement in Vietnam receding and with Washington and Beijing moving toward larger political and strategic understandings related to Taiwan, the United States shifted to a "one and a half war" defense strategy, effectively removing China from detailed U.S. military planning in East Asia. Planning for Korean contingencies remained a partial exception to this development. For all practical purposes, however, China was no longer deemed a plausible U.S. adversary, a trend immeasurably strengthened by the normalization of Sino-American relations at the end of 1978, the withdrawal of the residual U.S. military presence from Taiwan, and China's demilitarization of the coastal regions opposite Taiwan. Thus, Chinese military power had ceased to be a major preoccupation for American defense planners.

The accommodation between the United States and China and the growing American realization of the backwardness of China's defense technology base meant that Chinese military capabilities did not pose an inherent or insuperable risk to American regional security interests. If anything, a weaker China was deemed adverse to U.S. security interests, since Beijing was then presumably far more vulnerable to Soviet pressure or outright coercion. China therefore served as a tacit ally of the United States during the 1980s, with Washington actively facilitating China's scientific and technological advancement, including the Reagan Administration's decision to directly assist China's military modernization in four separate mission areas. In a remarkable display of historical amnesia, this entire history went unmentioned in the Cox Committee report of 1999, charged with investigating allegations of illicit Chinese acquisition of American high technology and nuclear weapons design data.[3] The report's authors chose to ignore the fact that the enhancement of Chinese technological and defense capabilities *was* deemed directly beneficial to American national security interests for more than a decade, by Republican and Democratic administrations alike. With the United States intent on cultivating China as a counterweight to Soviet power in Asia (or at least hoping to render China a substantial, continuing preoccupation for Soviet military planners), few officials in Washington considered whether or how China might adversely affect American regional security interests at some future date.

China's military development during the 1970s and 1980s proceeded at a desultory pace, and was judged either inconsequential or marginally advantageous to American security interests. China's military capabilities (though not its weapons sales, involvement in missile proliferation or nuclear technology transfers to Pakistan) were considered largely tangential to U.S. national security interests. With China's predominant energies focused on economic development and threat reduction with its neighbors, there seemed little reason to modify American policy. Deng Xiaoping's strategic reassessment of 1985 reinforced these judgments.[4] China's leaders no longer characterized major war (let alone global war) as inevitable, and China's future military development was explicitly subordinated to the

---

[3] Jonathan D. Pollack, "The Cox Report's 'Dirty Little Secret'," *Arms Control Today,* April/May 1999, pp. 26–27, 34.

[4] See in particular Deng Xiaoping's remarks to an Enlarged Meeting of the Party's Central Military Commission, June 4, 1985, in *Foreign Broadcast Information Service Daily Report-China,* June 12, 1985, pp. K1–2.

requirements of economic modernization. Though some senior leaders still expressed concerns about China's relative weakness, the implications for military modernization were largely deferred to a later date. For Washington, China's future military development was a decidedly back-burner issue. For Beijing, America's future military development (beyond concerns about U.S. arms sales to Taiwan) barely registered on the radar screen. By the end of the decade, however, these benign assumptions began to erode, posing the issue of whether these strategic judgments were ever fully rooted in either system.

The 1990s: American and Chinese Strategies Redefined

At the end of the 1980s and in the early 1990s, major domestic and international upheavals disrupted the policy framework governing Sino-American relations. The largely benign assumptions of defense planners in both systems shifted in significant ways, altering prevailing assumptions about the behavior and intentions of both states. These developments were sequential and cumulative, not immediately causal; political factors unrelated to national security also influenced the choices of both leaderships. I will briefly note the most important factors, and then identify some of the implications for security planning.

Domestic developments within China were among the primary triggers of change. The Tiananmen crisis of 1989 abruptly altered expectations of the continued maturation of U.S.-China military to military relations, and American programs for military technology transfer were soon cancelled. Within months of the cessation of American technological assistance, Liu Huaqing, one of China's highest ranking officers who had been educated in the Soviet Union in the 1950s, visited Moscow to initiate discussions on the resumption of Soviet military deliveries to China after a three decade hiatus, a step that would have previously been considered unimaginable. The earliest negotiations (and subsequent agreements) focused on purchase of advanced combat aircraft (the Su-27), whose capabilities vastly surpassed any aircraft in China's inventory. The aircraft's range and lethality would for the first time enable China to extend the reach of its air power beyond the mainland. With China prepared to enter into long-term defense collaboration with the Soviet Union, and with Moscow prepared to respond to such needs, the door had opened to the first meaningful enhancement of Chinese military capabilities in decades.

It is unclear whether American planners fully anticipated these developments; no doubt the post-Tiananmen freeze in military to military relations denied the United States vital information about these possibilities. Though the George H.W. Bush Administration sought to preserve as much of the political relationship with Beijing as possible, the value that both leaderships attached to close Sino-American relations had diminished. The administration's decision to approve the sale of 75 F-16 aircraft to Taiwan in the midst of 1992 Presidential election was in part explained by the ample electoral vote count in Texas, where the aircraft were provided, but the initial reports of Su-27 sales to China were also decisive in shifting the center of gravity in U. S. policy debate.[5] The Bush Administration decided to undertake a large-scale arms sales decision that (absent the larger deterioration in bilateral relations) might not have transpired. It also provoked major reactions from Beijing. With the United States no longer upholding the letter and spirit of the 1982 arms sales communiqué, Chinese leaders crossed thresholds of their own through sales of M-11 missiles to Pakistan and initial planning for the reintroduction of Chinese military capabilities opposite Taiwan.

Two additional factors loomed especially large in U.S. and Chinese security deliberations: the dissolution of the Soviet Union at the end of 1991; and far-reaching advances in the application of advanced technologies to modern warfare. The collapse of the U.S.S.R marked

---

[5] James Mann, *About Face: A History of America's Curious Relationship with China from Nixon to Clinton* (New York: Alfred A. Knopf, 1999), pp. 254–273.

the final end of a half century of superpower rivalry; as a consequence, the United States abruptly lacked a global adversary that had enabled it to justify, maintain, and "size" its military forces. The initial post-Soviet defense policy review (undertaken by the U.S. Department of Defense in 1992) devoted preponderant emphasis to the U.S. capability to project military power against a variety of regional threats, which still seemed credible in the aftermath of Operation Desert Storm.[6] Senior U.S. defense planners therefore characterized security threats from Iraq, Iran, and North Korea as the primary "force sizing constructs" in U.S. global strategy.

But there were other straws in the wind. DoD planning papers leaked to the press in early 1992 argued for open-ended American global predominance against any prospective major power adversary, but defined this objective in generic terms, without reference to any specific country.[7] The controversies engendered by these policy documents led to the shelving of this strategy; it would not be until the George W. Bush administration that these ideas again surfaced, and with far greater momentum. A threat-based logic remained the hallmark of U.S. defense planning in the early 1990s, focused predominantly on regional adversaries, thereby preserving America's commitment to global power projection capabilities. U.S. force reductions from the levels of the latter Cold War era still remained relatively modest.

China was not a significant factor in these policy deliberations, quite possibly reflecting its post-Tiananmen retrenchment and its still very tentative advances in military modernization. For example, had DoD been more concerned about the potential enhancement of Chinese military power, the Pentagon would have been far less likely

---

[6] Richard Cheney, *Defense Strategy for the 1990s: The Regional Defense Strategy* (Washington, DC: Office of the Secretary of Defense, January 1993).

[7] Relevant portions of the draft Defense Planning Guidance of 1992 are excerpted in the *New York Times,* March 8, 1992.; see also Barton Gellman, "Keeping the U.S. First: Pentagon Would Preclude a Rival Superpower," *Washington Post,* March 11, 1992.

to assent to the closure of U.S. bases in the Philippines in the early 1990s. The renewed surge in China's economy was in its early stages, and was only beginning to garner attention in the United States. Plans for the augmentation of Chinese military forces opposite Taiwan were not well advanced, inasmuch as cross-trait relations had yet to deteriorate sharply. The normalization of Sino-Russian relations also highlighted that China (not unlike the United States) no longer had a central defining threat around which to organize its military forces. Chinese defense planning was beginning to chart a different course, but in the early 1990s internal vulnerabilities and political pressures remained paramount. If Beijing identified a major U.S. threat to China at the time, it was more ideological than military (i.e., America's supposed pursuit of a "peaceful evolution" strategy designed to undermine the Communist Party's hold on power).

But PLA strategists had also begun to focus attention on the profound changes in warfare for which Chinese forces were woefully ill-prepared.[8] Modern information technologies had begun to transform the battlefield, rendering industrial age military forces ever more vulnerable. Chinese assessments of U.S. military capabilities prior to Operation Desert Storm were well wide of the mark, with many in the PLA anticipating a protracted conflict and significant U.S. combat losses. The stunning successes of American forces triggered an internal reassessment within the Chinese military that continues to the present day. The PLA leadership sought to accelerate acquisition and integration of advanced technologies into Chinese military research and development. These technological needs were also reflected in doctrinal reassessments and important organizational reforms, including continued reductions in the size of the armed forces and increased professionalization of the officer corps. Having long emphasized mass, redundancy, and defense of the homeland,

---

[8] For an overview of Chinese policy responses to these changes in warfare, consult James C. Mulvenon and Richard H. Yang (eds.), *The People's Liberation Army in the Information Age* (Santa Monica: RAND, CF-145-CAPP/AF, 1999).

PLA commanders embarked on gestational changes that have achieved far greater fruition over the past decade.[9]

Though the PLA remained a predominantly land-oriented force, national security was for the first time being viewed in a more extended light. An enhanced capacity to assert and protect China's declared national security interests (though still justified by an official defense policy characterized as wholly defensive) would require a much broader spectrum of military capabilities designed to ensure "a favorable peripheral environment," not simply defend the mainland. Indeed, Beijing's modernization efforts appeared largely congruent with the modernization programs underway elsewhere in East Asia, including Japan, South Korea, and (not least) Taiwan. For China, these developments presupposed more advanced air, naval, missile, communications, and intelligence assets, and increased competence and experience in utilizing these capabilities.

With China moving toward a more comprehensive concept of national security, the most pressing threats to Chinese interests were no longer those associated with direct military attack. But some defense planners called attention to how an adversary's military reach and technological advantage could put the mainland's economic and strategic assets at risk and challenge Chinese sovereignty. The PLA's efforts were now focused on the range, lethality, and accuracy of Chinese weapons systems, and preliminary efforts at realizing a modicum of "jointness." Without such advanced capabilities and experience in working with them, senior commanders contended, China could be left in a passive position, unable to protect its vital interests. Senior political leaders found these arguments increasingly persuasive, and as China's rapid economic growth was sustained, the leadership allocated increased funds toward military modernization goals. None of these concerns presumed a decision to employ such power; rather, these were deemed capabilities that China as a modernizing state could not do without. Having long been subordinate

[9] Dennis J. Blasko, *The Chinese Army Today-Tradition and Transformation for the 21st Century* (London and New York: Routledge, 2006).

in the resource allocation decisions of the reform era, the PLA had begun to develop a more compelling rationale and logic for longer-term military development that civilian leaders were prepared to support.

Absent a specific threat, however, these efforts lacked urgency, direction, and momentum. The sharp deterioration in cross-strait relations occasioned by Taiwan President Lee Teng-hui's visit to the United States in 1995 provided all three.[10] The PLA's exercises opposite Taiwan in 1995 and 1996 furnished the proximate opportunity to display China's nascent military capabilities. Leaders in Beijing were intent on demonstrating that the PLA was prepared (at least in a provisional sense) to exercise its increased combat power. The testing of unarmed short-range ballistic missiles launched from locations in Fujian Province (the first military batteries had been introduced to Fujian during 1994) provoked major military responses by the United States. Washington's deployment of two carrier battle groups east of Taiwan did not prefigure an imminent major crisis. However, it signaled then (and since) that the United States had recalibrated its security assumptions in relation to China, with a prospective Taiwan contingency again introduced into American defense planning.

The events of 1995–96 thus set in train longer-term effects in the defense bureaucracies of both states that reverberate to the present day. For Chinese planners, it validated the belief that the United States was still prepared to interject its military power into an issue of defining importance to Chinese interests. China therefore had to plan for two classes of scenarios involving Taiwan: those where American power was a major factor and those where it was not. This reassessment did not make the United States an avowed Chinese adversary, but it hugely sobered leaders in both states about the risks and potential consequences of a renewed crisis. U.S.-Chinese leadership interactions in President Bill Clinton's second term in office

---

[10] Robert L. Suettinger, *Beyond Tiananmen-The Politics of U.S.-China Relations 1989–2000* (Washington, DC: Brookings Institution Press, 2003), pp. 243–263.

therefore devoted ample political efforts to stabilizing bilateral relations. But the events of 1995 and 1996 set in motion longer-term changes in defense planning that are far more fully materialized today, with particular attention to China's building of "anti-access" capabilities directed against forward-deployed American maritime power.[11] The PLA did not obscure the perceived necessity to build such capabilities, nor does it do so today.

Although Beijing had never precluded non-peaceful means to achieve unification, for most of China's post-1949 history the use of force against Taiwan (as distinct from actions undertaken against various offshore islands) was a ritualized slogan, devoid of operational significance. In the aftermath of 1995–96, the prospective use of force, even if characterized as an option of last resort, had achieved greatly increased prominence in Chinese policy deliberations. The scope and scale of Chinese exercises opposite Taiwan increased measurably, and there was a surge in the enhancement of short range ballistic missiles (SRBMs) at coastal locations that has been sustained for a full decade. (According to late 2006 estimate from the Defense Intelligence Agency, the total number of SRBMs deployed opposite Taiwan numbers approximately 900; recent estimates from officials on Taiwan are closer to 1,000. OSD also reports that land-attack cruise missiles (LACMs) designed for precision strike against hard targets are also in development.[12]) Air, naval, and air defense acquisitions from Russia also grew both quantitatively and qualitatively, with the "Taiwan scenario" the defining rationale for Chinese military modernization.

The PLA asserted that its enhanced capabilities could advance a wide spectrum of objectives, including political deterrence, the

---

[11] James C. Mulvenon et al., *Chinese Responses to U.S. Military Transformation and Implications for the Department of Defense* (Santa Monica: RAND, MG-340-OSD, 2006); *Annual Report to the Congress-Military Power of the People's Republic of China-2007* (Washington, DC: Office of the Secretary of Defense, 2007), pp. 15–18.

[12] Ibid., p. 17.

demonstration of resolve in crisis and non-crisis, the forestalling of additional moves toward Taiwanese independence, and (not least) the use of force against Taiwan, should Beijing conclude that it had no other means to prevent the island's permanent political separation from the mainland. But the parallel need to plan against the possibility of third party intervention (and the capabilities deemed necessary to deny an external force the ability to intervene, either directly or indirectly) was fraught with far larger risks and consequences, and with ample potential for misperception and miscalculation. There were no operational precedents in China's post-1949 history for the large-scale employment of military force in and across the Taiwan Strait, and Chinese military forces had not engaged in significant armed conflict since the border war against Vietnam in 1979. Political leaders in Washington and Beijing were intent on defusing the possibility of renewed crisis, but military policy makers were simultaneously given increased latitude to plan for Taiwan contingencies. With the heightened attention to the potential for a major crisis in the Taiwan Strait, a major threshold had been breached, thereby reshaping the contours of military power and policy in both systems, but especially in China. To more fully elucidate these possibilities, we need to turn to how China and the United States are conceptualizing their respective defense objectives in the early 21st century, and weigh the potential consequences for future bilateral relations.

China and America: Planning for the Longer-Term

At the start of the George W. Bush Administration, the outlook for Sino-American relations seemed highly problematic, with senior U.S. officials determined to revisit; U.S. the policies of the Clinton Administration, including military to military relations with Beijing and U.S. arms sales to Taiwan. Though the worst fears of a sharp deterioration in relations did not materialize, major uncertainties and potential divergence persist in national security interactions between Washington and Beijing. Indeed, some analysts argue that

September 11 constituted only a momentary hiatus in what is destined to emerge as the defining interstate rivalry of the 21st century.[13] Longer-term wariness and suspicion within both systems about the "strategic intentions" of the other is now a commonplace feature in policy debate and in the comments of senior officials on both sides.

Chinese policy makers nevertheless remain largely focused on a "lower volume" strategy toward the United States, contesting major differences with Washington, but with a minimum of the stridency that once routinely characterized Chinese policy statements. The 2007 ASAT test constitutes a rare episode of demonstrating advanced military capabilities designed to caution and thereby deter the United States from courses of action in space deemed overtly inimical to Chinese security interests. But American policy makers view the ASAT test in far more worrisome terms.[14] A less overtly contentious relationship with Washington preserves the ability of both capitals to collaborate where necessary and feasible, without in any way inhibiting Beijing's pursuit of autonomous power goals, including a noticeable acceleration of its military development since the late 1990s. The essential paradox of contemporary Sino-American relations is the unprecedented expansion of bilateral ties, simultaneous with the development of military policies, programs, and activities that could skew future ties in much more adversial directions. Defense planning (though subject to political direction in both countries) often assumes a life of its own.

As major powers, China and the United States have also undertaken heightened efforts to justify and legitimate their national defense strategies, hoping to gain broader international support of declared policy goals while building and maintaining domestic

---

[13] Jonathan D. Pollack (ed.), *Strategic Surprise?-U.S.-China Relations in the Early 21st Century* (Newport: Naval War College Press, 2004).

[14] For an explicit and forceful presentation by a leading Chinese defense strategist, see Bao Shixiu, "Deterrence Revisited: Outer Space," *China Security,* Winter 2007, pp. 2–11.

support for national defense expenditure.[15] But this is predominantly the presentational side of military planning. It affords at best partial insight into the long-term factors that will shape the strategies, forces, and future conduct of both nations' military forces. Moreover, the seeming parallelism in such policy documents obscures the profound differences in the strategic circumstances and political and bureaucratic processes of the two countries. As an emergent power whose military modernization has accelerated significantly in recent years, China has sought to reassure others of its larger domestic preoccupations, while also asserting that its military development is appropriate for its growing economic and political prominence. This has obligated China to increased disclosure about the purposes and dimensions of its military development.

China has released five biannual Defense White Papers since 1998. The newest version, released in December 2006, reiterates a set of generic national security concerns that call primary attention to the longer-term requirements of Chinese security. These include: (1) the prevention of national separation and the promotion of reunification; (2) the defense of national sovereignty, territorial integrity and maritime rights and interests; (3) the coordinated development of economic development and overall capabilities; and (4) defense modernization in accord with China's domestic conditions and the enhancement of operational self-defense capabilities appropriate to the information era. These goals are sufficiently elastic that they can incorporate and justify a very wide range of modernization programs.

Beijing's latest White Paper (though offering important indications of modernization priorities) failed to mollify those seeking a fuller rendering of goals, programs, and capabilities. But the document

---

[15] For relevant examples, see *Report of the 2006 Quadrennial Defense Review,* February 6, 2006, available at www.defenselink.mil/pdfs/QDR20060203. pdf; and *China's National Defense in 2006* (Beijing: Information Office of the State Council of the People's Republic of China, December 29, 2006).

contained ample confirmation that the PLA aspires to a more technology-intensive force appropriate to 21st century strategic realities, premised on the increased "informationalization" of warfare. It posits the need for major enhancements in "firepower, assault, mobility, protection, and information," all premised on "major breakthroughs" in joint operations and inter-service integration. In the ground forces, these will be geared toward "trans-regional mobility ... air-ground integrated operations, long-distance maneuvers, rapid assaults, and special operations." The PLA Navy will emphasize "gradual extension of the strategic depth for offshore defensive operations ... and capabilities in integrated maritime operations and nuclear counterattacks." The PLA Air Force will undertake a "transition from territorial air defense to both offensive and defensive operations," including "air strike, air and missile defense, early warning and reconnaissance and strategic projection." The Second Artillery (i.e., the missile forces) will emphasize enhanced "capabilities in strategic deterrence and conventional strike," with Chinese nuclear doctrine premised on "a self-defensive nuclear strategy ... and counterattack in self-defense." At the same time, the White Paper acknowledged average annual increases in military expenditure between 1990 and 2005 (after allowing for increases in the consumer price index) of 9.64 per cent, still well below prevailing external estimates but far more congruent with the heightened priority of defense modernization.[16]

The U.S. Defense Department's latest assessment of China's military power, released in early 2007. The 2005 and 2006 DoD reports in particular take explicit issue with more relaxed characterizations of Chinese modernization goals. Both the 2005 and 2006 DoD reports offer far more worrisome assessments of Chinese plans and intentions, calling particular concern to the scale and breadth of various weapons development programs across the full spectrum of military operations, including what the reports deem a major investment in power-projection capabilities. In DoD's view, Chinese

[16] Ibid.

investment strategies portend "a force capable of prosecuting a range of military operations in Asia-well beyond Taiwan." Though the 2007 assessment adopted a more measured tone than the documents of the two preceding years, it identified a broadening range of Chinese capabilities that could purportedly be utilized in various "non-Taiwan contingencies" involving neighboring states.[17] These programs portend capabilities that "go beyond a Taiwan scenario" and "put regional balances at risk . . . potentially posing a credible threat to modern militaries operating in the region." DoD also faults China for a highly constricted approach to military transparency, including a supposed reliance on strategic deception, a penchant for extreme secrecy, a significant understatement of the budgetary resources allocated to national defense, and obscurity on how the PLA might employ force in a future crisis.

However, the Pentagon also acknowledges that Chinese programs and strategies are designed to counter major U.S. advances in information dominance and deep strike capabilities-i.e., the precise assets that the PLA would need to impede or undermine in a major crisis related to Taiwan, which DoD continues to characterize as the predominant focus of China's modernization programs. By implication, if not by explicit admission, the Pentagon report concedes that modernization activities undertaken by China cannot be understood apart from the capabilities that the PLA believes it could well confront. Thus, military planning (though a "stand alone" activity undertaken by both the United States and China) assumes primary meaning in relation to perceptions of the capabilities and future behavior of potential adversaries. In this regard, does China have any more assurance about future U.S. behavior and intentions than the United States has about China's? Under such circumstances, does either state have particular incentives for full information disclosure, even assuming that either could fully specify the scope and scale of longer-range military requirements and strategic intentions? Would not

---

[17] *Annual Report to the Congress-Military Power of the People's Republic of China–2007*, pp. 22–23.

these judgments derive in significant measure from the environment that China believes it could confront?

In this respect, DoD to a certain extent is hoist on its own petard. Since the onset of the Bush Administration, senior defense officials have routinely asserted that the U.S. no longer subscribes to "threat-based planning," opting instead for what it has described as "capability-based planning" that identifies how U.S. forces could be placed at risk, but does not identify the source of that threat. With the conspicuous exception of counteracting potential terrorist activities and an array of threats emanating from instability in the Islamic world, this claim seems suspect. The inherent character of contingency planning mandates that the specific circumstances (i.e., locale, forces, etc.) be the primary shapers of force requirements. Moreover, various characterizations in the Quadrennial Defense Reviews of 2001 and 2006 leave little to the imagination. In the 2001 document, DoD noted the prospect of a prospective threat in Asia from "a military competitor with a formidable resource base" that was China in all but name.[18] In the 2006 document, China is identified explicitly as the state with "the greatest potential to compete militarily with the United States and could over time field disruptive military technologies that could over time offset traditional U. S. military advantages.[19]" The report further highlights the goal of "shaping the choices of countries at strategic crossroads . . . [while] creat[ing] prudent hedges against the possibility that cooperative approaches by themselves may fail to preclude future conflict." Putting aside the question of what major power (including the United States) is *not* at a "strategic crossroads," the DoD report draws attention to three states: China, India, and Russia. But the characterization of China's current capabilities and longer-term power potential is qualitatively different in emphasis and implication.

---

[18] *Quadrennial Defense Review Report* (Washington, DC: Office of the Secretary of Defense, September 30, 2001), p. 4.

[19] *Report of the 2006 Quadrennial Defense Review,* p. 29.

Beijing also seems to subscribe (at least for representational purposes) to a concept akin to capability-based planning. For both states, there is a somewhat contrived quality to capability-based justifications of defense strategy. In the Taiwan case, however, Chinese military planners recognize that specific contingencies are largely driving modernization plans and acquisition priorities. But prominent Chinese strategic analysts also acknowledge that China's defense modernization has assumed increased pride of place in national priorities; there is now "coordinated development of economic construction and national defense and army building." This new circumstance – i.e., the need for Beijing "to build a powerful military force matching its international status"- requires a more compelling justification of the purposes underlying China's future political and security roles. Without such a rationale, some strategic observers note, China could trigger heightened wariness on the part of established powers, or even "serious conflict and confrontation," thereby directly undermining the larger "strategic opportunity" of advancing China's development goals by keeping free from embroilment in crisis or armed conflict.[20] This is compelling China's military leadership to articulate a more compelling and candid justification of its future force requirements.

Refreshingly, Chinese strategists are not speaking with one voice on these issues. Alternative possibilities loom as China contemplates the next stage of its military development, with pronounced distinctions between interest-driven definition of future military needs (much of this geared to China's economic and energy interests), as distinct from forces explicitly required for potential armed conflicts. Some leaders hope to evolve a rationale that is not threat-driven, and would enable China to avoid a longer-term confrontation with

---

[20] The above quotations are drawn from Yang Yi, "Adhere to Peaceful Development, Safeguard the Period of Strategic Opportunity," *Xiandai Guoji Guanxi*, September 20, 2006, pp. 40–42. Rear Admiral Yang is Director of the Institute of Strategic Studies, National Defense University.

U.S. power. The development of more autonomous capabilities that moves China (literally and figuratively) into uncharted waters looms as an ever more realistic prospect, with prominent voices (including the leadership of the PLA Navy) vigorously urging heightened attention to Chinese maritime development.[21] Yet others voice concern that China's reach could exceed its grasp, or that Beijing's growing attention to maritime power could distract the nation from more its enduring economic and security concerns as a land power.[22] Ye is a Professor in the School of International Studies at Peking University. Additional prospective paths could entail far broader Chinese involvement in disaster relief, humanitarian operations, and peace keeping as part of a larger Chinese "stakeholder" role in the global system. Others urge collaborative maritime security arrangements to guard against the disruption of global commerce or any impediments to the safe movement of energy resources. Without question, the debate over China's longer-term strategic horizons has been joined.

All these prospects will unfold in the context of the future Sino-American relationship. We therefore return full circle. Characterizations of potential threat derive in significant measure from perceptions and strategic judgment. The 2006 Quadrennial Defense Review and the 2006 National Security Strategy state that the United States hopes that China will emerge as a "responsible stakeholder," while the U. S. simultaneously "hedge[s] against other possibilities.[23]" Such dualism may well be inherent in long-term U.S. strategy toward China, but by so declaring hasn't the question of identifying a threat

[21] See in particular Wu Shengli and Hu Yanlin, "Building a Powerful People's Navy That Meets the Requirements of the Historical Mission for Our Army," *Qiushi*, July 16, 2007. Admirals Wu and Lin are respectively the Commander and Political Commissar of the PLA Navy.

[22] For one such provocative statement, see Ye Zicheng, "Geopolitics From A Greater Historical Perspective," *Xiandai Guoji Guanxi*, June 20, 2007.

[23] *Report of the 2006 Quadrennial Defense Review, p. 28; The National Security Strategy of the United States of America* (Washington, DC: The White House, March 2006), pp. 41–42.

been asked and answered? What policy responses does the United States expect to elicit from China in return? Configurations of long-term strategy are very much a two-way street. Where and how might Washington and Beijing meet on this street?

The longer-term capabilities, strategic orientations and mutual perceptions of the United States and China therefore underlie all these questions. The larger implications of China as an arrived power have yet to be fully evaluated. Does Beijing deem U.S. military power in the West Pacific an inherent threat to Chinese interests? Does Washington deem China's continued military enhancement an inherent threat U. S. interests? If not, what does the United States deem an appropriate level of capability, involvement, and responsibility for China as a reemerged major power in the Asia-Pacific region? Is there an underlying basis for Washington and Beijing to serve as simultaneous "responsible stakeholders," even as both pursue autonomous capabilities and national strategies? Or do both states (and their respective military bureaucracies) retreat into self-protective stances that leave both powers and the region less secure? Absent the serious, sustained attention of civilian and military leaders on both sides of the Pacific, the long-term viability of a reconfigured regional security order seems far from assured. A long-term policy agenda confronts the United States and China. It remains for both to grasp it fully.

Permissions and Acknowledgements

Every effort has been made to contact owners of copyright material. The Publisher shall be pleased to include further notices as advised by rights holders in subsequent printings.

1 **Why Study Military History?**
Gray RAF, Peter W. 'XII. Why Study Military History?' *Defence Studies*, Vol 5, No1 (2005), 151–164.
Online publication date: 1 March 2005.

2 **Why Strategy is Difficult**
Gray, Colin S., 'Why Strategy is Difficult', *Joint Force Quarterly* (Spring 2003), 80–86.
Published by the Institute for National Strategic Studies.

3 **General William T. Sherman and Total War**
Walters, John Bennett, 'General T. Sherman and Total War', *Journal of Southern History*, XIV, No.4 (November 1948), 447–480.
Copyright 1948 by the Southern Historical Association. Reprinted by permission of the Editor.

4 **Disjointed Allies: Coalition Warfare in Berlin and Vienna, 1914**
Herwig, Holger H., 'Disjointed Allies: Coalition Warfare in Berlin and Vienna, 1914', *The Journal of Military History*, Vol 54, No.3 (July 1990), 265–280.
Published by the Society for Military History.

5 **'Freies Deutschland' Guerilla Warfare in East Prussia, 1944–1945: A Contribution to the History of the German Resistance**
Biddiscombe, Perry, '"Freies Deutschland" Guerilla Warfare in East Prussia, 1944–1945: A Contribution to the History of the German Resistance', *German Studies Review*, Vol 27, No.1 (February 2004), 45–62.
Reproduced with kind permission of the *German Studies Review*.

6 **Revolutions in Warfare: Theoretical Paradigms and Historical Evidence –
The Napoleonic and First World War Revolutions in Military Affairs**
Liaropoulos, Andrew N., 'Revolutions in Warfare: Theoretical Paradigms
and Historical Evidence – The Napoleonic and First World War
Revolutions in Military Affairs', *The Journal of Military History*, Vol. 70,
No. 2 (April 2006), 363–384.
Published by the Society for Military History.

7 **Atrocity, War Crime, and Treason in the English Civil War**
Donagan, Barbara, 'Atrocity, War Crime, and Treason in the English Civil
War,' *The American Historical Review*, Vol. 99, No. 4 (October 1994),
1137–1166.
Published by the American Historical Association.

8 **Shell-shock and the Cultural History of the Great War**
Winter, Jay, 'Shell-shock and the Cultural History of the Great War',
Journal of Contemporary History, Vol. 35, No. 1, Special Issue:
Shell-Shock (January 2000), 7–11.
Copyright © 2000 SAGE Publications.
Reprinted by permission of SAGE.

9 **War Casualties, Policy Positions, and the Fate of Legislators**
Gartner, Scott Sigmund, Gary M Segura, Bethany A. Barratt, 'War
Casualties, Policy Positions, and the Fate of Legislators', *Political
Research Quarterly*, Vol. 57, No. 3 (September, 2004), 467–477.
Published by Sage Publications, Inc., on behalf of the University of Utah.

10 **Chinese Military Power: What Vexes the United States and Why?**
Pollack et al., 'Chinese Military Power: What Vexes the United States and
Why?' *Orbis: A Journal of World Affairs*, Vol. 51 (2007), 635–350.
Reproduced by permission of Elsevier.